CONTEMPORARY
BLACK AMERICAN
FICTION WRITERS

Writers of English: Lives and Works

CONTEMPORARY BLACK AMERICAN FICTION WRITERS

Edited and with an Introduction by

Harold Bloom

CHELSEA HOUSE PUBLISHERS
New York   Philadelphia

Jacket illustration: Fred Brown, *Stagger Lee* (1984) (courtesy of the National Museum of Art, Washington, D.C./Art Resource, New York).

CHELSEA HOUSE PUBLISHERS

Editorial Director Richard Rennert
Executive Managing Editor Karyn Gullen Browne
Picture Editor Adrian G. Allen
Copy Chief Robin James
Art Director Robert Mitchell
Manufacturing Director Gerald Levine
Assistant Art Director Joan Ferrigno

Writers of English: Lives and Works

Senior Editor S. T. Joshi
Series Design Rae Grant

Staff for CONTEMPORARY BLACK AMERICAN FICTION WRITERS

Assistant Editor Mary Sisson
Research Robert Green
Picture Researcher Pat Burns

First Printing

1 3 5 7 9 8 6 4 2

Library of Congress Cataloging-in-Publication Data

Contemporary black American fiction writers / edited and with an introduction by Harold Bloom.
    p.   cm.—(Writers of English)
    Includes bibliographical references.
    ISBN 0-7910-2212-9.—ISBN 0-7910-2237-4 (pbk.)
  1. American fiction—Afro-American authors—History and criticism. 2. American fiction—Afro-American authors—Bio-bibliography. 3. American fiction—20th century—History and criticism. 4. American fiction—20th century—Bio-bibliography. 5. Afro-Americans in literature. I. Bloom, Harold. II. Series.
PS374.N4C66 1994
813'.5409896073—dc20   94-5883
[B]   CIP

◼ Contents

▨ User's Guide

THIS VOLUME PROVIDES biographical, critical, and bibliographical information on the twelve most significant contemporary black American fiction writers. Each chapter consists of three parts: a biography of the author; a selection of brief critical extracts about the author; and a bibliography of the author's published books.

The biography supplies a detailed outline of the important events in the author's life, including his or her major writings. The critical extracts are taken from a wide array of books and periodicals, from the author's lifetime to the present, and range in content from biographical to critical to historical. The extracts are arranged in chronological order by date of writing or publication, and a full bibliographical citation is provided at the end of each extract. Editorial additions or deletions are indicated within carets.

The author bibliographies list every separate publication—including books, pamphlets, broadsides, collaborations, and works edited or translated by the author— for works published in the author's lifetime; selected important posthumous publications are also listed. Titles are those of the first edition; variant titles are supplied within carets. In selected instances dates of revised editions are given where these are significant. Pseudonymous works are listed, but not the pseudonyms under which these works were published. Periodicals edited by the author are listed only when the author has written most or all of the contents. Titles enclosed in square brackets are of doubtful authenticity. All works by the author, whether in English or in other languages, have been listed; English translations of foreign-language works are not listed unless the author has done the translation.

The Life of the Author
Harold Bloom

NIETZSCHE, WITH EXULTANT ANGUISH, famously proclaimed that God was dead. Whatever the consequences of this for the ethical life, its ultimate literary effect certainly would have surprised the author Nietzsche. His French disciples, Foucault most prominent among them, developed the Nietzschean proclamation into the dogma that all authors, God included, were dead. The death of the author, which is no more than a Parisian trope, another metaphor for fashion's setting of skirt-lengths, is now accepted as literal truth by most of our current apostles of what should be called French Nietzsche, to distinguish it from the merely original Nietzsche. We also have French Freud or Lacan, which has little to do with the actual thought of Sigmund Freud, and even French Joyce, which interprets *Finnegans Wake* as the major work of Jacques Derrida. But all this is as nothing compared to the final triumph of the doctrine of the death of the author: French Shakespeare. That delicious absurdity is given us by the New Historicism, which blends Foucault and California fruit juice to give us the Word that Renaissance "social energies," and not William Shakespeare, composed *Hamlet* and *King Lear*. It seems a proper moment to murmur "enough" and to return to a study of the life of the author.

Sometimes it troubles me that there are so few masterpieces in the vast ocean of literary biography that stretches between James Boswell's great *Life* of Dr. Samuel Johnson and the late Richard Ellmann's wonderful *Oscar Wilde*. Literary biography is a crucial genre, and clearly a difficult one in which to excel. The actual nature of the lives of the poets seems to have little effect upon the quality of their biographies. Everything happened to Lord Byron and nothing at all to Wallace Stevens, and yet their biographers seem equally daunted by them. But even inadequate biographies of strong writers, or of weak ones, are of immense use. I have never read a literary biography from which I have not profited, a statement I cannot make about any other genre whatsoever. And when it comes to figures who are central to us—Dante, Shakespeare, Cervantes, Montaigne, Goethe, Whitman, Tolstoi, Freud, Joyce, Kafka among them—we reach out eagerly for every scrap that the biographers have gleaned. Concerning Dante and Shakespeare we know much too little, yet when we come to Goethe and Freud, where we seem to know more than everything, we still want to know more. The death of the author, despite our current resentniks, clearly was only a momentary fad. Something vital in every authentic lover of literature responds to Emerson's battle-cry sentence: "There is no history, only biography." Beyond that there is a deeper truth, difficult to come at and requiring a lifetime to understand, which is that there is no literature, only autobiography, however mediated, however veiled, however transformed. The events of Shakespeare's life included the composition of *Hamlet,* and that act of writing was itself a crucial act of living, though we do not yet know altogether how to read so doubled an act. When an author takes up a more overtly autobiographical stance, as so many do in their youth, again we still do not know precisely how to accommodate the vexed relation between life and work. T. S. Eliot, meditating upon James Joyce, made a classic statement as to such accommodation:

> We want to know who are the originals of his characters, and what were
> the origins of his episodes, so that we may unravel the web of memory
> and invention and discover how far and in what ways the crude material
> has been transformed.

When a writer is not even covertly autobiographical, the web of memory and invention is still there, but so subtly woven that we may never unravel it. And yet we want deeply never to stop trying, and not merely because we are curious, but because each of us is caught in her own network of memory and invention. We do not always recall our inventions, and long before we age we cease to be certain of the extent to which we have invented our memories. Perhaps one motive for reading is our need to unravel our own webs. If our masters could make, from their lives, what we read, then we can be moved by them to ask: What have we made or lived in relation to what we have read? The answers may be sad, or confused, but the question is likely, implicitly, to go on being asked as long as we read. In Freudian terms, we are asking: What is it that we have repressed? What have we forgotten, unconsciously but purposively: What is it that we flee? Art, literature necessarily included, is regression in the service of the ego, according to a famous Freudian formula. I doubt the Freudian wisdom here, but indubitably it is profoundly suggestive. When we read, something in us keeps asking the equivalent of the Freudian questions: From what or whom is the author in flight, and to what earlier stages in her life is she returning, and why?

Reading, whether as an art or a pastime, has been damaged by the visual media, television in particular, and might be in some danger of extinction in the age of the computer, except that the psychic need for it continues to endure, presumably because it alone can assuage a central loneliness in elitist society. Despite all sophisticated or resentful denials, the reading of imaginative literature remains a quest to overcome the isolation of the individual consciousness. We can read for information, or entertainment, or for love of the language, but in the end we seek, in the author, the person whom we have not found, whether in ourselves or in others. In that quest, there always are elements at once aggressive and defensive, so that reading, even in childhood, is rarely free of hidden anxieties. And yet it remains one of the few activities not contaminated by an entropy of spirit. We read in hope, because we lack companionship, and the author can become the object of the most idealistic elements in our search for the wit and inventiveness we so desperately require. We read biography, not as a supplement to reading the author, but as a second, fresh attempt to understand what always seems to evade us in the work, our drive towards a kind of identity with the author.

This will-to-identity, though recently much deprecated, is a prime basis for the experience of sublimity in reading. *Hamlet* retains its unique position in the Western canon not because most readers and playgoers identify themselves with the prince, who clearly is beyond them, but rather because they find themselves again in the power of the language that represents him with such immediacy and force. Yet we know that neither language nor social energy created Hamlet. Our curiosity about Shakespeare is endless, and never will be appeased. That curiosity itself is a value, and cannot be separated from the value of *Hamlet* the tragedy, or Hamlet the literary character. It provokes us that Shakespeare the man seems so unknowable, at once everyone and no one as Borges shrewdly observes. Critics keep telling us otherwise, yet something valid in us keeps believing that we would know Hamlet better if Shakespeare's life were as fully known as the lives of Goethe and Freud, Byron and Oscar Wilde, or best of all, Dr. Samuel Johnson. Shakespeare never will have his Boswell, and Dante never will have his Richard Ellmann. How much one would give for a detailed and candid *Life of Dante* by Petrarch, or an outspoken memoir of Shakespeare by Ben Jonson! Or, in the age just past, how superb would be rival studies of one another by Hemingway and Scott Fitzgerald! But the list is endless: think of *Oscar Wilde* by Lord Alfred Douglas, or a joint biography of Shelley by Mary Godwin, Emilia Viviani, and Jane Williams. More than our insatiable desire for scandal would be satisfied. The literary rivals and the lovers of the great writers possessed perspectives we will never enjoy, and without those perspectives we dwell in some poverty in regard to the writers with whom we ourselves never can be done.

There is a sense in which imaginative literature *is* perspectivism, so that the reader is likely to be overwhelmed by the work's difficulty unless its multiple perspectives are mastered. Literary biography matters most because it is a storehouse of perspectives, frequently far surpassing any that are grasped by the particular biographer. There are relations between authors' lives and their works of kinds we have yet to discover, because our analytical instruments are not yet advanced enough to perform the necessary labor. Perhaps a novel, poem, or play is not so much a regression in the service of the ego, as it is an amalgam of *all* the Freudian mechanisms of defense, all working together for the apotheosis of the ego. Freud valued art highly, but thought that the aesthetic enterprise was no rival for psychoanalysis, unlike religion and philosophy. Clearly Freud was mistaken; his own anxieties about his indebtedness to Shakespeare helped produce the weirdness of his joining in the lunacy that argued for the Earl of Oxford as the author of Shakespeare's plays. It was Shakespeare, and not "the poets," who was there before Freud arrived at his depth psychology, and it is Shakespeare who is there still, well out ahead of psychoanalysis. We see what Freud would not see, that psychoanalysis is Shakespeare prosified and systematized. Freud is part of literature, not of "science," and the biography of Freud has the same relations to psychoanalysis as the biography of Shakespeare has to *Hamlet* and *King Lear,* if only we knew more of the life of Shakespeare.

Western literature, particularly since Shakespeare, is marked by the representation of internalized change in its characters. A literature of the ever-growing inner self is in itself a large form of biography, even though this is the biography of imaginary beings, from Hamlet to the sometimes nameless protagonists of Kafka and Beckett. Skeptics might want to argue that all literary biography concerns imaginary beings, since authors make themselves up, and every biographer gives us a creation curiously different from the same author as seen by the writer of a rival *Life.* Boswell's Johnson is not quite anyone else's Johnson, though it is now very difficult for us to disentangle the great Doctor from his gifted Scottish friend and follower. The life of the author is not merely a metaphor or a fiction, as is "the Death of the Author," but it always does contain metaphorical or fictive elements. Those elements are a part of the value of literary biography, but not the largest or the crucial part, which is the separation of the mask from the man or woman who hid behind it. James Joyce and Samuel Beckett, master and sometime disciple, were both of them enigmatic personalities, and their biographers have not, as yet, fully expounded the mystery of these contrasting natures. Beckett seems very nearly to have been a secular saint: personally disinterested, heroic in the French Resistance, as humane a person ever to have composed major fictions and dramas. Joyce, self-obsessed even as Beckett was preternaturally selfless, was the Milton of the twentieth century. Beckett was perhaps the least egoistic post-Joycean, post-Proustian, post-Kafkan of writers. Does that illuminate the problematical nature of his work, or does it simply constitute another problem? Whatever the cause, the question matters. The only death of the author that is other than literal, and that matters, is the fate only of weak writers. The strong, who become canonical, never die, which is what the canon truly is about. To be read forever is the Life of the Author.

⊠ *Introduction*

I CANNOT RECALL that any other contemporary writer of authentic eminence compares to Toni Morrison as having meditated in print, so extensively and profoundly, upon the processes of literary canon-making. One therefore ventures a canonical prophecy in regard to her work with a certain anxiety of wariness, yet of her six novels to date I greatly prefer *Song of Solomon* (1977) to the others. The success of *Beloved*, a decade later, doubtless had much to do with her Nobel Prize, and the recent *Jazz* has been extolled by H. L. Gates, Jr., our best-known African-American literary critic. Yet both *Beloved* and *Jazz* seem to me heavy with the cultural responsibilities that Morrison has assumed as the leading African-American writer since Ralph Ellison. Both novels are rather uneven, perhaps as a consequence of what I at least would regard as extraliterary pressures and considerations, admirable in themselves but not always relevant to Morrison's art as a novelist. Like Faulkner, Conrad, and Balzac, she essentially writes romance narratives that sometimes are disguised as societal analyses, though elements of fantasy tend to qualify the overt political and economic concerns. She herself insists that she be understood in the context of African-American literature, but she shares very little with Richard Wright or Zora Neale Hurston or Ellison, even though *Song of Solomon* does show traces of *Invisible Man's* effect upon her. Faulkner remains Morrison's nearest precursor for narrative stance and characterization, even as Virginia Woolf hovers as an undersong throughout Morrison's prose style.

Milkman Dead, the protagonist of *Song of Solomon*, is a true Faulknerian quester, driven by a metaphysical need for his true name, and for the transcendental folk-values that have been alienated from him because he has been "called out" of that name, as Keith Byerman observes. Milkman's search begins to find fulfillment only when he comes upon the appropriately named Circe, an aged black woman who incarnates a total rejection of all principles and standards that are not African. She sends him to his ancestral, American village, Shalimar, where initially he is resented almost as though he were wholly contaminated by the dominant white culture. Later, when he has been accepted and learns his family identity, he undergoes a metamorphosis radical enough to justify Morrison's audacity in naming her visionary crone as a Circe. There is nothing else in Morrison's work so magically strong (and indeed strongly magical) as Milkman's transformation. It is wholly persuasive, and achieves its aesthetic authority through a mythopoeic inventiveness that is independent of the moral fable that Morrison overtly seeks to tell. Milkman's obsessive intensity is like that of Sutpen or Joe Christmas or Darl Bundren, even though I suspect that Morrison meant him to resemble Ike McCaslin in "The Bear," a redeemed figure rather than a monomaniac or outcast. Morrison herself has argued that *Moby-Dick* has a hidden center in the trauma of white racism, and she knows that D. H. Lawrence preceded her in this argument. Lawrence, had he survived to read *Song of Solomon*, might have remarked that Milkman Dead is Toni Morrison's Captain Ahab, even as Sutpen was Faulkner's Ahab. The visionary novelist of *Song of Solomon* is still there in *Beloved* and *Jazz*, but is somewhat obscured by the spokesperson for her people. A romance consciousness of singular power, the story-teller and fantasist Morrison will return again, if I may risk the prophecy.

—H. B.

Toni Cade Bambara
b. 1939

TONI CADE BAMBARA was born Toni Cade on March 25, 1939, in New York City. She and her brother Walter were raised by their mother, Helen Brent Henderson Cade; her father seems to have abandoned the family shortly after her birth. Bambara attended various schools in New York and New Jersey before attending Queens College, receiving a B.A. in theatre arts and English in 1959. In that same year she won the John Golden Award for fiction from Queens College and the Pauper Press Award for nonfiction from the *Long Island Star*; she also published a short story, "Sweet Town," in *Vendome* magazine.

After graduation Bambara studied briefly at the University of Florence and the Ecole de Mime Etienne Decroux in Paris before enrolling in an American fiction program at the City College of New York, from which she received a M.A. in 1964. Both in and out of school Bambara held a wide array of positions with various organizations, such as the Colony House in Brooklyn, the Metropolitan Hospital, the Equivalency Program, the Veteran Reentry Program, the 8th Street Play Program, and the Tutorial Program at the Houston Street Public Library. These positions reflected her desire to improve social and educational conditions for the black community. In later years she has been an instructor or artist in residence at various universities, including Rutgers, Stephens College, and Spelman College.

During the 1960s Bambara continued to write short stories, which appeared in such publications as the *Massachusetts Review, Prairie Schooner,* and *Redbook*. She also pursued an interest in dance, studying at various schools (including the Katherine Dunham Dance Studio) throughout the decade.

In 1970 Bambara edited an anthology of black American writing entitled *The Black Woman*. This volume, which contained writings by Nikki Giovanni, Alice Walker, Paule Marshall, and others, was an outgrowth of her work with the SEEK program at the City College of New York. A second anthology followed in 1971, *Tales and Stories for Black Folks*. This anthology, like its predecessor, cut across lines of age and class and showed Bambara's increasing interest in personal and communal history. From an early age she was fascinated with her own family history, and in 1970 she adopted the family name Bambara when she found it scrawled on a sketchbook belonging to her great-grandmother.

In 1972 Bambara's first collection of short stories, *Gorilla, My Love*, appeared. This volume gathered most of her stories published between 1959 and 1970. The settings and characters were greatly influenced by her childhood wanderings, and a major concern of the collection is the role of black women in the family and the community. Reviewers received the collection with enthusiasm.

In 1973 Bambara went to Cuba, where she studied living and working conditions of Cuban women. She was much impressed by the power Cuban women had claimed through organization and solidarity. Bambara next visited Vietnam and finally landed in Atlanta, where she settled with her daughter Karma. Once again she became active in local affairs, as a founding member of the Southern Collective of African-American Writers and the Neighborhood Cultural Arts Center.

The Sea Birds Are Still Alive (1977), Bambara's second collection of stories, is marked by her interest in community affairs. The settings also move at times to the rural South and also overseas. Bambara was somewhat disappointed with the collection, and she promptly began work on a novel; *The Salt Eaters* appeared in 1980. Set in Georgia, the novel examines the workings of the black community and its relationship to other minority groups.

Most recently, Bambara has written for film and television, writing a number of screenplays for documentaries on black issues as well as a film adaptation of Toni Morrison's novel *Tar Baby* (1984). Three of her own short stories have been adapted as films.

▩ *Critical Extracts*

JUNE JORDAN   In *Gorilla, My Love*, Toni Cade Bambara sure have made it wonderfully clear where her affections truthsay/lie and signify, and how she have the altogether craft, the, well, the mastery, in fact, to snatch us happy and believing right into the heart of things: Black heart of Black things ordinary, strange, amazing, crazy, typical, peculiar, everyday on streets on city roof or countrified in fields and flower gardens by the wood porch of her dynamic, Granddaddy Cain. ⟨. . .⟩

For me, *Gorilla, My Love* standing up right next to Richard Wright's *Uncle Tom's Children*. No lie; except my copy moving around so much so fast among my friends who pass it on that, see, it be hard to hold things up and draw what you might call comparisons.

But let me try one minute; do you/can you remember how *Uncle Tom's Children* made you know and grieve and understand a new way? (Blew my mind, entirely.) Well, here is *Gorilla, My Love*, ranging through the tall tale, kitchen skinny, photographic/phonographic real, and also through the mythopoeic, dreamer, facts-be-facts, material of our experience and it is beautiful, this ranging, this embrace by Sister Toni Cade Bambara: she is teaching beautiful plus make you laugh out loud. Or hurt. As hard as hurt can be to handle when that's what it's about ⟨. . .⟩

⟨. . .⟩ And when she does that special thing she does, that thing of speaking as a Black child probably talk and think and turn and jump, distinct from grown-up people, then I can't think of no one near to how she does that; she be doing it so persuasive you rejuvenated down to nine-years-old and digging it, the world, from there. But check it out; go get *Gorilla, My Love*: it's some natural sugar, overdue.

June Jordan, [Review of *Gorilla, My Love*], *Black World* 22, No. 9 (July 1973): 80

JOHN WIDEMAN The novel's ⟨*The Salt Eaters*⟩ strengths are related to its weaknesses. Velma's trouble is obviously more than an individual neurosis, but how well do we get to know *her*, her plight, its resolution? Luminous moments imprint Velma's reality on the reader's consciousness, but do the scattered moments ultimately fuse, coalesce, so that we know and care who Velma is? Yes, we're all on this contaminated, exploited earth together and will have to learn to eat a lot of salt together before things get better, if they ever do, but does this truth justify the novelist's tendency to include all the woes besetting us? Digressions may be a way to achieve a panoramic, comprehensive overview, but they stretch the fabric of the narrative dangerously thin. The baroque convolutions of individual sentences, the proliferations of character and incident sometimes seem forced, detracting from the forward flow of the book.

Yet this demanding, haunting, funny, scary novel is persuasive. The words that open the book, the words Minnie Ransom addresses to Velma Henry as the two women perch on stools in the Southwestern Community Infirmary—"Are you sure, sweetheart, that you want to be well?"—ask a question of all of us. Getting well entails risk, honesty, a commitment to struggle, a collective effort that Toni Cade Bambara documents with the voices and lives of the Southwest Community's people. She makes us understand that what is at stake in Velma Henry's journey back to health is not only one woman's life but the survival of the planet: "tap the brain for any knowledge of initiation rites lying dormant there, recognizing that life depended on it, that initiation was the beginning of transformation and that the ecology of the self, the tribe, the species, the earth depended on just that."

John Wideman, "The Healing of Velma Henry," *New York Times Book Review*, 1 June 1980, p. 28

TONI MORRISON   Toni Cade Bambara has written two collections of short stories and one novel. She is a New Yorker, born and educated in that city with an intimate and fearless knowledge of it, and although the tone of most of her stories is celebratory, full of bravura, joyfully survivalist, the principal fear and grief of her characters is the betrayal of an adult who has abandoned not the role of providing for, but the role of advisor, competent protector. Of the sixteen stories in *Gorilla, My Love*, only two stories cannot fit that description. And one of the two, "The Survivor," describes a girl going to the country for help, succor, and regeneration at the hands of an elderly aunt who lives up to the demands of an ancestor exactly. ⟨. . .⟩

In "The Survivor," a rural story, Jewel, pregnant and reeling from an unfortunate marriage, has traveled from New York to her grandmother in a small town. When they first meet they stand in a field: "Miss Candy dainty but sinewy and solid, never hid from weather of any kind." And when she stoops to touch some roots, remarking on the need for rain, she "traced the travels of the tree roots barely bulging beneath the bristly grass. 'A good woman does not rot,' she said on her haunches like some ancient sage.'" Jewel has gone there because

> family ties [are] no longer knitted close and there was no one to
> say let's get our wagons in a circle when someone was in a crisis.

So she'd come to M'Dear, Miss Candy, the last of that generation who believed in sustaining.

In her novel, *The Salt Eaters,* the theme is totally explicated. A would-be suicide is literally and metaphorically healed by the ancestor: the witch woman, the spiritual sage, the one who asks of this oh so contemporary and oh so urban daughter of the sixties, "Are you sure you want to be well?" Here is the village, its values, its resources, its determination not to live, as Stevie Wonder has put it, "just enough for the city," and its requisites for survival only. The village is determined to flourish as well, and it is that factor that makes it possible for Velma to rise from the ancestor's shawl and drop it to the floor "like a cocoon."

Toni Morrison, "City Limits, Village Values: Concepts of the Neighborhood in Black Fiction," *Literature and the Urban Experience: Essays on the City and Literature,* ed. Michael C. Jaye and Ann Chalmers Watts (New Brunswick, NJ: Rutgers University Press, 1981), pp. 40–41

CLAUDIA TATE   C.T.: What determines your responsibility to yourself and to your audience?

BAMBARA: I start with the recognition that we are at war, and that war is not simply a hot debate between the capitalist camp and the socialist camp over which economic/political/social arrangement will have hegemony in the world. It's not just the battle over turf and who has the right to utilize resources for whomsoever's benefit. The war is also being fought over the truth: what is the truth about human nature, about the human potential? My responsibility to myself, my neighbors, my family and the human family is to try to tell the truth. That ain't easy. There are so few truth-speaking traditions in this society in which the myth of "Western civilization" has claimed the allegiance of so many. We have rarely been encouraged and equipped to appreciate the fact that the truth works, that it releases the Spirit and that it is a joyous thing. We live in a part of the world, for example, that equates criticism with assault, that equates social responsibility with naive idealism, that defines the unrelenting pursuit of knowledge and wisdom as fanaticism.

I do not think that literature is *the* primary instrument for social transformation, but I do think it has potency. So I work to tell the truth about people's lives; I work to celebrate struggle, to applaud the tradition of struggle in our community, to bring to center stage all those characters, just ordinary folks on the block, who've been waiting in the wings, characters we thought we had to ignore because they weren't pimp-flashy or hustler-slick or because they didn't fit easily into previously acceptable modes or stock types. I want to lift up some usable truths—like the fact that the simple act of cornrowing one's hair is radical in a society that defines beauty as blonde tresses blowing in the wind; that staying centered in the best of one's own cultural tradition is hip, is sane, is perfectly fine despite all claims to universality-through-Anglo-Saxonizing and other madnesses.

It would be dishonest, though, to end my comments there. First and foremost I write for myself. Writing has been for a long time my major tool for self-instruction and self-development. I try to stay honest through pencil and paper. I run off at the mouth a lot. I've a penchant for flamboyant performance. I exaggerate to the point of hysteria. I cannot always be trusted with my mouth open. But when I sit down with the notebooks, I am absolutely serious about what I see, sense, know. I write for the same reason I keep track of my dreams, for the same reason I meditate and practice being still—to stay in touch with me and not let too much slip by me. We're about building a nation; the inner nation needs some building, too. I would be writing whether there were a publishing industry or not, whether there were presses or not, whether there were markets or not.

Claudia Tate, "Toni Cade Bambara," *Black Women Writers at Work* (New York: Continuum, 1983), pp. 17–18

RUTH ELIZABETH BURKS   ⟨. . .⟩ while Bambara uses language to capture the speech patterns of the characters she idiomatically places in their time and space, Bambara eschews language, words, rhetoric, as the modus operandi for the people to attain their freedom. For Bambara, an innate spirituality, almost mystical in nature, must be endemic to the people if they are to have success. Her works juxtapose the inadequacy of language and the powers of the spirit, which needs no words to spread its light among the masses.

Words are only barriers to communication, here, in Bambara's first collection of short stories, *Gorilla, My Love*; a smile, a howl, a touch, a look, a hum, are the instruments with which her characters play in an attempt to communicate their joy, frustration, pain, confusion, and alienation.

These stories are all female ones, almost sung by Bambara in a first-person narrative voice reminiscent of the Negro spirituals with their strongly marked rhythms and highly graphic descriptions. Standard English is not so much put aside as displaced by constant repetition, a repetition bringing to mind the speech habits of a child who in just learning language constantly repeats himself, not fully convinced that language alone can communicate those needs and feelings so recently and so effectively expressed in tears and smiles.

And the childlike voices seem right here, and belong here, for each story is a vernal one—even those told by women who have long ceased to be girls—because each story is of initiation, of baptism, where the narrator is schooled in the ways of a world often cruel, more often disinterested, and rarely fair. ⟨. . .⟩

The paradoxical nature of Bambara's fictions manifests itself again when one realizes that, although each of these stories is narrated by a female, the pivotal character is male. Even in "The Lesson," where an individual male's action does not provoke the narration of the tale, "the man" as entity strikes the discordant note in the soul of a young Black girl, when a community worker forces her to visit F. A. O. Schwarz and to see with her own eyes what words cannot communicate—the needless oppression of her people by the white man.

Ruth Elizabeth Burks, "From Baptism to Resurrection: Toni Cade Bambara and the Incongruity of Language," *Black Women Writers (1950–1980): A Critical Evaluation*, ed. Mari Evans (New York: Anchor Books/Doubleday, 1984), pp. 49–51

KEITH E. BYERMAN   Toni Cade Bambara's stories focus on the ways gender roles, ideology, family, and community condition the experiences of black women. She portrays initiation as a painful but frequently rewarding ritual. Like ⟨James Alan⟩ McPherson, she seeks to take her characters from a state of certainty to a state of doubt, but unlike him, she does not so clearly define the conventions of that certainty. She implies that the realm of woman is more organic and less overtly confrontational than that of man. Nonetheless, a dialectic is clearly at work, one that is in some ways more complex since it adds to generational, racial, and cultural oppositions the polarity of male-female. While Bambara says that she is "much more concerned with the caring that lies beneath the antagonisms between black men and black women," she does repeatedly examine the nature of those antagonisms. Moreover, like ⟨Ernest J.⟩ Gaines and McPherson, she finds in folk material the means for her characters to resist fixed, dehumanizing identities, whether sexual, racial, or cultural. And also like these male writers, she tends to leave her characters at the edge of some new experience rather than with a sense of the completion of action and thus the resolution of oppositions.

"My Man Bovanne," the initial story in *Gorilla, My Love* (1972), links sexual and ideological conflicts. It tells the story of Hazel, a middle-aged black woman whose behavior scandalizes her ideologically correct children:

> "And you going to be standing there with your boobs out and that wig on your head and that hem up to your ass. And people'll say, 'Ain't that the horny bitch that was grindin with the blind dude?'
>
> "And then there's the drinkin. Mama, you know you can't drink cause next thing you know you be laughin loud and carryin on," and he grab another finger for the loudness. "And then there's the dancin. You been tattooed on the man for four records straight and slow draggin even on the fast numbers. How you think that look for a woman your age?"

The children, in their ideological purity, seek to eliminate the individuality and freedom of the mother. They implicitly fix the definitions of *mother* and *black* so as to satisfy the necessities of their political efforts. They justify those efforts in the name of "the people," and thus public recognition of the "grass roots," as Hazel calls herself, is mandatory. But the reality of those grass roots must be suppressed if the ideological system is to function efficiently. They rationalize such suppression as necessary to the struggle against the oppressor, the white social structure. Paradoxically, the children must control the mother because they see her as fitting the white society's stereotype of the licentious, irresponsible black woman. In the place of that image they would impose the image of the serious, puritanical mother. As Hazel understands, either imposition is a form of repression: "Felt just like the police got hold to me."

Keith E. Byerman, "Women's Blues: The Fiction of Toni Cade Bambara and Alice Walker," *Fingering the Jagged Grain: Tradition and Form in Recent Black Fiction* (Athens: University of Georgia Press, 1985), pp. 105–6

GLORIA T. HULL   ⟨In *The Salt Eaters*⟩ Bambara struggles with the problem of finding words and ways to communicate these forms of knowledge for which we, as yet, have no adequate vocabulary. Readers most versed in these spiritual arts (and in this new age, that number is growing) understand the work most deeply. The fact that The Master's Mind wears yellow and white works on a generally symbolic level, but resonates on other frequencies if one considers that yellow is the hue of intellect and a saint's nimbus and that white is the harmonious blending of all colors. The basic meaning of the number twelve will be easily grasped; but everyone will not know to reduce the year 1871 (when the Infirmary was built) and the 107 years it has been standing to their root "8," which signifies worldly involvement and regeneration. Then, there is Cleotus Brown, "The Hermit." Porter is planning to study with him when he is killed; Doc Serge directs Butch to him for answers to his impertinent questions; he himself appears incognito/ in disguise to Jan (with Ruby), eerily reminding her of something she should/ does know but cannot quite remember. He is the arcane figure from the Tarot (which Jan reads), who symbolizes the right, initiatory path to real knowledge and truth. These three slight examples suggest how the entire novel can be annotated in this manner. Integrally related here, too, are the recurring symbols of mud, blood, salt, circles, mirrors, sight, water (rain), fire, snakes, and serpents.

Devising a vocabulary and symbology for communicating spiritual matters is only one aspect of Bambara's general quest for an adequate language and structure. She says: "I'm just trying to tell the truth and I think in order to do that we will have to invent, in addition to new forms, new modes and new idioms." The process is an arduous one, beginning with the word, the first unit of meaning:

> I'm trying to break words and get at the bones, deal with symbols
> as though they were atoms. I'm trying to find out not only how a
> word gains its meaning, but how a word gains its power.

It is further manifested in the overall composition of the book, Bambara's "avoidance of a linear thing in favor of a kind of jazz suite." Predictably, this approach results in a novel of extraordinary brilliance and density that swirls the reader through multiple layers of sound and sense.

The literal plot, which takes place in less than two hours, is almost negligible. However, while Velma and Minnie rock on their stools, other characters are proceeding with their lives. We follow first one and then another of them through the twelve chapters of the book. The effect is to recreate the discretely random, yet touching, simultaneity of everyday existence. A unifying focus—something shared in common by everyone— is the annual spring festival of celebration and rebirth. This basic structure, though, is complicated further by the near-seamless weaving in of flashbacks, flashwords, dreams, and visions.

> Gloria T. Hull, " 'What It Is I Think She's Doing Anyhow': A Reading of Toni Cade Bambara's *The Salt Eaters*," *Conjuring: Black Women, Fiction, and Literary Tradition*, ed. Marjorie Pryse and Hortense J. Spillers (Bloomington: Indiana University Press, 1985), pp. 220–21

ELLIOTT BUTLER-EVANS   The nationalist-feminist ideology in *Seabirds* is not solely generated by depictions of characters. It is reinforced by narrative texture and form. As a body of race- and gender-specific narratives, these stories draw on various Afro-American cultural practices—the oral storytelling tradition, the use of folklore, and the reinscription of Afro-American music forms. The incorporation of these practices is evident in the narrative structure, point of view, and semiotic texture of the stories.

Bambara has spoken and written extensively on the influence of Afro-American music on her work. What is most striking about her appropriation of jazz in *Seabirds*, however, is its role in emphasizing and reinforcing the ideology of the text. Jazz performances generally begin with a statement of theme, are followed by improvisations or extreme variations, and conclude with reiteration and resolution. An analogous pattern structures each of the stories in this collection. In "The Apprentice," for example, the narrative begins with the narrator's anxiety about her mission, moves to an encounter between a young Black man and a white policeman, then moves to a senior citizen's complex, and finally to a Black restaurant. It then refocuses on the narrator's concerns and reveals her resolution to remain committed to political engagement. In "Witchbird," each fleeting reflection of Honey's extended blues solo constitutes a comment on some aspect of her life—her career, her past relationships with men, and her overall perception of herself. And in "Christmas Eve at Johnson's Drugs N Goods," Candy begins by reflecting on Christmas and a possible visit from her father, moves on to individual episodes largely focused on characterizations of the store's customers, and concludes with accepting Obatale's invitation to a Kwanza celebration.

This mode of narration serves a significant ideological function. In its highlighting and summarizing, as well as its glossing over certain episodes, the text produces its ideological content largely through clusters of events. Hence, in "Broken Field Running," the renaming process by which Black children discard their "slave names" and appropriate African names to define themselves with the context of Black culture, the police harassment symbolized by the police car cruising in the Black community, and the destructive effect of ghetto life depicted in the criminal activities of Black males form a montage, a cluster of images each one of which might be said to encode a particular aspect of ideology. 〈. . .〉

Narrative structure and perspective are further complemented by the semiotic texture, or strategies of sign production, that inform the ideological context of the work. Since the major thrust of the collection is the awakening of cultural nationalist and feminist consciousness, clusters of signs keep the text grounded in those ideologies. The linguistic subcode itself, a reified construction of "Black English," becomes the sign of difference from the dominant culture and unity with the alternative Black community.

Elliott Butler-Evans, *Race, Gender, and Desire: Narrative Strategies in the Fiction of Toni Cade Bambara, Toni Morrison, and Alice Walker* (Philadelphia: Temple University Press, 1989), pp. 119–21

MARTHA M. VERTREACE   Bambara's stories present a decided emphasis on the centrality of community. Many writers concentrate so specifically on character development or plot line that community seems merely a foil against which the characters react. For Bambara the community becomes essential as a locus for growth, not simply as a source of narrative tension. Thus, her characters and community do a circle dance around and within each other as learning and growth occur.

Bambara's women learn how to handle themselves within the divergent, often conflicting, strata that compose their communities. Such learning does not come easily; hard lessons result from hard knocks. Nevertheless, the women do not merely endure; they prevail, emerging from these situations more aware of their personal identities and of their potential for further self-actualization. More important, they guide others to achieve such awareness.

Bambara posits learning as purposeful, geared toward personal and societal change. Consequently, the identities into which her characters grow envision change as both necessary and possible, understanding that they themselves play a major part in bringing about that change. This idea approximates the nature of learning described in Paulo Freire's *Pedagogy of the Oppressed*, in which he decries the "banking concept," wherein education becomes "an act of depositing, in which the students are the depositories and the teacher is the depositor." Oppressive situations define the learner as profoundly ignorant, not possessing valuable insights for communal sharing.

Although many of Bambara's stories converge on the school setting as the place of learning in formal patterns, she liberates such settings to admit and encourage community involvement and ownership. Learning then influences societal liberation and self-determination. These stories describe learning as the process of problem solving, which induces a deepening sense of self, Freire's "intentionality."

> Martha M. Vertreace, "Toni Cade Bambara: The Dance of Character and Community," *American Women Writing Fiction: Memory, Identity, Family, Space*, ed. Mickey Pearlman (Lexington: University Press of Kentucky, 1989), pp. 155–56

JACQUELINE DE WEEVER   The "psychic set," the psychological territory of both protagonists and antagonists, becomes very important for understanding the metaphors used, and determines, in the majority of cases, the outcomes of the plots ⟨in black women's fiction⟩. The images that build the metaphors are culled from nature, from creatures of the earth in most cases, with creatures of the air—the bird for example— used occasionally. The capacity of metaphor to illuminate "untranslatable experiences" is startlingly borne out in the metaphors of insects and animals. ⟨. . .⟩

Toni Cade Bambara uses the spider metaphor for describing Minnie Ransom, the healer who presides over the birth of Velma's sanity at the Southwest Community Infirmary in a ritual of healing:

> Minnie Ransom, the legendary spinster of Claybourne, Georgia, spinning out a song, drawing her of all people up. . . . Velma caught, caught up, in the weave of the song Minnie was

humming, of the shawl, of the threads, of the silvery tendrils that extended from the healer's neck and hands disappeared into the sheen of the sunlight.

As the embodiment of the power that transforms Velma, Minnie is a "spinster," one who spins. Thus the first sentence of the passage establishes her function in the novel. The sustained metaphor of the spider represents Minnie's wisdom, derived from her spirit guide, an old conjure woman named Karen Wilder. Minnie is a kind of shaman, meditating between the visible and invisible forces that have created the tensions in Velma's soul. In close touch with her spirit-guide, Minnie is a medial woman; she calls forth or evokes the inner spirit. The feminist theologian Mary Daly sees the work of woman as spinster thus: "Spinsters spin and weave, mending and creating unity of consciousness. In doing so we spin through and beyond the realm of multiple split unconsciousness. In concealed workshops, Spinsters unsnarl, unknot, untie, unweave. We knit, knot, interlace, entwine, whirl, and twirl."

Minnie is such a spinster. It is her job to unravel the snakes in Velma's head, to bring her back to lucidity. Nor Hall writes that "it is the medial woman's function to be of assistance in time of difficult passage. As midwife to the psyche she is constellated in 'emergency' situations where a spirit, a song, an alternative, a new being is emerging. . . . She has not only the power to inspire but also the power to intoxicate or induce stupor and sleep." Velma sinks into a kind of sleep as her state begins to change. Minnie says:

> "You'll have to choose, sweetheart. Choose you own cure."
> "Choose?" Sleepriding and sleeptalking, not sure where she was, Velma felt herself sinking.

The depiction of Minnie as a spider not only delineates her function and relationship to Velma in her madness but also the possibility of Velma's cure. And where the spider hangs, the snake waits. As Velma slowly becomes aware of the Minnie the spinster, she who spins, she also sees the bandages "unraveled and curled at the foot of the stool like a sleeping snake." By linking spider and snake at the beginning of the work, Bambara establishes a therapeutic connection, maintained throughout, between Minnie and the patient who has snakes in her head. The diverse meanings elicited by the emblem of the spider and snake show the complexity of the symbol. 〈Toni〉 Morrison uses it to depict the differences in the essences of the two friends in the life paths they choose, while Bambara shows the interdependence of Minnie and Velma as they face each other as healer and patient. Minnie's spirit-guide says to her: "You and that gal on the stool cut from the same cloth."

Jacqueline de Weever, *Mythmaking and Metaphor in Black Women's Fiction* (New York: St. Martin's Press, 1992), pp. 62, 82–83

Bibliography

The Black Woman: An Anthology (editor). 1970.

Tales and Stories for Black Folks (editor). 1971.

Gorilla, My Love. 1972.

The Sea Birds Are Still Alive: Collected Stories. 1977.

The Salt Eaters. 1980.

Raymond's Run. 1990.

Daughters of the Dust: The Making of an African American Woman's Film (with Julie Dash and bell hooks). 1992.

Samuel R. Delany

b. 1942

SAMUEL RAY DELANY, JR., was born in New York City on April 1, 1942, the son of Samuel R. Delany, a funeral director, and Margaret Boyd Carey Delany, a library clerk. He sporadically attended City College (now part of the City University of New York) in 1960 and in 1962–63, and in 1961 he married his high school girlfriend Marilyn Hacker, with whom he had a daughter. That same year he wrote *The Jewels of Aptor* (1962), the first of a string of novels that earned him an admiring readership in the science fiction community. In the process, he became the first important black science fiction writer.

After producing the epic but unextraordinary trilogy *The Fall of the Towers* (*Captives of the Flame*, 1963; *The Towers of Toron*, 1964; *City of a Thousand Suns*, 1965), Delany progressed to stake out his own literary territory. Books like *The Ballad of Beta-2* (1965), *Empire Star* (1966), and the Nebula Award–winning novels *Babel-17* (1966) and *The Einstein Intersection* (1967) incorporated new intellectual concerns into science fiction, such as linguistic theory and structuralist literary analysis. *Nova* (1968) was one of the central works of science fiction's New Wave, infusing the stuff of space opera with new mythopoeic sophistication.

While laboring over his next SF novel, Delaney published the short story collection *Driftglass* (1971) and the pornographic *The Tides of Lust* (1973). In 1970 and 1971 he edited the *QUARK* anthology series with Hacker, who had become a celebrated poet. Delany and Hacker were separated in 1974; he has since identified himself as gay. The long-awaited *Dhalgren* appeared in 1975. This immense experimental novel aroused a storm of controversy over its dense style and enigmatic narrative; it became Delany's first mainstream best-seller. *Triton* (1976), the story cycle *Tales of Nevèryon* (1979) and its sequel *Neveryóna* (1983), and *Stars in My Pocket Like Grains of Sand* (1984) confirmed and furthered Delany's literary reputation.

In recent years Delany has turned to the writing of poststructuralist criticism, including *The Jewel-Hinged Jaw: Notes on the Language of Science*

Fiction (1977), *The American Shore* (1978), and *Starboard Wine: More Notes on the Language of Science Fiction* (1984). He has also written two memoirs, *Heavenly Breakfast* (1979) and *The Motion of Light in Water* (1988). He taught at the State University of New York in Buffalo in 1975, was a senior fellow of the Center for Twentieth Century Studies in 1977, and in 1987 was a senior fellow at the Society for the Humanities at Cornell University. Since 1988 he has been professor of comparative literature at the University of Massachusetts at Amherst. He lives in New York City.

◈ *Critical Extracts*

SANDRA MEISEL   Samuel R. Delany is one of the pre-eminent mythopoets in speculative fiction today. Nowhere has he used myth with more originality than in his latest novel *Nova*. He also applies traditional mythologies in a distinctive way. He is not directly retelling a particular myth like C. S. Lewis's *Till We Have Faces*, nor faithfully transposing like Cordwainer Smith's Instrumentality stories, nor borrowing images like Roger Zelazny's *Lord of Light*, nor even reassembling mythic elements into a new linear story like Poul Anderson's *Broken Sword*. Instead Delany treats myth as "meta-communication." Intense concern about the practice and theory of communication pervades all his work. The object of communication—and therefore of all art—is the reconciliation of divergent perceptions into one vision shared by artist and audience. Not surprisingly Delany's paramount myth is the harmony of opposites.

In *The Einstein Intersection* Delany maintains that myths need not be eternally recapitulated; therefore, he never hesitates to use conflicting correspondences simultaneously or construct fresh patterns. His fondness for perplexing symmetries is amply displayed in *Nova*, a novel as maddeningly fluid, elusive, and complex as its Indian and Celtic sources.

The theme of *Nova* is power—physical, social, political, economic, artistic, intellectual, sexual—as *Babel-17*'s theme is communication. All Delany's novels are quests. *Nova* is based on the Quest par excellence, the legend of the Holy Grail. He stresses his model repeatedly, but the obscurity of some of his referents may unduly puzzle the reader. The style as well as the substance of his mythmaking needs elucidation.

The Grail mythos is not just one component of the Matter of Britain; it is an assemblage of fertility motifs related as an initiatory scenario. This blend of extremely ancient Sumero-Semite and Indo-European elements springs from the very sources of Western civilization. Beyond its specifically Christian associations with the Last Supper and the Crucifixion in the Arthurian cycle, the Holy Grail symbolizes the Source of Life/Grace/Power. To seek the Grail is to seek the ultimate experience of reality and to attain complete fullness of being. The specific task of the Grail quester is to restore the Wasteland, ravaged by the incapacity of its King.

In this novel the quest for the Grail is a quest for an Illyrion-bearing nova. Illyrion, the collective name for a series of extraordinarily rare superheavy elements, is the galaxy's fundamental power source. The "psychophysics" of this "heterotropic" substance straddles a deliberately obscure line between mysticism and sober scientific explanation. However, Delany departs from tradition in motives and time sequence. Revengeful quester Lorq Von Ray fights to *avert* the wasting of his part of the galaxy by breaking an industrial monopoly. (Contemporary galactic culture also seems sterile.) After initial dislocations his drastic increase of the Illyrion supply will inaugurate a new era of abundance and unified culture.

Sandra Meisel, "Samuel R. Delany's Use of Myth in *Nova*," *Extrapolation* 12, No. 2 (May 1971): 86–87

GERALD JONAS *Dhalgren*, by Samuel R. Delany is the long-awaited major novel by a writer who won four Nebula Awards in the 1960's and who was undoubtedly the most interesting member of that group of S.F. mavericks known collectively as the New Wave. His last novel appeared in 1968. Since then, by all accounts, he has been hard at work on a truly big book, his magnum opus. In some S.F. circles, Delany's project has been treated as the equivalent of Norman Mailer's self-touted major novel—the book that Mailer insists will prove to the world that he belongs in the same room with Mr. Tolstoi and Mr. Dostoevsky.

It takes a writer of unusual gifts to make a work-in-progress seem more interesting than most published novels. The world is still waiting for Mailer's big one. Delany, at the age of 32, has now delivered. The cover copy of *Dhalgren* includes the tag: "Bantam Science Fiction." But from the first page, Delany lets the reader know that his ambitions extend even beyond challenging Mr. Wells and Mr. Verne.

Dhalgren is 879 pages long. Its form is unmistakably circular. The first words in the book—"to wound the autumnal city"—seem to be the end of a sentence, and the last words of the book—"I have come to"—seem to be the beginning of the same sentence. This obvious echo of *Finnegans Wake* is both daring and defensible. It is Delany's way of flagging his intent, of proclaiming the standards he wishes to be judged by. Among science fiction fans, his book is bound to set off a new round of that interminable debate over what is S.F. and what isn't S.F. Delany himself is on record as preferring the label "speculative fiction."

One thing is certain: *Dhalgren* is not a conventional novel, whether considered in terms of S.F. or the mainstream. But since a great deal of science fiction falls into the sub-category of "space opera"—callow adventure stories that use outer space and the far future as convenient backdrops—perhaps *Dhalgren* can best be classified as a "space-time opera." If the book can be said to be *about* anything, it is about nothing less than the nature of reality.

> Gerald Jonas, [Review of *Dhalgren*], *New York Times Book Review*, 12 February 1975, pp. 27–28

ROBERT SCHOLES and ERIC S. RABKIN   Samuel R. Delany (b. 1942) grew up in New York and attended the Bronx High School of Science. He is something of a prodigy and a polymath as well as a very prolific witer. His first work of any size was of considerable size, three volumes, and was completed by early 1964, when he was barely over twenty-one years old. (*The Jewels of Aptor*, 1962, is a short novel written even earlier.) His *Fall of the Towers* trilogy leans toward Sword and Sorcery. But in *Babel-17*, which won a Nebula Award from the Science Fiction Writers in 1966, Delany used his considerable knowledge of linguistics and semiotics to write a novel about language and communication. Though the story has elements of whirlwind adventure and exotic decor in the ⟨Alfred⟩ Bester manner, the attention to language and nonverbal communication is Delany's own. In particular, the implications of a character being conditioned to speak in a computer language which lacks the pronouns "I" and "you" are worked out with ingenuity and emotional power. *The Einstein Intersection*

(1967, another Nebula) was in the pseudo-mythic mode favored by Zelazny, but with the insertion of fragments from the author's journal among other epigraffiti to the chapters. Strange, in a work of science fiction, to encounter the breaking of illusion, to find the author, a young, black American discussing this task of writing the book while on a Grand Tour of the Mediterranean world. In *Nova* (1968) Delany set out deliberately to pay homage to Bester by imitating *The Stars My Destination*, but again with features that made the work his own. Where Bester had introduced elements from Blake's romantic poetry and Rimbaud's derangement of the senses, Delany gives us the modern story of a young man learning how to be the writer who can write the story we are reading. As *Babel-17* was about communication, *Nova* is about art. In both these excellent novels, the protagonists are artists. Rydra Wong of *Babel-17* is a poet as well as a cryptographer, and the two young men through whose eyes we follow the adventures of Captain Von Ray in *Nova* are a prodigious note-taker who wants to write an old-fashioned novel and an almost instinctive performer on the "sensory-syrinx," which is a kind of musical instrument that projects images that are apprehensible by human sight, sound, and smell. Attached to the physical adventures of Von Ray are the intellectual and emotional adventures of the two artists, whose attempts to understand one another make a kind of allegory of the growth of a literary artist, who needs the spontaneity of "the Mouse" and the thoughtfulness and learning of Katin to do his work properly. In *Babel-17* and *Nova*, Delany showed that he could tell a rousing popular adventure story in the Bester manner, introducing serious questions of his own—a considerable achievement. But he was not content to rest there. ⟨. . .⟩

His latest novel, *Triton* (1976), is subtitled "An Ambiguous Heterotopia"—which is an oblique reference to the subtitle of Le Guin's *The Dispossessed*; "An Ambiguous Utopia." *Triton* is closer to traditional science fiction than *Dhalgren* was, in that it is set clearly in a future, on a satellite of Neptune, and involves the examination of alternatives to the social structures we all know. But it is in no way a retreat from Delany's progress toward his own vision. His characters are richer, more human, than ever, more individualized and less mythic, and above all freer and more responsible than ever. This, too, is a story about communication, and about love, and it is more somber and more moving than Delany's pre-*Dhalgren* work. The protagonist, Brom Helstrom, has problems loving and communicating—and nothing, including a complete change of sex, changes the problems. The novel is richly documented, presenting its future society with great solidity, and raising important questions about the nature of sexuality and sex roles among many other things. It is an impressive addition to an impressive career, by a writer still under thirty-five when it was published. Though entirely unique as a writer, Delany's ability to combine formal experiment with social vision makes his work a perfect example of what people ought to mean when they speak of a New Wave of science fiction.

Robert Scholes and Eric S. Rabkin, *Science Fiction: History, Science, Vision* (New York: Oxford University Press, 1977), pp. 94–96

PATRICK PARRINDER   These books ⟨*The Jewel-Hinged Jaw* and *The American Shore*⟩—as the author warns prospective readers—are not introductions to their subject. Nor are they easy to introduce to those who do not yet know them. Intricate, uneven, often infuriating, and at the same time highly perceptive, Delany's criticism demands the fullest attention of its readers. As a critic-novelist of SF, he subsumes and goes beyond the two modes of critical discourse that have best served the genre in the past: the unlocking of a few pearls from the hoard of the writer's wisdom (in the manner of Heinlein or Le Guin), and the impassioned defense of the higher reaches of the SF ghetto from the hordes below (in the manner of "Atheling" ⟨James Blish⟩ or Damon Knight). One does not readily imagine those writers giving their days to the invention of new critical terminology and their nights to the study of Parisian semiotics. Delany, however, is an avowed theoretician for whom the critical activity is as arduous and intricate as a process of scientific discovery. This is not to say that he is much concerned with the accumulation of knowledge about the literary history and cartography of SF, which has played so large a part in the study of the genre by academics trained outside it. If the process of scholarship is like the building of some vast pyramid—in which far more workers are needed around the base than can ever aspire to the construction of the apex—Delany's concern is more with the elaboration of a series of prisms, whose main property is that they refract and resolve the light played upon them from outside. Not all his prisms have equal refractive powers, yet to have looked into them is to have glimpsed some new and dazzling configurations in the SF he discusses.

The Jewel-Hinged Jaw is a retrospective collection of essays, some of which (such as the classic "About 5,750 Words") will be already familiar to *Science-*

Fiction Studies readers. The essays, however, have all been slightly revised, and the longest and most forceful of them—an examination of Le Guin's *The Dispossessed*, 〈. . .〉, appears for the first time. *The American Shore* is a prolonged sequence of meditations on and around a single SF story, "Angouleme," from the *334* series by Thomas M. Disch. The format of this volume is indebted to Barthes' *S/Z*, though Delany artfully hints that its predecessors might also include Nabokov's *Pale Fire*. Still earlier precedents might be found in James Joyce, and Delany seems to envisage the kind of intense, pedantic scrutiny that present-day Joyceans bring to the text of *Finnegans Wake* as a viable method for SF studies. *The American Shore* is a painstaking and praiseworthy demonstration of such a critical method, which does, however, put severe constraints on a free-ranging intelligence such as Delany's. His best essays, in *The Jewel-Hinged Jaw*, are those in which he begins with large questions rather than small textual units, and is able to play the hare as well as the academic tortoise.

Patrick Parrinder, "Delany Inspects the World Beast," *Science-Fiction Studies* 6, No. 3 (November 1979): 337

SETH McEVOY   What is *Dhalgren*'s story then?

If we ignore some of the side questions, the story is quite simple: a young man enters a city somewhere in the American midwest during the mid 1970's. Some kind of unknown disaster has affected the city, and most of the people of the city have gone elsewhere.

The young man cannot remember his own name or much about himself, but he is given the name Kid by one of the first people he meets. He then encounters many other people in the city and learns how the people there are coping with the changes that have happened in the city as a result of the disaster. The Kid is a writer, and he becomes the leader of the Scorpions, a gang who runs through the city doing, essentially, what they want. He becomes their leader, not because he is a writer, but because he can lead. The Kid becomes a celebrity in the city when his book of poetry is published, and then, the Kid leaves the city.

One cannot be sure of the eventual outcome because the book does not end. It does not matter for this book is about the daily events of life, not the final outcomes. What excites the reader who likes *Dhalgren* is the *way* the Kid and other characters act. This manner of action can be summarized in one word: freedom. ⟨. . .⟩

What is different about *Dhalgren* is not the theme, but the way of depicting the theme. In terms that do apply, Delany had "let it all hang out." Instead of having a Jon Koshar questing for political and emotional freedom, one now has a Kid who is questing for total freedom of *anything*.

This determination by Delany to produce a book that finally answers the questions of "how can a person be totally free?" was what made him spend so much time on creating *Dhalgren*. He had played with themes before, but had not carried them out to their ultimate conclusions. This made all his works fit together into a logical pattern, and made *Dhalgren* the masterpiece it is because Delany had worked on these ideas for many years until he found the perfect manner to present them in a complete package.

Furthermore, he had written about matters that were important to himself before, such as myths of culture and triple relationships, but had only skimmed the surface.

Delany's earlier books had been short and accessible, but had not gone deeply enough. But with the length and depth of *Dhalgren*, something else had changed. Was the work still science fiction?

The answer is yes.

If Delany had not been a science fiction writer and had not read so much science fiction, *Dhalgren* would have been very different, because there is a second reason to enjoy *Dhalgren*.

This second reason can be called "the science fiction puzzle" approach. One thing that science fiction readers have loved since the beginning of the field is the idea of the reader solving a mystery, one that involves science.

Once the reader gets past the first ten pages of *Dhalgren*, many, many mysteries are presented to the reader. These ten pages, by the way, prepare the reader for the structure of the puzzle. Sentences are presented to the reader, tiny pieces of the world that the reader will be entering, but the tiny pieces are not explained. This prepares the reader for the parts that follow, where whole scenes are presented, but the links between the scenes are not explained. One must view *Dhalgren* as a puzzle, and prepare one's mind to accept that the story will not be told in a normal way.

Seth McEvoy, *Samuel R. Delany* (New York: Frederick Ungar Publishing Co., 1984), pp. 105–6, 111–12

GREG TATE   Besides being black Delany is gay, and in his books sexual preference figures as prominently as racial identity, if not more so. Delany's love interest in the new novel ⟨*Stars in My Pocket Like Grains of Sand*⟩ is Rat Korga, former slave and lone survivor of a mysterious annihilated world, who has been computed by the Web to be Dyeth's perfect erotic object out to a few decimal places. The Web, by the way, is one of three political factions waging the Information Wars over the 6000 planets in the novel's galaxy. The Family and the Sygn are the other two. Their enmity stems from a longstanding dispute: "The Family trying to establish the dream of a classic past . . . on a world that may flower." And the Web, an arm of the Sygn, being the interstellar agency in charge of the general flow of information about the universe. The Web manages this flow through a technique called GI—General Information—which maps and circuits synapses, then accesses them to a vast galactic computer library. Among the features of this system are instantaneous reading and comprehension of poetry and the option of calling up data to fill the gaps when communication bogs down between you and an alien.

That all this makes the book seem less like some futuristic homoerotica, or Toni Morrison in the 28th century, and more like the science-fiction novel as semiotics enterprise will come to no surprise to those readers who know that besides being black, gay, and a feminist to boot, Delany is a structuralist critic. He speaks of science fiction not as a genre but as a form of *paraliterature*, and has written a book, *The American Shore*, that's a 300-page exegesis on a 20-page short story by Thomas Disch. (When I told him his various philosophies convey the sense that he's out to become the ultimate ghetto writer, he replied that his mother was always saying he had a ghetto mentality.) Delany uses the cold war between the Family and the Sygn to signify on two systems of dictatorship—one authoritarian, one libertarian—and how they structure human and alien possibility. Asked if he felt a kinship with Eastern European writers because of their treatment of cultural alienation, Delany said he was more intrigued by their depiction of how social engineering inevitably leads to social decay. He felt this brought a sense of reality to their fiction missing from traditionally utopian American SFs.

Given his concern for the dialectics of social organization, a case can be made for Delany the Marxist. His work has always seemed to play with one of Uncle Karl's more famous dicta—to wit, the future of woman will be a future of class struggle. My favorite Delany novel, *Nova*, besides being a space-opera reworking of *Moby Dick* and the quest for the Holy Grail, presents future societies full of class divisions and class antagonisms. Following his own belief that SF doesn't so much represent reality as misrepresent it, Delany makes cultural rather than economic oppression the cause of those antagonisms. ⟨. . .⟩

The specter of racism rears up in the book's third person prologue, which describes Rat Korga's years as a slave on Rhyonon before the planet was immolated. One of the intriguing things about this chapter is how similar Delany's satirical handling of slavery and slave mentality is to Ishmael Reed's and Ralph Ellison's. Just check the book's opening—"Of course, you will be a slave . . . but you will be happy with who you are and with the tasks the world sets before you." Korga hears this from the doctor who gives him the synapse-snipping operation known as Radical Anxiety Termination, which not only makes for happy slaves but slaves incapable of reasoning, information processing, or self-preservation. Korga nearly incinerates himself walking across the hot side of his planet when one of his masters misdirects him there. He also lets two other slaves fester and die because RAT's can't handle inductive reasoning or emotional identification with other slaves. For his negligence he's beaten unmercifully with a steel pipe by one of his female masters, while sympathetic males cower in revulsion. A scene which ain't exactly what you'd call an endorsement of the sexually liberated female—but then one of the subtexts of the novel is that black women are going to be the folk who conquer the stars and gonna bust some balls along the way doing it.

> Greg Tate, "Ghetto in the Sky: Samuel Delany's Black Whole," *Voice Literary Supplement*, February 1985, pp. 12–13

ROBERT ELLIOT FOX   One might say that Delany's works offer an implicit answer to a question raised (not merely rhetorically) by ⟨Amiri⟩ Baraka: "What are the Black purposes of space travel?" It is not simply a matter of replacing flights to Canada with flights to the stars (although it is worth recalling that Reed's Raven makes his journey on a 747; technology does get you there—but where?). The fact that many of Delany's characters are genetically black to one degree or another demonstrates that mankind as a whole has moved out into the universe, not just one race or nation. He does not depict a future Earth as a planetary ghetto for people of color.

"Space is the place. Black folks is the space race" ⟨Clay Goss⟩. If black writers have mapped the darkness, so to speak, of their people's invisibility, of that cultural and racial territory exploited but never truly seen by the white world, science fiction provides maps which precede the territory, opening space(s) for us to continually reimagine our becoming. ⟨. . .⟩

Delany uses the traditional motifs of science fiction in new, highly sophisticated ways ("the seim anew," as Joyce wrote). His novels through *Nova* (1968) embody the theme of heroic epic; thereafter, the quest turns inward until the appearance of the Nevèryon stories, when the heroic asserts itself again, though now solidly within the context of the psychosocial. (Both "nova" and "novel" are derived from the Latin *novus*, new. Lorq von Ray's quest for the nova and Katin's quest for his novel are each transformative, although the former is a quest for power, the latter for understanding. However, power destroys, and understanding is necessarily incomplete, which is why *Nova* breaks off in mid sentence, an appropriately open ending to a book which is the denouement of the first stage of Delany's career.) Considering the difficulties Delany must have had as a black, dyslexic homosexual, it is not surprising that his works generally privilege the viewpoint of minority characters, often with an emphasis on loneliness and separation. Outsiders—frequently artists and criminals (sometimes they are both the same person)—are important for Delany because they present a challenge to, and critique of, society's values; they test its limits. This need to call into question the givens of a particular reality is perfectly in keeping with the kind of challenges that Reed and Baraka have hurled at Eurocentrism, with its presumption of "universality." What is significant about myths, then—the stories man has made about the past—is how in large measure they have predicated what we are now living through in the present. Delany, Reed, and Baraka read back into our cultural textus in order to untangle the knots that tie us to our confusions and (self)enslavements.

> Robert Elliot Fox, "Samuel R. Delany: Astro Black," *Conscientious Sorcerers: The Black Postmodernist Fiction of LeRoi Jones/Amiri Baraka, Ishmael Reed, and Samuel R. Delany* (Westport, CT: Greenwood Press, 1987), pp. 93–94, 96

SAMUEL R. DELANY   On the day before Christmas Eve, a City College companion, who shared both my Speech and my Art classes and whom I'd nicknamed "Little Brother" when we became friends in the first

days of school, came over to spend the night with me at my mother's apartment. At about three o'clock in the morning, an hour after we'd stopped talking and were, presumably, asleep he suddenly sat up in his underwear at the edge of his bed and said, "I have to go home . . ."

"Hm?" I said, sleepily, from mine. "Why . . .?"

"Because if I don't," he said, "I'm going to try to get in bed with you."

"That's okay," I said. "Come on."

"I don't think you understand," he said softly. "I want to go to bed with you."

"Sure I do." I held back the covers for him. "I want to go to bed with you, too. Come on. Get in."

And, a moment later, he slid down beside me.

The next afternoon, when he left, I wrote some dozen rather jejune sonnets about it all—though I did not see him again for some three or four years. When the Christmas break was over, he did not return to school.

Christmas passed, and on that snowy New Year's Eve, I went to a party at a young musician and composer's, Josh Rifkin's, where the two of us went upstairs and, secreted in Josh's room, listened to carefully and analyzed for hours the Robert Craft recording, just released, of the complete works of Anton Webern, while people celebrated downstairs.

Midnight passed.

In January 1961, I began my second term at City, continuing with Latin and Greek, dropping English, Speech, and Art, and adding History, Calculus Two (I'd received advanced placement in math, allowing me to skip Calculus One), and an obligatory Physical Education course. I became *The Promethean*'s poetry editor. 〈. . .〉

In May, I cut all my final exams. Unofficially, I had dropped out of school. (I managed, however, to fulfill my duties on the magazine.) Over the previous six months I had written a number of short novels, with titles like *The Flames of the Warthog, The Lovers*, and *The Assassination*. Along with some earlier novels, I regularly submitted these to a number of New York publishers—by whom they were regularly rejected.

In June Marilyn 〈Hacker〉 became pregnant with our second sexual experiment.

In the first week of July, after *Perseus* closed, banjo-playing Pete and I drove up to the Newport Folk Festival, where we attended concerts in the evening and slept on the beaches at night with the thousands of other young people. The notebook I filled up over the four days was typed up over the next month to become an eighty-page memoir of the trip, whose title, "The Journals of Orpheus," I rolled around on my tongue for weeks, for months. A week later, on my own, I took a bus up to the Newport Jazz Festival.

Back in New York, after the festival, I went with Marilyn to rent a four-room apartment on the Lower East Side.

In August, with a loan from another old high school friend, Sharon, Marilyn and I took a three-day trip to Detroit, Michigan, where we were married.

At the beginning of September, I got a job at Barnes & Noble on Fifth Ave and Eighteenth Street as a stockclerk, in time for the September textbook rush. Two weeks later, Marilyn got a job as an editorial assistant at Ace Books, a paperback house.

In October, almost exactly a year after my father's death, Marilyn miscarried. Probably within a week (certainly no more than ten days), after a set of obsessively vivid dreams, I began what, a little more than a year later, would be my first published novel, *The Jewels of Aptor*.

> Samuel R. Delany, "Sentences: An Introduction," *The Motion of Light in Water: Sex and Science Fiction Writing in the East Village 1957–1965* (New York: Arbor House, 1988), pp. xiv–xvi

---

DAMIEN BRODERICK   For all its faults ⟨. . .⟩ *The Einstein Intersection* is a model of (at least one kind of) writing and reading sf. Its most notable failure as an adequate allegory of reading sf is, absurdly enough, its lack of science, either as plot motivation or decorative iconography—unless one is prepared to accept as pivotal the epistemological-cum-ontological pretext of Spider's lecture on Gödel. This last, though, proves finally no better than a pretext: the same end might have been reached by an invocation of paranormal phenomena, say, or the disruptive interpenetration of "a higher dimension". Still, the discourse of reductive science is clearly under attack, no less than the discourse of reductive myth. The book is thus itself, to the extent that it works, perhaps a new myth of deconstructive scientific discourse, as disseminative as Gillian Beer's readings of Charles Darwin.

Later Delany texts venture even more forcefully into sf's vocation. *Nova*, for example, employs no less mythic substructures in its use of Tarot and

Grail, Kennedy's death and the Cold War, but does so within an explanatory frame—historical models of society, cybernetic reconstructions of work and subjectivity, the search for rare energy sources—consistent with sf's cognitively elaborated requirements. In these later texts, Delany's trajectory marks a path at once idiosyncratic and curiously exemplary of mature sf as "high" paraliterature at a pivotal moment: when it veers toward and across postmodernism in just the ways Theresa Ebert terms "transfiction", the kind of textual intersection of principled relativism and a more drastic uncertainty which *The Einstein Intersection* prefigured as allegory and allography.

> Damien Broderick, "Allography and Allegory: Delany's SF," *Foundation* No. 52 (Summer 1991): 38

▨ *Bibliography*

The Jewels of Aptor ⟨with *Second Ending* by James White⟩. 1962, 1976.

Captives of the Flame ⟨with *The Psionic Menace* by Keith Woodcott⟩. 1963, 1968 (as *Out of the Dead City*⟩.

The Towers of Toron ⟨with *The Lunar Eye* by Robert Moore Williams⟩. 1964.

City of a Thousand Suns. 1965.

The Ballad of Beta-2 ⟨with *Alpha Yes, Terra No!* by Emil Petaja⟩. 1965.

Empire Star ⟨with *Tree Lord of Imeten* by Tom Purdom⟩. 1966.

The Fall of the Towers: A Classic Science Fiction Trilogy ⟨*Out of the Dead City*, *The Towers of Toron*, *City of a Thousand Suns*⟩. 1966.

Babel-17. 1966, 1969.

The Einstein Intersection. 1967, 1972.

Nova. 1968.

QUARK/1 (editor; with Marilyn Hacker). 1970.

QUARK/2 (editor; with Marilyn Hacker). 1971.

QUARK/3 (editor; with Marilyn Hacker). 1971.

Driftglass: Ten Tales of Speculative Fiction. 1971.

QUARK/4 (editor; with Marilyn Hacker). 1971.

The Tides of Lust. 1973.

Dhalgren. 1975, 1977.

Triton: An Ambiguous Heterotopia. 1976.

The Jewel-Hinged Jaw: Notes on the Language of Science Fiction. 1977, 1978.

The American Shore: Meditations on a Tale of Science Fiction by Thomas M. Disch—"Angouleme." 1978.

Empire: A Visual Novel (with Howard V. Chaykin). 1978.

Heavenly Breakfast: An Essay on the Winter of Love. 1979.

Tales of Nevèryon. 1979.

Fundamental Disch by Thomas M. Disch (editor). 1980.

Nebula Winners Thirteen (editor). 1980.

Distant Stars. 1981.

Neveryóna; or, The Tale of Signs and Cities. 1983.

Starboard Wine: More Notes on the Language of Science Fiction. 1984.

Stars in My Pocket Like Grains of Sand. 1984.

Flight from Nevèryon. 1985.

The Complete Nebula Award–Winning Fiction. 1986.

The Bridge of Lost Desire ⟨Return to Nevèryon⟩. 1987.

Wagner/Artaud: A Play of 19th and 20th Century Critical Fictions. 1988.

The Motion of Light in Water: Sex and Science Fiction Writing in the East Village 1957–1965. 1988.

The Star Pits ⟨with Tango Charlie and Foxtrot Romeo by John Varley⟩. 1989.

The Straits of Messina. 1989.

We, in Some Strange Power's Employ, Move on a Rigorous Line ⟨with Home Is the Hangman by Roger Zelazny⟩. 1990.

They Fly at Ciron. 1993.

Silent Interviews: On Language, Race, Sex, Science Fiction, and Some Comics: A Collection of Written Interviews. 1994.

Ernest J. Gaines
b. 1933

ERNEST JAMES GAINES was born on January 15, 1933, on a plantation in Oscar, Louisiana, to Manuel and Adrienne Gaines. Gaines's earliest education probably came from his family and their stories. In 1948, he moved with his family to Vallejo, California, where he attended Vallejo Junior College. He served in the army for two years before entering San Francisco State College, by which time he was already writing short stories. In 1956 his first story was published in a small magazine in San Francisco called *Transfer*. After graduating in 1957, Gaines attended a creative writing program at Stanford University for one year.

Gaines's first novel, *Catherine Carmier* (1964), is set, like most of his work, in the rural South. Gaines derived much inspiration from Russian writers such as Tolstoy, Turgenev, and Gogol, and this novel seems based upon Turgenev's *Fathers and Sons* in its depiction of a young black man who returns to his native plantation after gaining an education in the city and who falls in love with the daughter of a black Creole farmer. Gaines is concerned with the complex relationship between rural and urban living, and the economic and social effects of changing agrarian lifestyles. His South is a South in transition. He captures the cadences of black, Creole, and Cajun dialects while examining a variety of personal and communal relationships. Gaines frequently writes about women, as in the case of the eponymous Catherine Carmier. His women are generally older, strong-willed, religious, and, perhaps, unprepared for social change.

Gaines did not receive much public attention until his second novel, *Of Love and Dust,* appeared in 1967. This work, narrated in the first person, is more concerned with black/white relations than its predecessor and, in the end, is a clear condemnation of the traditional racism of the Old South. A collection of stories, *Bloodline* (1968), succeeded *Of Love and Dust,* containing five long stories, three of which were published prior to *Catherine Carmier;* one of these, "A Long Day in November," was issued separately in 1971. In that year Gaines's most successful novel, *The Autobiography of*

Miss Jane Pittman, was published. This work—based in part upon one of the stories in *Bloodline*, "List Like a Tree"—is a folk history of black experience from the Reconstruction to the civil rights era, as told by the elderly Jane Pittman. It received enormous popular and critical acclaim. Gaines contributed to a television adaptation, which, however, was toned down for white audiences, inviting criticism from the black community; nevertheless, the adaptation won nine Emmy Awards. Gaines's next two novels, *In My Father's House* (1978) and *A Gathering of Old Men* (1983; adapted for television in 1987), were critically well received but did not win as much attention as *The Autobiography of Miss Jane Pittman.*

Gaines has served as a writer in residence at Denison University, Stanford, and Whittier, and since 1983 he has been a professor of English and writer in residence at the University of Southwestern Louisiana. He has received honorary degrees from Denison, Brown, Bard College, Louisiana State, and other universities. After a decade in which he published little, Gaines in 1993 issued his sixth novel, *A Lesson Before Dying*, which became a best-seller.

▧ *Critical Extracts*

GRANVILLE HICKS   Each of these stories ⟨in *Bloodline*⟩, it may be noted, is told in the first person, though in the fifth there are several "I's" and not just one. It is not surprising that Gaines likes the first person, for he uses colloquial language effectively and has a strong feeling for the rhythms of speech. For example, the boy in "The Sky Is Gray" tells how his mother beat him when he refused to kill two redbirds he and his brother had trapped: "I'm still young—I ain't no more than eight; but I know now; I know why I had to do it. (They was so little, though. They was so little. I 'member how I picked the feathers off them and cleaned them and helt them over the fire. Then we all ate them. Ain't had but a little bitty piece each, but we all had a little bitty piece, and everybody looked at me 'cause they was so proud.) Suppose she had to go away like Daddy went away? Then who was go'n look after us? They had to be somebody left to carry on." ⟨. . .⟩

I first came across "The Sky Is Gray" in *American Negro Short Stories,* edited by John H. Clarke, and "A Long Day in November" in Langston Hughes's *The Best Short Stories by Negro Writers,* and I was impressed by both. In spite of my reservations about the endings, they are strong stories, and so are the others in the collection. Gaines knows how to create living characters and to set them against a rich and vivid background. Now, if I ever get a chance, I will read his two novels. If they are anywhere near as good as the stories, he is one of the young writers—he was born in 1933— who will help to form the American literature of the future.

Granville Hicks, "Sounds of Soul," *Saturday Review,* 17 August 1968, pp. 19–20

ALICE WALKER   Because politics are strung throughout this rich and very big novel ⟨*The Autobiography of Miss Jane Pittman*⟩, it will no doubt be said that Gaines's book is about politics. But he is too skilled a writer to be stuck in so sordid, so small a category. ⟨. . .⟩

Gaines somehow manages to show that there is more even to a redneck than his racism. Racists are dangerous, unstable, vicious individuals, but never that alone. They are people, fully realized in Gaines's fiction, and have a haggard futility, a pale and shrieking dullness, a pained unsatisfiedness that makes them appear wounded and deficient and far less complete than the blacks they attempt to intimidate.

Gaines's people are never completely wiped out by whites, even when they are killed by them. They are too large and the whites around them too small. His heroes would fight to walk uprightly through a hurricane. They do no less when confronted with a white world intent on grinding them down. They fight to maintain small human pleasures and large human principles in a hostile and morally degenerate world. They have seen the level to which humankind can sink and have managed to remain standing all these many years.

Gaines is much closer to Charles Dickens, W. E. B. Du Bois, Jean Toomer and Langston Hughes than he is to Richard Wright or Ralph Ellison. There is nothing in Gaines that is not open—to love or to interpretation. He also claims and revels in the rich heritage of Southern black people and their customs; the community he feels with them is unmistakable and goes deeper even than pride. Like the beautifully vivid, sturdy and serviceable language of the black, white and Creole people of Louisiana, Gaines is mellow with

historical reflection, supple with wit, relaxed and expansive because he does
not equate his people with failure.

Alice Walker, [Review of *The Autobiography of Miss Jane Pittman*], *New York Times
Book Review*, 23 May 1971, pp. 6, 12

SHERLEY ANNE WILLIAMS   In the works of Ernest Gaines,
the efforts of the individual to broaden or break out of narrow traditional
ways are couched in terms of the conflict between the old and the new.
Even though his themes are, in some measure, those which have concerned
many Black writers (masculinity, dignity and the effort to align one's personal
concept of self with the dominant society's view of one's group identity and
experience), his deepest concern is centered on this clash between youth
and age, between those who adhere to the patterns which have made it
possible for Black people to survive in the past and the young people
who are disenchanted with these values. The subsequent attempts of these
younger people to erect new values and find new ways of making it through
the world provide the framework for many of his stories.

Gaines uses the rural Louisiana countryside as the setting for most of his
stories. The countryside and most particularly, the quarters, those ancient
structures which have served as homes for generations of Black people back
to the times of slavery, are captured in a purposely ill-defined time between
the Second World War and the present, a time not quite yesterday, not
quite today. The struggle for ascendency in the small Southern backwater
Gaines has created is not between white and Black. The racial order, with
the Blacks who are on the bottom, rich white people who are on the top
and the Cajuns (the descendants of the white Arcadians who were resettled
in Louisiana by the British after the close of the French and Indian Wars
in the late eighteenth century), who, no matter how high their income,
are not quite as good, at least in the eyes of Blacks, as the Anglican whites,
but no matter how poor, are at least one step above the Blacks, is slowly
changing. But change, in an overtly racial manner, seldom moves beyond
the periphery of Gaines's attention. His concern is for the ways in which
people attempt to hold on to or break from the past, adjust to the present
or influence the future. Thus, his major theme, in its broadest sense, is the
clash between the old and the new, the past and the future. The old is
violated by the new, not out of wanton destruction; rather it is attacked in

an attempt to wrench new definitions, new images of manhood and dignity, new realities out of the old. This is the struggle which comprises the title story from Gaines's volume of short stories, *Bloodline*, for Cooper Laurent, the hero, is determined to claim his birthright from the tradition which had denied him one.

Gaines's older characters seem, at first glance, Faulknerian caricatures who, like the Black servant, Dilsey, in *The Sound and the Fury*, "attempt to hold the white family together . . . [who are] the foundations of a dying institution." Some of the characters are set very firmly in this image but it is a mistake to dismiss any of them as mere stereotypes. There are variations and gradations in Gaines's characterizations. Bishop, in *Of Love and Dust*, for example, blames the troubles of his master, Marshall Herbert, on the convict Marcus. Marcus, literally and figuratively, sticks his foot in the door of the Big House that slavery built, and in Bishop's opinion, a Black person who has the nerve to do that "would do almost anything." Herbert, whom he has served as faithfully as he served the father before him, can do no wrong; he will always be the master to Bishop.

> Sherley Anne Williams, *Give Birth to Brightness: A Thematic Study in Neo-Black Literature* (New York: Dial Press, 1972), pp. 169–71

JERRY H. BRYANT   There is an air of the American classic writer about Ernest J. Gaines. Like Twain and Faulkner, he has maintained a close identificatin with a region of America from which myths may be drawn, in his case south Louisiana. Like Hemingway, he works meticulously at perfecting a simple, lucid style. And, like all of our classic writers from Cooper to Heller, he has that talent for creating a character who has a broad visceral appeal— who embodies a wide range of complex historical meaning while at the same time speaking to a heterogeneous audience on a highly personal level in an eccentric but profoundly moral language. Huckleberry Finn does this, and so does Miss Jane Pittman, the title character of Gaines's latest novel.

Gaines has that combination of moral—sometimes political—commitment and aesthetic distance that characterizes the classic American writer. A black man himself, he has taken up the familiar themes of contemporary black fiction: the tyranny of whites over blacks, the rebellion of blacks against that tyranny. But he has avoided any close political or social ties that would induce him to violate his artistic independence. He does not level any accusations, reflect any specific ideology, idealize any black revolutionary type. He suggests that rebellion against tyranny is necessary, and that the system must be changed. But what makes his fiction special is the way he expresses his position, his humanity, humor, breadth of vision.

> Jerry H. Bryant, "Ernest J. Gaines: Change, Growth, and History," *Southern Review* 10, No. 4 (October 1974): 851

FRANK W. SHELTON   In *In My Father's House* Gaines again focuses on two themes implicit in all his earlier works: the nature of black manhood and the relationship of fathers and sons. He includes his familiar deterministic explanation of why black men cannot assume their responsibilities and be men. ⟨Philip⟩ Martin tells his illegitimate son, " 'It took a man to do these things, and I wasn't a man. I was just some other brutish animal who could cheat, steal, rob, kill—but not stand. Not be responsible. Not protect you or your mother. They had branded that in us from the time of slavery. [To have acted any differently would have been] to break the rules, rules we had lived by for so long, and I wasn't strong enough to break them then.' " Like some other Gaines male characters, Martin moves toward manhood and indeed does assume responsibility for family, church, and community. But when encountering the virtually wordless accusations of his son, he is forced to wonder if he has truly escaped his past.

We must give Martin due credit. Challenged by his son, he does not turn away from him; instead he searches his memory and, in a trip to Baton Rouge, actually revisits the past. He is not without courage and honesty. Yet we must also notice other character traits he displays. Gaines has said, "I like pride in people," and certainly his most memorable characters—the mother in "The Sky Is Gray," Marcus in *Of Love and Dust*, Jane and Joe Pittman, Ned and Jimmy in the *Autobiography*—all possess it in abundance. Gaines has long acknowledged his interest in Greek tragedy and its influence on his works. Of all his novels, *In My Father's House* perhaps best fits the pattern of classical tragedy in its concern for determinism and free will and for excess pride in its consequences. For what becomes clear in the course of the novel is that beneath the veneer of piety, there is a hard core of egotism in Philip Martin's character, a determination to follow his own desires, a certainty that he knows what is best for everyone, and a disregard for other people.

Frank W. Shelton, "*In My Father's House*: Ernest Gaines After Jane Pittman," *Southern Review* 17, No. 2 (Spring 1981): 342–43

CRAIG HANSEN WERNER   For Ernest Gaines, ⟨James⟩ Joyce provided an escape from Faulkner. Gaines acknowledges that Faulkner strongly influenced his own early novels, *Catherine Carmier* and *Of Love and Dust,* both of which share the classic inability to resolve contradictions. Unable to endorse Faulkner's commitment to the old aristocratic South, Gaines shares Faulkner's distrust of the new order. Only in *Bloodline* does he resolve this tension—not by abandoning the Faulknerian influence, but by revaluing it using Joycean techniques. Commenting on Jerry Bryant's discussion of the influences on his early novels, Gaines observes: "I don't think it's possible for me to break away from the influence of jazz or blues or Negro spirituals or Greek tragedy or James Joyce or Tolstoy." In another interview, Gaines includes both *Dubliners* and *Ulysses*, the two Joyce works most often claimed by the realists, on a list of the books which have most influenced his writing.

Joyce's obsession with the Dublin of his youth attracts Gaines, who himself returns time after time to Bayonne, the Louisiana setting which provides the most obvious unifying device for *Bloodline*. Most immediately, however, Faulkner's Yoknapatawpha County rather than Joyce's Dublin appears to have inspired Gaines's conception of Bayonne. A more distinctive Joycean contribution to *Bloodline* lies in Gaines's juxtaposition of the perspectives of the five stories to clarify his attitude toward Faulkner's historical nostalgia. Gaines begins *Bloodline* with a naive limited narrator in "A Long Day in November" and gradually expands to the seemingly omniscient manipulative narrator of "Just Like a Tree." ⟨. . .⟩

"Just Like a Tree," if read with an awareness of the unambiguous rejection of Anne-Marie Duvall's code in the preceding stories, resolves *Bloodline*. The shifts in point of view within the story indicate that no one character can resolve the issues. In fact, Gaines's resolution hinges on the juxtaposition of Emmanuel and Aunt Fe, the only two major characters whose thoughts he does not portray directly. William Burke argues that this silence underlines the opposition of the old black matriarchy and the new "masculine" black revolution. It seems more logical, however, to invert this assumption and see Fe's and Emmanuel's actions as aspects of a coherent movement which both understand.

Fe's declaration that "I ain't leaving here tomorrow" implies that she wills her own death. Her final blessing on Emmanuel indicates her understanding of his determination to act despite white retaliation. Symbolically representing the old order willing itself out of existence, her death grants the future to the "soldier" who, unlike General Christian Laurent, can act with practical goals in view. In addition, her death withholds a negative symbol from those who desire to retreat from the confrontation and accept the Faulknerian code. Abandoning her roots would appear to provide further proof of black weakness, perpetuating the code which lies not only behind the gift of the scarf but also behind the bombings. Her death, then, serves both as a symbol of support for Emmanuel and as a realistic action pledging that "Just like a tree that's / planted 'side the water. / Oh, I shall not be moved."

Gaines, then, manipulates his perspective to transform a Faulknerian statement on the passing of the Old South into a call for commitment to the new order. The silence of two major characters stresses the insufficiency of individual perspectives (such as Anne-Marie Duvall's) either within the story or within the book as a whole. Aunt Fe's death is an epiphany which completes the *Dubliners*-style development of *Bloodline*.

Craig Hansen Werner, "Dublin(er)'s Joyce: Ernest Gaines, Flannery O'Connor, Russell Banks," *Paradoxical Resolutions: American Fiction Since James Joyce* (Urbana: University of Illinois Press, 1982), pp. 35–36, 39–40

LOYLE HAIRSTON   ⟨. . .⟩ Gaines is one of the few black writers whose fiction is not mired in racial parochialism. He writes about Blacks and whites equally well, avoiding stereotypes in strong, sensitive characterizations that are rendered with warmth and compassion. But A *Gathering of Old Men* misses its chance to be outstanding fiction by its lack of profundity and fresh insight into the quality of black and white relations in the old and "new" South. I found myself yearning for more than a superficial rehash of black victimization at the familiar hands of racists. Excessive violence, in its banality, tends to obscure the more profound, more subtle nuances in the dynamic of human relations. ⟨. . .⟩

But in its way, *A Gathering of Old Men* is a delightful, very amusing novel that will leave the reader smiling and yet thoughtful. Moreover, it is a refreshing departure from the gloomy, pessimistic, embittered moralizing of some recent novels. Gaines has managed to depict the ordeal of black and white folk without sinking into despair, not least among the reasons why he is one of my favorite writers.

Loyle Hairston, " 'New South' Tragi-Comedy," *Freedomways* 24, No. 1 (First Quarter 1984): 59–60

BLYDEN JACKSON   Gaines takes care, with some significant and highly visible signals at the beginning of his book ⟨*The Autobiography of Miss Jane Pittman*⟩, to make of Jane's memoir, for all of his emphasis upon Jane's independent contribution to it, a collaborative act of composition. Jane's amanuensis, for instance, the aforesaid teacher of history who seeks her out, driven by a sense of professional duty honed to an extra edge of keenness, it is not difficult to see, both by his appreciation of Jane's venerability and his own simple curiosity, is white. He will, through his many weeks of association with Jane, record not only what Jane tells him, but also what some of Jane's friends, speaking in Jane's stead, assure him, under Jane's supervision, Jane might well have said to him to fill in lacunae left by her in her confessions to him. Moreover, when Jane dies some months after his last interview with her, this white historian checks Jane's story with surviving neighbors of hers who, he thinks, should be able to verify or supplement Jane's legacy of anecdotes to him. Thus, in one quite discernible manner Jane's individual testimony acquires something of the character and force of the voice of a community—a community, moreover, with decidedly a distinctive identity and a strong sense of solidarity—discoursing about itself. There is, too, in the voices other than Jane's in *Pittman*, as a complementary value certainly not to be taken lightly, a reminder of an important auxiliary to the action often to be found in ancient Greek tragedy. This notable auxiliary is the chorus, which has given surely many moments of exquisite pleasure to scholars and other lovers of the drama of Old Hellas. For, frequently, this Greek tragic chorus does more than say in effect, "Look, if you do not know it, this is what is going on in this play." Frequently this faithful band of devoted onlookers goes beyond its possible other functions to comment on the action in the very play it accompanies. What a sense of universality thus may be imparted to any playwright's utterance! Men do puzzle over their own lives and other human lives of concern to them, and when they do, often it is within a context of their most profound and comprehensive musings about the nature and eschatological implications of their experience of life—in other words, within a frame of reference for their thought which attention solely to an individual self could not satisfy. The voices, then, of Jane's coadjutors in her autobiography do play a role, impressively, in making of her autobiography more of the history of an entire people than her autobiography, but for them, otherwise might be.

> Blyden Jackson, "Jane Pittman through the Years: A People's Tale," *American Letters and the Historical Consciousness: Essays in Honor of Lewis P. Simpson*, ed. J. Gerald Kennedy and Daniel Mark Fogel (Baton Rouge: Louisiana State University Press, 1987), pp. 255–56

MARY ELLEN DOYLE   ⟨Gaines⟩ has always insisted that no black writer influenced him. By the time he went to San Francisco State, Wright and Baldwin were available, and *Invisible Man* had just been published. But neither these nor any other earlier black writers were taught in the classroom or recommended to his reading. That may or may not be regrettable: the reading of black writers just might have fogged his clear vision of his own materials and goals, but from the white authors he always knew he was learning skills of narration and not a way of seeing his own world. He acknowledges some impact from reading Zora Neale Hurston, but that is all. Jean Toomer's *Cane*, he says, would have influenced him had he known it, by its subject (the rural black South) and its structure (short pieces combined into a novel). But he did not know *Cane*, and any resemblance now is coincidental or due to the authors' similar experiences.

Gaines's education in the fifties may have left him uninfluenced by black writers, but beginning publication in the militant sixties subjected him to the demand on black writers to write for social and political goals. Resistance was not easy. California especially was seething with hippies and protest; other young writers thought him out of touch at best, and at worst, an Uncle Tom. Gaines has recognized that had he been in Louisiana, not California, during the Civil Rights era, he might, like his fictional Jimmy, have died on the streets of his home town. But militant words and acts were not what he had experienced "at home"—not even demonstrations.

And he believed that the way to force reluctant white recognition of black humanity was to "do something positive . . . to use the anger in a positive way, to create a lasting punch, one that will have a longer effect than just screaming" or calling obscene names. And so, as the violence escalated, he kept writing. On a day of bad news, he would sit still till he had written a perfect page. He would prove to the Wallaces, Connors, and Faubuses of the South that he could take the letters given by *their* ancestors and use them better, could do more with them to help his race than they could do to destroy it. And he would do it his way, by telling his people's story. He would "write black" indeed, but *his* black, that of his people; and he would write not only about his black people in the quarters but his multi-ethnic people, the Creoles, Cajuns, and landowner whites—all their interaction as he knew it, as it had been seared into his memory and carved onto his heart, during the first fifteen years of his life. For his choice of subject, the heart had its reasons which no reasons of any political or aesthetic movement could shake. In his territory, he needed no one to free him.

> Mary Helen Doyle, "Ernest Gaines' Materials: Place, People, Author," *MELUS* 15, No. 3 (Fall 1988): 90–91

MARCIA GAUDET and CARL WOOTON   MG: What about your work in progress? Can you tell us anything about it?

GAINES: I can say that it deals with a teacher who visits a guy on death row. That has been said in the opening chapter, when the defense is trying to get something less than the death penalty for him.

This guy is going into a bar. He's as broke as anything. He doesn't have any money, and he's going into this bar, and it's probably cold weather like this. Two guys come along and say, hey, man, do you want a ride? He says, all right. So he gets into the car with them, and these guys start talking about how we need a bottle, want some booze. Let's go over to the old man. We've spent our money there all the time, and he should be able to let us have a pint until grinding, until the sugarcane-cutting time.

When they go into the store, the old man's there all by himself, and this guy, this third guy, goes along in that store with them. The old man knows them and speaks to them the way he does all the time, saying hello and how's your family and all that kind of stuff. One of them speaks to him and he says, we want a bottle of wine. The old man says, OK, give me your money. When they put the money on the counter, he knows there's not enough money. He says, no, no, no, you bring your money, then you'll get your bottle. They say, come on, you know we're good for it. The old man says, no, no, so one of the guys starts going around the counter. He's going to take it. The old man says, hey, don't come back here. I told you already, you must bring the money. The guy is walking toward him, so the old man breaks toward his cash register where he has a gun.

This guy standing back doesn't know what the hell is going on around him. All of a sudden, there is shooting all around. When he realizes what has happened, the old man is dying, and these two guys are dead. And then he doesn't know what to do. He hears this voice calling him and calling him, and he doesn't know what to do. Finally he goes around the counter. The old man is dying, and the guy feels, "God, he knows I was here and now he's going to blame me for all this. He's going to tell."

He doesn't know what he's doing. He just grabs a bottle and he starts drinking. He's looking at this man and drinking and drinking and drinking like this. And as he turns he sees the cash register is open from when the old man grabbed the revolver, and he grabs the money. He says, "I need money." By now the old man has died.

This is told from a teacher's point of view—who knows nothing about any of this. I get all of this later. As he starts out, two men come into the place. Now, you see this kind of action during the trial. This happens in the forties. That's why I wanted to see the local prisons where the executions went on at that time. The trial goes on. The jury is made up of twelve white men, and this kid is sentenced to death, although he says he had nothing to do with it. But the prosecutor says, wait awhile. He went there with those guys. He's telling us he had nothing to do with it. We don't know that. We know that everybody's dead except him, and he came out of the place with a bottle and money in his pocket.

So [this] convinces the jury, and he's sentenced to die. The court-appointed defense attorney tries to get him off by saying this is not a man. This is a fool. You wouldn't call him a man. This boy has no idea what size his clothes are. He doesn't know Christmas from Fourth of July. He doesn't know a thing about Keats. He doesn't know Byron or the Bill of Rights. He can't plan any murder or robbery. He didn't do any of this. Finally he says, I'd just as soon tie down some kind of animal in the electric chair, a hog or something like that. Nevertheless, he's sentenced to die for this crime.

Now, his grandmother, or his *nanane*, or his auntie, or whoever she is, approaches this schoolteacher. She tells him: "I don't know how much time he has left—I don't know whether it's a year, several months, several weeks. Whatever, I want you to approach him and bring him to the level of a man. Then let him die as a man. That's what I want."

And this is where I am now.

> Marcia Gaudet and Carl Wooton, *Porch Talk with Ernest Gaines: Conversations on the Writer's Craft* (Baton Rouge: Louisiana State University Press, 1990), pp. 132–33

VALERIE MELISSA BABB   The power to act, "to be identified," "to be caught up forgetfully and exultingly in the swing of events" is central to Gaines's final novel, *A Gathering of Old Men,* originally titled "The Revenge of Old Men." In this text, too, action is power. Men who for many years have waited as silent brutes at long last discard their yokes and seize power over their lives. They become men who "do things," and in a single act of courage reaffirm their manhood and humanity. Having tacitly supported a social order that relegated them to a subhuman existence, in their twilight years they realize the opportunity an act of murder provides them to salvage their dignity.

The old men reside in and around Marshall Quarters. Although the action takes place in the 1970s, social conventions change so slowly in Marshall that the novel could have taken place anytime during the period of tenant farming. Marshall is the remnant of a plantation in which "[T]here were nothing but old people. . . . The young ones had all gone away." Their exodus is caused by the same Cajun infringement Gaines delineates in other novels. Here again, the Cajuns overtake, in one character's words, "[T]he very same land we had worked, our people had worked, and our people's people had worked since the time of slavery." Because the Cajuns have so thoroughly subjugated the blacks of Marshall plantation, it comes as a shock to this community when a Cajun overseer is shot by a black man. The entire populace is left wondering how, on a plantation where there are only old men too bound to a system to change it, such a murder could take place. Shock turns to perplexity when *all* the elderly black men of the plantation claim responsibility for the killing. Participating in a scheme devised by the young white overseer, Candy Marshall, these men have vowed to hide the identity of the true killer and execute their final act of pride and dignity, confessing to the shooting of Beau Boutan.

Though only one man has actually shot Beau, each black man in the work has committed the same murder at one point, in his heart, in his mind. While he is only one white man, Beau represents all the white men who have disdained their existence and all the injustices that have been heaped upon them their entire lives. To claim to be Beau's killer provides each man with the opportunity to gain revenge against a society that has abused him and told him he is worthless. The men successfully fool the officials enforcing the rules of their society and subsequently cause a revolution through confusion.

Valerie Melissa Babb, Ernest Gaines (Boston: Twayne, 1991), pp. 113–14

CARL SENNA   Despite the novel's ⟨A Lesson Before Dying⟩ gallows humor and an atmosphere of pervasively harsh racism, the characters, black and white, are humanly complex and have some redeeming quality. At the end, Jefferson's white jailor, in a moving epiphany, is so changed that he suggests the white-black alliance that will emerge a generation later to smash Jim Crow to bits.

The New England abolitionist preacher William Ellery Channing observed just before the Civil War that "there are seasons, in human affairs, of inward and outward revolution, when new depths seem to be broken up in the soul, when new wants are unfolded in multitudes, and a new and undefined good is thirsted for." A Lesson Before Dying, though it suffers an occasional stylistic lapse, powerfully evokes in its understated tone the "new wants" in the 1940's that created the revolution of the 1960's. Ernest J. Gaines has written a moving and truthful work of fiction.

Carl Senna, "Dying Like a Man," New York Times Book Review, 8 August 1993, p. 21

🔶 Bibliography

Catherine Carmier. 1964.
Of Love and Dust. 1967.
Bloodline. 1968.

A Long Day in November. 1971.
The Autobiography of Miss Jane Pittman. 1971.
In My Father's House. 1978.
A Gathering of Old Men. 1983.
Porch Talk with Ernest Gaines: Conversations on the Writer's Craft (with Marcia
       Gaudet and Carl Wooton). 1990.
A Lesson Before Dying. 1993.

Alex Haley
1921–1992

ALEXANDER PALMER HALEY was born on August 11, 1921, in Ithaca, New York, where his father, Simon Haley, was a graduate student at Cornell University and his mother, Bertha Palmer Haley, was planning to enter a musical conservatory. After Alex's birth, his parents took a hiatus from their studies and returned to Bertha's hometown of Henning, Tennessee, where they had two more sons. Young Alex was quite close to both his maternal grandparents, Will and Cynthia Palmer. He had a special fondness for his grandmother, who along with her sisters would entertain him by reciting their family's history back to the first family member to arrive in America from Africa.

Bertha Haley was never in good health and died when Alex was ten. Two years after her death, Haley's father married Zeona Hatcher, and the couple had a daughter. Although Haley did well in school, graduating from high school at age fifteen and then completing two years of college, his youth and his degenerating relationship with his father impelled him to drop college and join the Coast Guard. During his twenty years in the Coast Guard, Haley honed his writing skills, first as a ghostwriter of love letters for fellow shipmates and then as a public relations officer in New York and San Francisco. He began to sell stories (usually about the Coast Guard) to men's adventure magazines and in 1954 sold an article to *Reader's Digest*.

Haley took early retirement from the Coast Guard in 1959 and became a writer. Continuing his work for *Reader's Digest*, in 1960 Haley conducted the first of what would be many interviews with a controversial minister of the Nation of Islam named Malcolm X. His reputation as a journalist continued to grow as he conducted a widely read series of interviews with prominent black Americans for *Playboy*. In early 1963, Haley began to interview Malcolm X for *The Autobiography of Malcolm X*, published in 1965. Despite Malcolm X's initial distrust of his interviewer, respect and confidence eventually developed between the two men, and the book remains important both as a personal history of the militant preacher (assassinated two weeks after the completion of the manuscript) and as a powerful influence on the civil rights movement.

Haley began research for the book that was to become *Roots* in the early 1960s, envisioning it as a much smaller project that would tell of his family's rise from slavery in the United States. The project quickly expanded, however, and Haley spent more than a decade researching his family's history in the United States, Europe, and Africa. The resulting book (completed ten years after the publisher's deadline) was published in 1976 and became an instant best-seller as well as a critical success. Haley won a special Pulitzer Prize in 1977, the same year that the television miniseries, "Roots: The Triumph of an American Family," was aired. The miniseries remains one of the most-watched television shows in the United States and was followed the next year by "Roots: The Next Generation." *Roots* was not without controversy, however. Various sources criticized Haley's scholarship, and more damagingly, the novelist Harold Courlander took Haley to court on charges of plagiarism (Haley settled against the advice of his publishers).

The success of *Roots* resulted in both wealth and celebrity for Haley. Unfortunately, the resulting demands on his time and energy effectively ended his career as a writer. He published a Christmas story, *A Different Kind of Christmas*, in 1988, but produced no more books during his lifetime. He began research into the family history of his paternal grandmother, exploring his family's Irish roots, but died suddenly of a heart attack on February 10, 1992, before completing the project. The book was assembled and in part written by David Stevens and published posthumously in 1993 as *Queen*.

◈ *Critical Extracts*

ALEX HALEY   The old *griot* ⟨Gambian oral historian⟩ had talked for nearly two hours up to then, and perhaps fifty times the narrative had included some detail about someone whom he had named. Now after he had just named those four sons, again he appended a detail, and the interpreter translated—

"About the time the King's soldiers came"—another of the *griot's* time-fixing references—"the eldest of these four sons, Kunta, went away from his village to chop wood . . . and he was never seen again. . . ." And the *griot* went on with his narrative.

I sat as if I were carved of stone. My blood seemed to have congealed. This man whose lifetime had been in this back-country African village had no way in the world to know that he had just echoed what I had heard all through my boyhood years on my grandma's front porch in Henning, Tennessee . . . of an African who always had insisted that his name was "Kin-tay"; who had called a guitar a *"ko,"* and a river within the state of Virginia, "Kamby Bolongo"; and who had been kidnaped into slavery while not far from his village, chopping wood, to make himself a drum.

I managed to fumble from my dufflebag my basic notebook, whose first pages containing grandma's story I showed to an interpreter. After briefly reading, clearly astounded, he spoke rapidly while showing it to the old *griot*, who became agitated; he got up, exclaiming to the people, gesturing at my notebook in the interpreter's hands, and *they* all got agitated. ⟨. . .⟩

Later the men of Juffure took me into their mosque built of bamboo and thatch, and they prayed around me in Arabic. I remember thinking, down on my knees, "After I've found out where I came from, I can't understand a word they're saying." Later the crux of their prayer was translated for me: "Praise be to Allah for one long lost from us whom Allah has returned." ⟨. . .⟩

My mind reeled with it all as we approached another, much larger village. Staring ahead, I realized that word of what had happened in Juffure must have left there well before I did. The driver slowing down, I could see this village's people thronging the road ahead; they were waving, amid their cacophony of crying out something; I stood up in the Land-Rover, waving back as they seemed grudging to open a path for the Land-Rover.

I guess we had moved a third of the way through the village when it suddenly registered in my brain what they were all crying out . . . the wizened, robed elders and younger men, the mothers and the naked tar-black children, they were all waving up at me; their expressions buoyant, beaming, all were crying out together, *"Meester Kinte! Meester Kinte!"*

Let me tell you something: I am a man. A sob hit me somewhere around my ankles; it came surging upward, and flinging my hands over my face, I was just bawling, as I hadn't since I was a baby. *"Meester Kinte!"* I just felt like I was weeping for all of history's incredible atrocities against fellowmen, which seems to be mankind's greatest flaw.

Alex Haley, *Roots* (Garden City, NY: Doubleday, 1976), pp. 679–81

JAMES BALDWIN   The world of Alex Haley's book ⟨*Roots*⟩ begins in Gambia West Africa in 1750 with the birth of one of his ancestors, Kunta Kinte, born of Omoro and Binta Kinte, of the Mandinka tribe, and of the Muslim faith. In the re-creation of this time and place, Haley succeeds beautifully where many have failed. He must have studied and sweated hard to achieve such ease and grace, for he would appear to have been born in his ancestral village and to be personally acquainted with everybody there. The public ceremonies of this people are revealed as a precise and coherent mirror of their private and yet connected imaginations. And these ceremonies, imaginations, however removed in time, are yet, for a black man anyway, naggingly familiar and present. I say, for a black man, but these ceremonies, these imaginations are really universal, finally inescapably as old and deep as the human race. The tragedy of the people doomed to think of themselves as white lies in their denial of these origins: they become incoherent because they can never stammer from whence they came. ⟨. . .⟩

We know that Kunta will be kidnapped, and brought to America, and yet, we have become so engrossed in his life in the village, and so fond of him, that the moment comes as a terrible shock. We, too, would like to kill his abductors. We are in his skin, and in his darkness, and, presently, we are shackled with him, in his terror, rage, and pain, his stink, and the stink of others, on the ship which brings him here. It can be said that we know the rest of the story—how it turned out, so to speak, but frankly, I don't think that we do know the rest of the story. It *hasn't* turned out yet, which is the rage and pain and danger of this country. Alex Haley's taking us back through time to the village of his ancestors is an act of faith and courage, but this book is also an act of love, and it is this which makes it so haunting.

> James Baldwin, "How One Black Man Came to Be an American," *New York Times Book Review*, 26 September 1976, pp. 1–2

L. D. REDDICK   The publication of Alex Haley's *Roots* is a political event, even more than a cultural achievement. It is seldom that a Black man gets to the stage where the nation, including the government itself, will be listening to what he has to say. Usually the crude or subtle "enemies" of black people hold that stage, and even when a reform crusade comes along, it's a Harriet Beecher Stowe who makes the plea that the nation hears. ⟨. . .⟩

How did *Roots* happen? What does it have to say to millions who will read its words or perceive the faces and voices that will enact the scenes on stage and screen? Will it, for example, counter-balance *Gone with the Wind* that went around the world? Or did *Tobacco Road* do that?

In the first place, externally, *Roots* is a marketing success, demonstrating great professional skill. It is packaged to reach a universal audience. It is deliberately not a Black book. Its title is not *Home to Africa* or even *Black Roots*. Its dedication is not to "my people" but to "my country." It has no pictures. There are no barriers against every reader identifying in his own way with the heroes and victims. It is, thus, not obviously very specially "ours"; rather, it is, as somebody said, "a book for mankind." Let's debate it: is this what one *must* do—especially in these "blacklashing times"?

In the second place, *Roots* is a literary masterpiece. Alex Haley is a superb story teller and the flow of the narrative, despite a few sluggish pages, is so easy and natural that few will lay it down without finishing it. ⟨. . .⟩

The heart of the Haley story is that it establishes in the public mind the link of Afro-Americans with their homeland and that this link, though hammered and hidden, psychologically has never been broken. There is indeed a basic continuity. In many moments of crisis, this bond is most reassuring, though Africans have blended with other peoples and cultures— often by force, sometimes by choice. There does seem to be a quality of humanity about the sons and daughters of the idealized motherland that explains, in part at least, their survival in the past and the possibility of their prevailing in the post-industrial future.

L. D. Reddick, "Our Own Story—At Last!," *Freedomways* 16, No. 4 (Fourth Quarter 1976): 253–54

MARK OTTAWAY   If there is any element of truth in ⟨the griot Kebba⟩ Fofana's story one question remains: who then was the Kunta Kinte who allegedly disappeared from Juffure? Once again, we move into speculation. But the probabilities that he disappeared much later than 1767, that he was never shipped as a slave to America, and that he was not an ancestor of Haley far outweigh any possibilities that he did or was.

For a start the generations do not match. Haley is a seventh generation American. By the same reckoning Kebba Kinte of Juffure, who is roughly the same age as Haley, is the fourth generation descendant of the brother of the Kunta Kinte, according to Fofana's archive statement.

This is not the only indication that Fofana's Kunta Kinte disappeared later than the Kunta Kinte of *Roots*. Fofana says in his archive statement that when Kunta was missed his family believed that he had either been eaten by hyenas or had got lost. But then his brother, Suwandi, had another idea. He decided to take his canoe and paddle across to James Island "because he had heard there were many people settled there," but unfortunately his canoe capsized and Suwandi drowned.

The significant point about this statement is that in 1767 the presence of white settlers on James Island was a dominant fact of life in Juffure, not merely a rumour. Indeed Suwandi need not have gone to James Island at all to make inquiries, because the people from James Island ran a virtual shuttle service to Juffure in their constant visits to the village. It was not until 1829 that the British abandoned the island and transferred their headquarters to Bathurst (now Banjul) at the mouth of the River Gambia. 〈. . .〉

Alex Haley admitted to me yesterday that, at one point, he found the African end of his inquiries so confusing, so obscured by contradictory statements from different sources, that he very nearly decided to make the African section, if not the entire book, a mere historical novel.

He concedes that, in retrospect, his reliance upon Fofana, the "griot" of Juffure, was perhaps an error, "and that it is possible I was misled. I have since discovered he was something of a playboy." Yet it was on the evidence of Fofana that Haley's claim to kinship with Kunta Kinte and much of the authority of *Roots* must stand or fall.

It is undoubtedly on the assumption of accuracy that the book's commercial success is founded. The blurb to the *Daily Express* serialisation, which began yesterday, proudly proclaimed, "The dialogue in this epic is imagined, but the events and characters are real . . . This is the true history of Haley's family."

But Haley still maintains, with some justification, that the "symbolic truth" of *Roots* remains untarnished. It is an acceptable generalisation on the appalling fate of thousands of Africans shipped into slavery. Men like Kunta Kinte did exist. The Mandinkas (or Mandingoes as they were known in the States) were highly prized by slavers. Many were captured up-river from James Island, and many must have been called Kinte since it is a common name in those regions. If his grandmother's story was correct, Haley has demonstrated his forefather was such a man. But he has not demonstrated that his name was Kunta Kinte, that he lived in Juffure, or that he was captured by slavers in 1767.

Mark Ottaway, "Tangled Roots," *Sunday Times* (London), 10 April 1977, p. 21

DAVID A. GERBER   Haley's rendering of family life and kinship relations among his slave ancestors ⟨in *Roots*⟩ fuses together ⟨the⟩ intersecting themes of bondage, vulnerability, and resilience, with intelligence and subtlety. Indeed, I believe it is here, in providing us with a sensitive and plausible view of the interior life of slaves, that he has made his most significant contribution. ⟨. . .⟩

A moment's reflection on the situation of Haley's slaves should be enough not only to suggest the depth of his portrayal of family life in all its varied forms, but to demonstrate the shallowness of the issue of their typicality. True enough Kunta Kinte is a coachman and his wife Bell, the Big House cook. They do no backbreaking field labor, by virtue of her position they eat well, have a relatively well-appointed cabin, and enjoy some opportunity for spatial mobility in the general vicinity of the plantation. ⟨. . .⟩ But they are nonetheless slaves: hemmed in, unpaid for their labor, lacking many fundamental choices, and treated more often than not as if they were incapable of choosing under any circumstances. Although their marriage helps to fill the emotional void a system of alienating labor and racist coercion particularly lends itself to, for all practical purposes marriage and the subsequent birth of their daughter end once and for all Kunta Kinte's hopes for escape to freedom. ⟨. . .⟩ The shallowness of their privileges, which Kunta Kinte himself realizes involve constant accommodation with a system he cannot ever morally accept, is never more starkly revealed than the morning when daughter Kizzy is summarily sold away for helping a young man in an unsuccessful attempt at escape. As Kizzy is dragged away, her parents, after decades of obedient service, watch with horror; though they offer some gestures at resistance, they are helpless to change her fate. ⟨. . .⟩

⟨. . .⟩ Much of the balance of *Roots* is the story of the struggles of ⟨Kizzy's son⟩ George and his now maturing and married children, led by son Tom a blacksmith, to keep together all of their related households during the waning years of slavery and into the troubled first years of freedom. George, who lives into his 80s, sees the family he has fought to preserve not only free and secure but even rather prosperous by the time of his death in 1890. Yet, while the television version was advertised as "the triumph of an American family," at least until well into the Reconstruction years (and thus through 95% of the book) *Roots* might better be described, as Philip Foner has said, as "the survival of an American family." Of course, under the circumstances of slavery and Reconstruction, perhaps "survival" did constitute a "triumph," and it would be both unfeeling and a misjudgment to fail to see the achievement of those slaves who did struggle for their loved ones against all of the odds they inevitably faced. But it is not until the late nineteenth century that Haley's people either achieve a position which might be called prosperous or which truly ensures their security and stability as a family.

> David A. Gerber, "Haley's *Roots* and Our Own: An Inquiry into the Nature of a Popular Phenomenon," *Journal of Ethnic Studies* 5, No. 3 (Fall 1977): 92–94

LESLIE FIEDLER   The image that possesses ⟨young black Americans⟩ is no longer that of the "good good nigger" as projected in Uncle Tom or of the "bad bad nigger" as embodied in Eldridge Cleaver, but of the "good bad nigger" as imagined by Malcolm X *after* his break with Elijah Muhammad. ⟨. . . Malcolm X's⟩ *Autobiography* was reconstructed by Alex Haley, a writer of fiction, who had to believe for reasons of his own that he was dealing with fact. A regular contributor to the *Reader's Digest,* his model not just for *The Autobiography of Malcolm X* but for *Roots* as well was that standard *Digest* piece, "The Most Unforgettable Character I Have Ever Known."

It is indeed his ability to make it at the heart of the white establishment, for twenty years in the Coast Guard and ten more in the mass media (including *Playboy,* for which he did a series of interviews), that qualified Haley to become the laureate of black-white relations in a time of accommodation. He is, in short, a "good good nigger," an "Uncle Tom," late twentieth-century style. At least that is what he seemed in Malcolm X's eyes—and reflexively in his own—at the moment of their first meeting. In any case, the epithet he avoided in *Roots* appears in Haley's description of that meeting. "We got off to a very poor start," Haley explains. "To use a word he likes,

I think both of us were a bit 'spooky' . . . I had heard him bitterly attack other Negro writers as 'Uncle Toms.' . . . . My twenty years in the military service and my Christian religious persuasion didn't help either." ⟨. . .⟩

⟨. . .⟩ throughout ⟨Roots⟩ Haley strives to portray his forebears even in Africa aspiring to a bourgeois life-style that would have pleased Mrs. Stowe. When Chicken George, for instance, prophesies for the benefit of his wife, Matilda, the domestic utopia which lies ahead for them after freedom, he does so in the following terms: "How you reckon you look settin' in yo' own house, yo' own stuffed furniture, an' all dem knickknacks? How 'bout Miss Tilda axin' de other free nigger womens over for tea in de mornin's, an' y'all jes' settin' 'roun talkin' 'bout 'rangin' y'all's flowers, an' sich as dat?"

It is, however, not that simple, since finally Roots is not really a Tom book, any more than it is an anti-Tom one. Yet, after the fact, Haley was much pleased by the critics who described it as "the most important book in terms of social change since Uncle Tom's Cabin." "If that is true," he is reported as saying, "I can only be humbled by that fact." It is an anti-anti-Tom book, and appropriately enough, its most memorable, which is to say, its only even approximately mythic character, Kunta Kinte, is an anti-anti-Tom: a noble African who after a symbolic castration and a happy marriage becomes a "good bad nigger," passing on the hope of freedom, but running away no more. ⟨. . .⟩ Kunta Kinte is less a portrait of Haley's first American ancestor, legendary or real, than of Malcolm X as Haley perceived him in guilt or envy.

Even as the living Haley ghostwrote the Autobiography, Malcolm X, from beyond the grave, ghostwrote what is most authentic and moving in Roots—the story of Kunta Kinte. Like Malcolm X, the Moslem Kunta Kinte rejects his white Christian name, dreams of a return to Africa not just for himself but for all black Americans, and is an old-fashioned sexist, believing that women should not be taught to read and that their place is in the home. He is, moreover, an inverted racist, convinced not only that all whites invariably do evil to all blacks but that they have an offensive odor and are properly classified not as humans but as toubab, "devils," who must be resisted unto death. Like the almost-white Black Muslim who possessed him, Haley is driven to euphemize Africa to the same extent he vilifies the American South. Though he perfunctorily admits to the existence of slavery on that continent and the complicity of black Africans in the slave trade, he manages to make them seem innocuous, as he does the prevailing violence of African life. If someone is forever beating someone else in Haley's Gambian village, it is *for their own good,* only white men presumably being capable of gratuitous brutality.

> Leslie Fiedler, "Alex Haley's *Roots:* Uncle Tom Rewrites *Uncle Tom's Cabin,*" *What Was Literature? Class Culture and Mass Society* (New York: Simon & Schuster, 1982), pp. 222–25

ALBERT E. STONE   Haley's book ⟨*The Autobiography of Malcolm X*⟩ deserves unstinting admiration, first of all, for recapturing both the vertical and horizontal axes of the unique yet deliberately representative life of a contemporary urban black man. "How is it possible to write one's autobiography in a world so fast-changing as this?" is Malcolm X's initial and ultimate question. Many celebrity autobiographies raise the same question, but Haley and his subject explore it with a terrible urgency. ⟨. . .⟩ Malcolm X comments to his collaborator on the radically different circumstances in his urban experience. "With the fast pace of newly developing incidents today, it is easy for something that is done or said tomorrow to be outdated even by sunset on the same day." "Sunset" indeed came while Malcolm X was in the throes of a rapid personal transformation. Before the assassination, however, he and Haley had fixed at least the outlines of a new identity born in the tumult of the 1960's. Yet this new self is also firmly anchored in the personal past. Malcolm X once remarked: "Why am I as I am? To understand that of any person, his whole life, from birth, must be reviewed. All of our experiences fuse into our personality. Everything that ever happened to us is an ingredient." Had Alex Haley not been at his side, Malcolm X might never have grasped the basic patterns and interactions of his violently changing inner and outer worlds.

To test this judgment, we must take note of the writer's crucial role as revealed in the biographical Epilogue. There Haley records not only Malcolm X's last months but traces in some detail the process of collaboration interrupted by the assassin's bullets. "Nothing can be in this book's manuscript that I didn't say," the subject insisted, "and nothing can be left out that I want in it." In return, Haley won an equally significant concession: "I asked for—and he gave—his permission that at the end of the book I could write comments of my own about him which would not be subject to his review." As Malcolm X pointedly remarked, "a writer is what I want, not an interpreter." But the Epilogue reveals that such a distinction is illusory. Though Haley made extraordinary efforts to subordinate himself to his partner and subject, his more vital achievement was to get Malcolm X to *see*, *say*, and *believe* the changes and continuities in his life and character which Haley had come to see. Such self-awareness is the crucial consequence, is it not, of any successful autobiographical act? How can we know that, even in the true autobiography, illumination has not come this way?

Their cooperation began coolly enough. Skepticism and mistrust abounded on both sides—as it also existed in many readers' minds of 1965—and perhaps still exists in 1981. For at the time of his death Minister Malcolm X of the Nation of Islam was widely (though falsely, as I think this book shows) depicted as a dangerous, rigid, and violent racist. For his part, Malcolm X was probably right to distrust Haley who, after all, was a thoroughly middle-class black, associated with white magazines whose viewpoints on race were little different from other mass media. Later, in their midnight sessions in Greenwich Village, Haley's adroit questioning gradually won over his suspicious subject while encouraging him to probe more deeply into the violent past and the problematic present. All the while, Malcolm X was living through the agony of his break with his leader and father-figure, the Honorable Elijah Muhammad. The temptation was great to revise the past just as it was being recovered. This Haley perceived as a great danger. Not only would it rob his story of dramatic interest and suspense, but would undermine the chief trait revealed in Malcolm's character: this ability to move and live fully in each stage and milieu of his life, his capacity to reenter each part of the past with sympathy yet with moral judgment. *Then* seen from *now* is, of course, the perspective of all autobiography. Haley succeeded brilliantly in getting Malcolm X to balance memories of his sinful past and his initial conversion in prison against more recent changes—including the hegira to Mecca and his second conversion there to a larger, raceless vision of mankind and society.

Albert E. Stone, "Collaboration in Contemporary American Autobiography," *Revue Française d'Etudes Américaines* No. 14 (May 1982): 159–61

HELEN CHAVIS OTHOW   In *Roots* a literary environment is established similar to that in Greek classical literature. The audience has prior knowledge of the story. Because of the prior speaking engagements, the reviews in journals and magazines, and finally the spectacular eight-day ABC television series of the story, the reader comes to the work with knowledge of the myth—the main characters, their trials, and outcomes. As one reads the story of Kunte and the other six protagonists, he knows that the main figure after Kunte is Alex because he is what his great-great-great-great-grandfather will become. It is as though each protagonist takes up the torch in the race of life from the other. In a sense, it is not their race alone, but Alex's race as he tries to run back in time to retrieve his heritage. In the end, it is the author who is the main hero. He is the author as hero. He has always been there throughout the story, although he enters into sharp focus at the end. ⟨. . .⟩

In the epic tradition, the hero discovers his opportunity for glory by the gods as in classical mythology; by Divine Providence as in the medieval epics; or by accident as in modern myth. Alex discovers his potential for understanding by stumbling across the Rosetta Stone in the London Museum, the stone from which the Egyptian characters had been deciphered by Jean Champollion for the first time. Then the thought occurred to him that his family's oral tradition could become alive and fructuating. Thus, the tradition becomes a talisman for success:

> Tom continued the tradition that had been passed down from the late Gran'mammy Kizzy and Chicken George, and there was much joking afterward that if ever anyone among them should neglect to relate the family chronicle to any new infant, they could surely expect to hear from the ghost of Gran'mammy Kizzy.

⟨. . .⟩ The aim of the author-hero's quest has been to finish the task begun by Kunte as he planted the seed of survival in Kizzy's ear. After many harsh, frustrating, and costly years of research, Alex returns with the Golden Fleece. He first returns to Africa (symbolic of the return of Kunte) where the ancient griot fills in the missing link of the prized possession. Like the mythical hero, he then returns to America where the nation shares in his triumphant victory. The trophy that he brings after twelve years of searching is a witness to the triumph of human perseverance. It is a relic, a book, and hope for the hungry masses of disenchanted people engulfed in secular and sometimes meaningless pursuits.

Helen Chavis Othow, "*Roots* and the Heroic Search for Identity," *CLA Journal* 26, No. 3 (March 1983): 313–16

SHERLEY ANNE WILLIAMS   Alex Haley's *A Different Kind of Christmas* is the sort of tale that asks to be read aloud. An adventure set during the days of the Underground Railroad, the elusive network of blacks and whites that helped Southern slaves escape to freedom in the North in the turbulent decades before the Civil War, it is the story of Fletcher Randall's conversion from scholarly defender of "his Southland" to avowed abolitionist and outlaw conductor on the legendary railroad.

The elements of a classic tale are here, the kind that warrants re-reading year after year because it affirms, without sentimentality, an uplifting sense of our national character and moral identity. Unfortunately, the master storyteller of *Roots* and the equally fine *The Autobiography of Malcolm X* is present only in sporadic flashes of style, and disturbing moral questions raised by his latest tale. ⟨. . .⟩

A Different Kind of Christmas is meant to delight and inspire "readers of all ages," as the publisher puts it, but Haley quickly abandons any real attempt to appeal to adult readers. The rich vocabulary of the opening pages, which evokes the 19th-Century setting and invites reading aloud to a favorite child, gives way to simple sentences and pat plottings likely to bore even younger readers. Haley's reliance on stock characters and descriptions vitiates the power of Fletcher's crisis and conversion and the suspense of his mission. The road between Princeton and Philadelphia, for example, is a "scenic way"; but we are given no hint of what the landscape looks like—whether wooded or open, flat or hilly.

The "ethnic diversity" of Philadelphia, which piques Fletcher's curiosity about different people, is suggested more in the repetition of that phrase than in descriptions of the look or sound of immigrants. Fletcher's politically ambitious father is given to "senatorial" warring, his mother to weeping. Our sympathy for these cardboard characters is almost non-existent, and our empathy for Fletcher's conflicting loyalties is likewise limited. Fletcher's own conversion from slaveholder to abolitionist is intellectualized, never dramatized or rendered for us. ⟨. . .⟩

Such conversions did take place during the abolitionist years, and hair-breadth escapes from slavery were not uncommon. Haley is due some credit for writing about an era, an institution whose heroism is too often ignored. In *A Different Kind of Christmas*, however, Haley has done little more than suggest the outlines of the classic tale that remains to be written about the Underground Railroad and its mystery train.

Sherley Anne Williams, "A Christmas Flight to Freedom," *Los Angeles Times Book Review*, 25 December 1988, pp. 1, 8

GARY JENNINGS   As a posthumous novel, *Queen* is something
of an oddity and, in its publisher's promotional puffery at least, something
of a scam. Not published until 15 months after Alex Haley's death and,
oddly, not until three months after it served as the basis for a CBS-TV
miniseries, it is touted in the jacket copy as Haley's "Final book . . . as only
Alex Haley could tell it."

However, screenwriter and playwright David Stevens—who rates very
low on the title page—takes full responsibility for the book's existence
(though not until the afterword, when a reader presumably has finished
reading what he took for a Haley creation). Stevens says he wrote it from
"a seven-hundred-page outline provided by Alex . . . some finished pages
. . . some scenes we wrote together" and adds that he is "keenly aware that
this is not the book Alex would have written." While left until rather too
late, this is a noble confession, because *Queen* is a slapdash job of work not
likely to enhance any author's reputation. ⟨. . .⟩

Unfortunately, though this book runs to a tad fewer pages than the
"outline" cited by Stevens, it remains just an outline, not a novel of fleshed-
out dimensions. We are taken to the scenes of many events, but too often
are only told about each event—"They aged, not in years, on their short
journey south, but with experience of the world"—seldom shown it or made
to feel we've been there. The characters, one and all, are likewise mere
outlines, containing no guts, emotions or vitality that would bring them to
life on the page, but only penciled-in descriptions of their traits, feelings
and reactions. It is hard to take any interest in, let alone care about, a
person presented as "a natural leader of men, a natural authority figure, but
with charm and good humor," who never manifests any of those qualities.

Gary Jennings, "*Queen*: Hardly Haley," *Washington Post*, 6 July 1993, p. C3

◈ *Bibliography*

The Autobiography of Malcolm X (with Malcolm X). 1965.

Roots. 1976.

A Different Kind of Christmas. 1988.

The Playboy *Interviews.* 1993.

Alex Haley's Queen: The Story of an African Family (with David Stevens).
    1993.

◈ ◈ ◈

Gayl Jones
b. 1949

GAYL JONES was born on November 23, 1949, the daughter of Franklin and Lucile (Wilson) Jones. She grew up in a segregated neighborhood in Lexington, Kentucky, where she was influenced by extant oral traditions—mostly in the form of street chatter and storytelling (both her mother and grandmother wrote stories and plays, sometimes solely for Gayl's amusement). Jones began writing at an early age, and even her early stories are full of the colloquial language of her neighborhood. She received a B.A. in English from Connecticut College in 1971; she then received an M.A. (1973) and D.A. (1975) in creative writing from Brown University. In 1975 she joined the faculty of the University of Michigan, attaining the rank of professor of English by the time she left in 1983.

Jones's first book was a play, *Chile Woman*, produced at Brown in 1973 and published in 1974. She then wrote two novels in quick succession—*Corregidora* (1975) and *Eva's Man* (1976)—followed by a collection of short stories, *White Rat* (1977). These fictions are distinguished for their uncompromising subject matter and their faithful and lyrical replication of the language of the street and the ghetto. *Corregidora* examines a brutal world of sexual violence and incest caused, primarily, by the slave system. In *Eva's Man* the sexual violence becomes more explicit, culminating in an act of dismemberment that lands Eva in prison. The novel, an explicit attack on male dominance, was not as well received as its predecessor. *White Rat* contains stories written and published between 1970 and 1977. Here the focus shifts to an intense examination of character, usually from within (most of the stories are written in the first person), occasionally with Gothic effects reminiscent of Poe or Kafka. This volume too received only mixed reviews, some critics complaining of its unrelenting grimness.

In recent years Jones has turned to poetry, producing three volumes, *Song for Anninho* (1981), *The Hermit-Woman* (1983), and *Xarque and Other Poems* (1985). These works reveal many of the same concerns as her fiction. *Song for Anninho* is a long narrative poem with an historical setting in seventeenth-century Brazil and tells the story of the troubled love of two fugitive slaves, Anninho and Almeyda. The poem is considerably more optimistic than Jones's previous works. She is now at work on another novel as well as a nonfiction study of Brazilian history in the sixteenth and seventeenth centuries; both these works appear to focus on Brazilian settlements for escaped slaves. In 1991 she published a critical work, *Liberating Voices: Oral Tradition in African American Literature*.

◈ *Critical Extracts*

JOHN UPDIKE   *Corredigora* persuasively fuses black history, or the mythic consciousness that must do for black history, with the emotional nuances of contemporary black life. The novel is about, in a sense, frigidity, about Ursa's inability to love. ⟨. . .⟩ Her interior monologues, where they do not concern Corregidora, are addressed to her first husband, Mutt, whose attempted domination of her, climaxed by her fateful fall down the stairs, nevertheless quickened a response she cannot give her second, gentle husband, Tadpole. Throughout the span of her life that is related—in the end she is forty-seven—Ursa rejects the advances made to her by her husbands, by amorous night-club clients, by lesbian sisters. Similarly, her mother, having rejected Martin, lives alone, spurning the courtship of a friendly neighbor. The interweave of past shame and present shyness gives the dialogue depth ⟨. . .⟩ The book's innermost action ⟨. . .⟩ is Ursa's attempt to "get her ass together," to transcend a nightmare black consciousness and waken to her own female, maimed humanity. She does it, in the end, with a sexual act that she imagines was what "Great Gram did to Corregidora"— an act combining pain and pleasure, submission and possession, hate and love, an act that says, in love, "I could kill you." This resolution is surprising but not shocking; one of the book's merits is the ease with which it assumes the writer's right to sexual specifics, and its willingness to explore exactly how our sexual and emotional behavior is warped within the matrix of family and race.

> John Updike, "Selda, Lilia, Ursa, Great Gram, and Other Ladies in Distress," *New Yorker*, 18 August 1975, pp. 81–82

DARRYL PINCKNEY   The men in this second novel ⟨*Eva's Man*⟩
complain of Eva's isolation, of her impenetrability. She constantly refuses
to explain herself to the men she encounters. She is utterly unwilling to
talk. Initially we see this as a defense against ruthlessness, but what is offered
the reader is somewhat insufficient: the torment she suffers as a woman is
not unusual, unfortunately, due to its frequency. No, this is not meant to
depreciate the daily nature of a woman's pain; but not all women become
schizophrenic, destructive. Both novels are relentlessly about fornication
and sex, as an act, as a burden, central to the plot of existence, a dialogue
between the deprived. The most private and reduced relations between the
characters is all that is needed to indicate their social oppression. There is
a continual sense of suffocation in these novels, as if their lives took place
in a closet. The stasis and isolation are haunting. Locations are ignored:
bus stops, taverns and cut-rate hotels all melted to a bleak, bare, unpaved
texture. There does not even seem to be a white side of town. No doubt
this is a source of the novels' power, as well as the distant and withheld
quality of the heroines. The wife, a woman, is a matter of possession and
property is always defined by the necessity for protection. Jealousy is a kind
of aggression and Gayl Jones' novels are, finally, indictments against black
men. The women are denied by convention what Angela Davis has called
"the deformed equality of equal oppression."

The imbalances in *Eva's Man* are discomforting. Fixations with menstrua-
tion, erections, even the treatment of the characters' diets—scrambled eggs,
onions, cooked sausage, cucumbers, cabbage, mustard, grease—create an
aversion, repulsion, as if the sensual were not a relief from existences misera-
ble and difficult, but a destiny bearing down without mercy. The skin of
her neighbor in jail is covered with scabs. A man is missing a thumb.
Women wear unnecessary amounts of perfume, cosmetics, jewelry. "You
just sitting right on the pot and scared to shit." Odors leap up from every
page. *Eva's Man*, then, is a tale of madness; one exacerbated if not caused
by frustration, accumulated grievances. Girlhood is reduced to incidents of
assault: little boys experiment on her with "a dirty popsicle stick," and
demand she fondle their genitals; old men accost and intimidate. Poverty
is not as evident in Eva's remembrance of New York slums as is another
kind of scarcity—women and men in doorways, under stairs; lurid remarks;
rape. ⟨. . .⟩

Gayl Jones places her heroines between victory and defeat where depriva-
tion is a narcotic. Though they are women of intense and complicated

feelings, their severity suggests an impasse. How does one sustain or add to the pitch of these books? There are hints of fragmentation and strain in the conception of *Eva's Man*. And there are risks in offering the novel as a forum for poetic and violent tirades of the solitary self: the limitations of tradition are exchanged for the narrowness of inaccessibility. Opaque, flat, peculiar, in her fiction Gayl Jones has presented problems that are living, historical and important additions to the current American—not just black—scene. These novels are genuinely imaginative creations.

Darryl Pinckney, [Review of *Eva's Man*], *New Republic*, 19 June 1976, pp. 27–28

JOHN WIDEMAN   Gayl Jones ⟨. . .⟩ exhibits debt to a literary tradi- tion, but it is a tradition including Wheatley and Pope, Faulkner and Ellison, a tradition richer in models and less foreign to American speech. The salient issue here is not the throng of influences on *Corregidora* which may be mustered from other works of literature, but rather the relationship between literature and oral traditions in Jones' novel. Gayl Jones is a member of a black speech community and this membership implicates a significant dimension of her literary style. In contrast to Wheatley for whom oral traditions black or white are negligible, the fluency of Jones in two language cultures permits her to create a considerable dramatic tension between them, a tension responsible for much of the novel's impact and uniqueness. One critic's comment that "The book is written with almost embarrassing power" is evidence of how difficult this tension is to resolve. In ⟨. . .⟩ *Corregidora* there is no hierarchical relationship between black speech and a separate literary language, no implicit dependency. The norms of black oral tradition exist full bodied in the verbal style of the novel: lexicon, syntax, grammar, attitudes towards speech, moral and aesthetic judgments are rendered in the terms of the universe they reflect and reinforce. Through the filter of the narrator's sensibility the entire novel flows, and Corregidora's sensibility is constructed of blocks of black speech, her own, her men's, the speech of the people who patronize Happy's bar, the voices of her mother and the dead black women keeping alive the memories of slavery. Black speech is allowed to do (the author insists that it can) everything any other variety of literary language can do. The message comes through loud and clear to the reader: there is no privileged position from which to view this fictional world, no terms into which it asks to be translated, its rawness is not incidental, not local color or exoticism from which other, more familiar voices will relieve you. A black woman's voice creates the only valid terms for Corregidora's world; the authority of her language is not subordinated to other codes; the frame has disappeared.

John Wideman, "Frame and Dialect: The Evolution of the Black Voice in American Literature," *American Poetry Review* 5, No. 5 (September/October 1976): 35–36

MICHAEL S. HARPER   [HARPER]: Do you have any models for artistic conception, literary, historical, or autobiographical?

[JONES]: I used to say that I learned to write by listening to people talk. I still feel that the best of my writing comes from having *heard* rather than having read. This isn't to say that reading doesn't enrich or that reading isn't important, but I'm talking about foundations. I think my language/ word foundations were oral rather than written. But I was also learning how to read and write at the same time I was listening to people talk. In the beginning, *all* of the richness came from people rather than books because in those days you were reading some really unfortunate kinds of books in school. I'm talking about the books children learned to read out when I was coming up. But my first stories were heard stories—from grown-up people talking. I think it's important that we—my brother and I—were never sent out of the room when grown-up people were talking. So we heard their stories. So I've always heard stories of people generations older than me. I think that's important. I think that's the important thing.

Also, my mother would write stories for us and read them to us. She would read other stories too, but my favorite ones were the ones she wrote herself and read to us. My favorite one of those was a story called "Esapher and the Wizard." So I first knew stories as things that were heard. That you listened to. That someone spoke. The stories we had to read in school— I didn't really make connections with them as stories. I just remember us sitting around in the circle and different people being called on to read a sentence. But my mother's reading the stories—I connected with that. And I connected with the stories people were telling about things that happened back before I was born.

When I was in the fifth grade, I had a teacher who would have us listen to music and then write stories. We had to write the stories that came to us while we were listening and then we would have to read the stories aloud to the whole class. I had started writing stories when I was in the second or third grade, when I was seven or eight, but didn't show them to anybody until her. Of course, my mother knew I was writing. Of course, I showed things to her. But my fifth-grade teacher was the first teacher I showed any work to. Her name was Mrs. Hodges. I remember I used to make stories and put the names of people in the class in them so that everybody would laugh. So then there was the music and the heard stories. It was an all-black school. I went to an all-black school until the tenth grade when there was integration. I say that because I think it's important. I think it's important about the music and the words, too.

A lot of connections I made with tradition—with historical and literary things—I started making later. I was writing stories in first-person before I made connections with the slave narrative tradition or the tradition of black autobiography, before "oral storytelling" became something you talked about. At first, I just felt that the first-person narrative was the most authentic way of telling a story, and I felt that I was using my own voice—telling a story the way I would talk it. I liked the way the words came out better than the way they came out in third-person. And I liked writing dialogue in stories, because I was "hearing" people talk. But I hadn't made any of the kinds of connections you make with your traditions other than the connections you make in living them and being a part of them. I didn't really begin to make the other kinds of connections till graduate school. I still don't like to stand away from the traditions, talking about them. You ought to be able to talk about them standing right inside them.

Michael S. Harper, "Gayl Jones: An Interview" (1977), *Chant of Saints: A Gathering of Afro-Amrican Literature, Art, and Scholarship*, ed. Michael S. Harper and Robert B. Stepto (Urbana: University of Illinois Press, 1979), pp. 352–53

DIANE JOHNSON   In the work of Gayl Jones one sees other literary influences—of Hemingway, perhaps, or Jean Rhys, highly wrought and economical—but also of those bus station thrillers in which a female narrator describes her loss of innocence, her sexual exploitation by a relentless string of single-minded lechers. The ancestress of Ursa Corregidora, the abused heroine of Jones's first novel, is the lusty, busty high-yellow beauty so beloved on paperback covers. The difference is that Jones's women, brutalized and dull, seem all too real. It is skillful expoitation of the stereotype.

The stories in her collection *White Rat* were written in some cases earlier than her novels, so they confirm one's sense of her direction and preoccupations: sex is violation, and violation is the principal dynamic of human relationships. In the sexual relation lies the struggle for power, the means of survival, the symbol of adulthood, the cause of suffering. Where ⟨Toni⟩ Morrison is an art novelist, who can invoke black speech for striking effect, Jones is a vernacular novelist with a marvelous ear, for whom black speech is the only medium. A boy says to the narrator of "The Women,"

> "You got a nice house," . . .
> "If you don't got to live in it."
> "Your mama keep things around."
> "What nots."
> "Yeah, my mama got those around too. She paint pictures and
> put them on the wall. Daddy tell her take 'em down. She say she
> don't like look at the bare wall."
> "Aw."

The monosyllables with which the characters conduct their lives suggest their defended isolation. It is as if there were only so much information to go around, and each person, jealous of the advantage it confers, is reluctant to share his. The jazzy banter that Morrison and ⟨James Alan⟩ McPherson both portray so well has the same back-to-the-wall quality. Though ignorance these days has lost much of its traditional status as a routinely stigmatized enemy of human happiness—indeed it is often admired—the plight of these characters renews one's sense of its virulence.

The women characters in Morrison are all eccentric, brave, and resolute. Gayl Jones presents women who are stunned and withdrawn. But both writers arrange their narratives in such a way as to avoid preachiness and, perhaps, to avert accusations of disloyalty. Morrison often lets a character have a say, like Lena, in *Song of Solomon*, who asks her brother "Where do you get the *right* to decide our lives? . . . I'll tell you where. From that hog's gut that hangs down between your legs. Well, let me tell you something, baby brother, you will need more than that."

Moral comment in Jones is more oblique. Ursa Corregidora, asleep, dreams resentfully of her possessive lover, "talking about *his* pussy. Asking me to let him see his pussy. Let me feel my pussy. The center of a woman's being. Is it?" When she wakes up she denies her resentment. "The shit you can dream." (His beatings have required her to lose her womb.) Because she writes entirely in the first person, Jones seems to record what people say and think as if it were no fault of hers, and Morrison seems to assert no more control over the exotic events of her narratives than the teller of a tall tale does. Perhaps art is always subversive in this way.

Diane Johnson, "The Oppressor in the Next Room," *New York Review of Books*, 10 November 1977, pp. 6–7

VALERIE GRAY LEE   Gayl Jones' *Corregidora* is another work by a black woman in which the womenfolk spend their time discussing the menfolk. Whereas the folktalk that Janie ⟨in Zora Neale Hurston's *Their Eyes Were Watching God*⟩ uses in discussing the men is romantic and Sula's ⟨in Toni Morrison's *Sula*⟩ is earthy, Ursa Corregidora's is downright bawdy. The four-letter sexual street language is in keeping with the trials and pathos of Ursa's story. Old Man Corregidora, the Portuguese slavemaster, mated with Ursa's grandmother and great grandmother. All of the flashbacks of the novel, all of Ursa's thoughts, revolve around Corregidora and what he did with his "womens." Ursa's great grandmother passed the story down from generation to generation so that there would always be evidence of what had gone on. According to Great Gran, Old Man Corregidora first "broke his womens hisself." She explained to Ursa over and over again the situation:

> "He liked his womens black, but he didn't wont us with no black mens. It wasn't color cause he didn't even wont us with no light black mens, cause there was a man down there as light as he was, but he didn't wont us with him . . . cause when he send them white mens in there to me he didn't look like that, cause he be nodding and saying what a fine piece I was, said I was a fine speciment of a woman, finest speciment of a woman he ever seed in his life."

There is nothing in the novel that does not connect to this sexual theme. Ursa has to come to grips with the story passed down by her ancestors before she can produce her own life story. Because of Ursa's hysterotomy, she is not able to make generations in the literal way that grandmothers and mother did. Instead she turns to folk music—the blues. The blues help her to explain what she cannot explain. They are the evidence that she leaves behind.

Just as Janie and Sula have best friends with whom they discuss "the menfolks," so does Ursa. Ursa tries to explain to Catherine ("Cat") some of her present problems with men. Ursa has an ex-husband and a lover who both claim to love her. Her husband, Mutt, unfortunately, does not view her as a whole person, but refers to her in a derogatory folk language as his "piece of ass." Ursa does not want to be a piece of anything. She dreams of telling Mutt off in a dirty-dozens duel. Mutt needs to realize that there will have to be some changes before Ursa takes him back.

The recurring question in *Corregidora* is, "What's a husband for?" Is he someone who literally knocks the womb out of his woman? Is he someone who owns her? Is he someone only to take care of her sexual needs? What's a husband for? The bawdy folk language captures, in a way that "conventional English" cannot, the answers to these questions. It does indeed make the work read like an extended blues lyric.

Valerie Gray Lee, "The Use of Folktalk in Novels by Black Women Writers," *CLA Journal* 23, No. 3 (March 1980): 270–71

JERRY W. WARD, JR.   In the American penal system, female prisoners are often subjected to more psychosexual abuse than their male counterparts. The same condition obtains, according to our most perceptive writers, in American society outside the prison walls. The abuse of women and its psychological results fascinate Gayl Jones, who uses these recurring themes to magnify the absurdity and the obscenity of racism and sexism in everyday life. Her novels and short fictions invite readers to explore the interiors of caged personalities, men and women driven to extremes. Her intentions seem less analytic than synthetic, the strategies of her fictions themselves being indices of contemporary disorder as norm rather than deviation. Throughout Jones's fictions, prisons and asylums function as settings for problematic narratives and as clues for the interpretation of outsideness. In the very act of concretizing these fictions as aesthetic objects, readers find themselves caught. The pleasure of experiencing such irony, and of gradually coming to know how accurately it confirms our habitation of an invisible penal colony, is justification for attending to Gayl Jones's achievement.

The unpredictable structures of *Corregidora* and *Eva's Man* and of the short fiction of *White Rat* provoke questions about how we construct meaning from allowing our minds to play through the texts. The author invites us into semantic realms for which we may have no guides other than cultivated literary competence, previous knowledge of other texts. We cannot begin to speak of the value of the experience until we understand how we have been seduced. Indeed, we may find ourselves posing unusual questions. What does it mean to think in fiction? Does thinking in a fiction lead us to experience states of mind ostensibly *represented* in the fiction? And how does one distinguish thinking in fiction from its mimesis? Where does such inquiry lead us? Does it offer any insights about qualitative differences between fictions by male and female writers?

Definitive, universal answers to such questions are unlikely. Yet raising them encourages us to think seriously about the verbal entrapment that is so pervasive a quality of modern fiction. Like the magic of Circe and Faust, modern fictions can transfom us—while we permit their influence—into the beings that our humanity disguises. As readers we begin to grasp that neither man nor woman is immune to the siren song of Jones's fictions.

Jerry W. Ward, Jr., "Escape from Trublem: The Fiction of Gayl Jones" (1982), *Black Women Writers (1950–1980): A Critical Evaluation*, ed. Mari Evans (New York: Anchor Books/Doubleday, 1984), pp. 249–50

KEITH E. BYERMAN   Gayl Jones, of all the writers discussed thus far, creates the most radiant worlds. Not only are the societies depicted the most thoroughly and correctly oppressive, but she also denies readers a "sane" narrative center through which to judge world and narrator. Most frequently, her narrators have already been judged insane by the society; and this assessment, given the teller's actions and obsessions, seems reasonable. But we cannot therefore assume that we have entered a Poesque world of confessors of personal guilt or madness, for it is equally apparent that society has its own obsessions and that its labeling of the narrators as mad facilitates evasion of the implications of those obsessions. ⟨. . .⟩

"Asylum" is an extreme case of Jones's attitude. The narrator, a young woman committed to an asylum because of her irrational behavior, refuses to allow the doctor to examine her genital area, yet she was admitted after deliberately urinating in the living room when her nephew's teacher visited their home. She explains to the reader (though not to the psychiatrist) her motive for the latter action: "She [the teacher] just sit on her ass and fuck all day and it ain't with herself."

Obsessed with acts of violation, whether sexual, intellectual, or psychological, she reveals her madness in rendering this sense of violation in graphic terms. Thus, her feeling that the teacher functions as an exploiter of children and thus provides a humanly worthless education is effectively expressed by presenting and using the family slop jar. Significantly, when the psychiatrist explains the means by which she is to be made "normal," she sees those means as schoolwork.

She considers the whole process of physical and mental examination to be rape. Whenever she has been examined, she sees a "big black rubbery thing look like a snake" emerging from either her vagina or her anus. Those examining her define her resistance and sensibility as narcissistic sexual obsession, needing correction by experts. What Jones accomplishes through selection of narrator is a rebuttal of such a reductive notion. Even if the narrator is insane, our access to her thoughts informs us that the probing and objectification of her by the doctors is woefully inadequate. The pain and disorder she experiences are unrelieved and even aggravated by such clinical clichés as: "libido concentrated on herself."

Moreover, she associates this reification and violence with whites. In a dream, the narrator sees the black nurse becoming "chalk white" when she assists in the examinations. More important, the narrator dreams that she herself takes on white characteristics and is thereafter unable to prevent the vaginal exploration.

The final conversation of the story suggests the dilemma facing the narrator:

> "What does this word make you feel?"
> "Nothing."
> "You should tell me what you are thinking?"
> "Is that the only way I can be freed?"

The asylum microcosm of the totalitarian state. Those in authority determine what constitutes sane behavior and thought. Not to speak is to condemn oneself to imprisonment as a mental incorrigible. But the act of speaking is collaboration in one's dehumanization since it leads to categorization and "treatment," which in effect is imposition of values and modes of behavior designed to make one a functioning cog in the social machine. In other words, there is no freedom, no escape from this "refuge."

Keith E. Byerman, "Beyond Realism: The Fictions of Gayl Jones and Toni Morrison," *Fingering the Jagged Grain: Tradition and Form in Recent Black Fiction* (Athens: University of Georgia Press, 1985), pp. 171–72, 176–77

RICHARD K. BARKSDALE   Two conclusions can be drawn from studying the patterns of sexual conflict in Jones's two novels. First, the roots of the black woman's sexual slavery are deeply buried in the physical violence and degradation of African chattel slavery. Here, too, are the roots of black concubinage, often incestuous and sadomasochistic. This lamentable side of black history in the diaspora has been widely documented. Dorothy Sterling, for instance, in a chapter entitled "Seduction, Rape, and Concubinage" in *We Are Your Sisters* (New York: Norton, 1984), shows how black women, entrapped and exploited in a violent system, resorted to desperate stratagems to survive and retain their sanity and their womanly self-esteem. As Sterling reports, sometimes, in their travail, black women in slavery sang:

> Rains come wet me
> Sun come dry me
> Stay back, white man
> Don't come nigh me.

Obviously a little song like this could not stop the savage whippings and the physical, mental and emotional indignities suffered by the black slave woman. For further documentation of her status, we have Frederick Douglass' tragic portrait of his mother (actually, his half-sister as well as his mother), who was driven to an early death by cruel and inhumane treatment.

The second conclusion to be drawn from the Jones novels is that, with slavery's end, black men like the Mutt Thomases of the world began to imitate the sexual behavior of their former masters. Stripped of political and economic power and harassed by a still-dominant white majority, they sought to enjoy their new freedom in whatever limited sense they could under the circumstances. Within this context they sought to hold sexual mastery over their women, and to some extent, unless a former master intervened, the black freedmen enjoyed and exploited this power. So over the years there occurred a mirror-imaging exchange of power, and in his sexual relations with his women the black man replaced his former master.

Richard K. Barksdale, "Castration Symbolism in Recent Black American Fiction," *CLA Journal* 29, No. 4 (June 1986): 406–7

MELVIN DIXON   The action in *Eva's Man* (1976) begins where *Corregidora* left off and envelops us in the despair of one woman's self-inflicted failure to achieve refuge or redemption. The unrelenting violence, emotional silence, and passive disharmony in *Eva's Man* are the undersides of the blues reconciliation and active lovemaking in *Corregidora*. Eva Medina Canada poisons her lover Davis Carter and castrates him with her teeth once he is dead. Important to our brief study here is that Eva never gains control over her voice, her past, her place, or her identity. Instead of wielding language as useful evidence for justice and regeneration as Ursa has done, Eva is defeated by words and brandishes first a pocket knife against Moses Tripp, then arsenic and teeth against Davis. Eva never comes to terms with her past; she chooses to embrace received images of women as *femmes fatales*. Ursa and Eva are further separated by their vastly different ability to experience love.

In view of Jones's concern with opening avenues for reconciliation between the sexes, it is important to see *Eva's Man* and *Corregidora* as companion texts. Primarily through the protagonists' attitudes toward language and their fluency with idioms necessary for personal deliverance, we encounter one woman's fall and another's rise. The clear contrast between them makes Ursa appear as Eva's alter ego and reveals Jones to be a gifted ironist: Eva, surnamed Canada, the promised land and refuge for fugitive slaves, contrasts with Corregidora, Brazilian slave master in one of the larger regions of New World slavery. Yet it is Ursa who frees herself from bondage and Eva who succumbs to it. Eva has chained herself to the debilitating stereotypes of Queen Bee, Medusa, and Eve long before she is locked away in prison for her crime. And Eva is only partly aware of her own responsibility in getting there. ⟨. . .⟩

Eva fails to deliver herself from the wilderness. She remains "looking like [the] wild woman" she first appeared to be in newspaper photos of her arrest, and she erroneously believes in the surface meaning of the blues song she hears, "Wild Women Don't Get the Blues." Eva misreads the song's irony and Ursa's example. Although Ursa inhabits an interior space of the past in her memory of Corregidora, she succeeds in breaking free. The mountain tunnel releases the train in her song. Ursa travels to another height of self-possession. The geography of the journey for Gayl Jones is both sexual and musical.

> Melvin Dixon, "Keep Me from Sinking Down: Zora Neale Hurston, Alice Walker, and Gayl Jones," *Ride Out the Wilderness: Geography and Identity in Afro-American Literature* (Urbana: University of Illinois Press, 1987), pp. 117, 120

FRANÇOISE LIONNET   ⟨. . .⟩ Eva's self-representation ⟨in *Eva's Man*⟩ as well as the way she feels about herself and her actions cannot be separated from the cultural images of women that are common currency around her. Consequently, when the psychiatrist who tries to "help" her asks her how she feels, she can only recall other instances of people asking her and other women how "it feels," for how is a woman supposed to feel about her own sexuality when its value is repeatedly denied, when she knows nothing about her own desires, and when male sexuality expresses itself in the form of sexual harassment? The doctor is an obvious composite of the male protagonists who have used her in the past: his name is David Smoot, recalling young Freddy Smoot as well as Davis Carter himself. In fact, just as Eva is made to represent a certain stereotype of fatal woman, all the men eventually merge into one single paradigm of male dominance, the voice of "all them Dr. Frauds" that, since Freud, keeps on interrogating femininity: "Why won't you talk about yourself?" "Why did you kill him?" "What did he do?" "What happened?" "Did you want to do anything you did?" This is the same voice that has always puzzled over "what a woman wants." ⟨. . .⟩ Eva refuses to explain herself: "I don't like to talk about myself," and this is the only way she has of resisting the dominant discourses that imprison her inside certain labels: "Her silences are . . . ways of maintaining . . . autonomy," Gayl Jones has said. Her seemingly passive compliance is a way of resisting the double bind, what ⟨Hélène⟩ Cixous has called the "phallocentric representationalism" that distorts and objectifies: "You keep all your secrets, don't you?" Davis says, when there are in fact no "secrets" to keep, only the impossibility for the woman to accede to the symbolic realm of language without simultaneously putting herself under erasure, risking misunderstanding, or confirming the patriarchal representations that preexist her speech: "A motive was never given. She never said anything. She just took the sentence." It is this apparent "serenity" that leads to the insanity plea: "When a woman done something like you done and serene like that, no wonder they think you crazy," as Elvira explains. Eva instinctively knows what the entire United States would be forced to watch during Anita Hill's testimony before the U.S. Senate in September 1991: that what a black woman might feel, and what she might want, are so inconceivable to the imagination of a patriarchal nation, so threatening, that she must be neutralized by stereotypical accusations of feminine instability and unreliability. ⟨. . .⟩

On a structural level, Jones makes no attempt to placate her readers; *Eva's Man* is a difficult book, a tale of great intensity that resists closure. ⟨. . .⟩ it is a story about men, about their obsessive sexuality and exploitative relationships. Eva's own personal story is not really told, since most of what we know of her is what the men in her life (Freddy, Mr. Logan, John Canada, Tyrone, Davis, Alfonso, Moses Tripp, James Hunn, and finally David Smoot) have done to the women she knows. The narrative shows how they have made Eva herself into a "little evil devil bitch," a "sweet [castrating] bitch." The narrative fragments do not add up to a coherent picture of the past, and the novel thematizes its structural discontinuities by stressing the gaps and the fissures in Eva's memory, by suggesting that it is thanks to those gaps that she can manage to slip out of the symbolic domain, and disrupt the culture's master narrative.

> Françoise Lionnet, "Geographies of Pain: Captive Bodies and Violent Acts in the Fictions of Myriam Warner-Vieyra, Gayl Jones, and Bessie Head," *Callaloo* 16, No. 1 (Winter 1993): 144–45

Bibliography

Chile Woman. 1974.
Corregidora. 1975.
Eva's Man. 1976.
White Rat. 1977.
Song for Anninho. 1981.
The Hermit-Woman. 1983.
Xarque and Other Poems. 1985.
Liberating Voices: Oral Tradition in African American Literature. 1991.

Terry McMillan
b. 1951

TERRY L. MCMILLAN was born October 18, 1951, in Port Huron, Michigan. Her parents, Edward McMillan and Madeline Washington Tillman, were uneducated laborers who had to support six children. This task was made more difficult by the fact that Edward McMillan was an alcoholic; his death when his daughter was sixteen created still more hardship for the family. Terry McMillan took a job at a library that year, which she credits with introducing her to literature.

After graduating from high school, McMillan traveled to Los Angeles to attend a community college; she later transferred to the University of California at Berkeley. While in college she discovered black literature and also met and befriended writer and critic Ishmael Reed, who enabled her to publish her first short story, "The End," in 1976. She graduated from Berkeley with a B.A. in journalism in 1979 and then briefly attended film school at Columbia University before dropping out. For the next few years she supported herself by word processing while attempting to publish various short stories and eventually being accepted into the Harlem Writers Guild.

In 1983, McMillan was accepted at the MacDowell artists colony and then the Yaddo writers colony, where she quickly produced the first draft of *Mama*, a highly autobiographical novel about a poor family's struggles to survive. When the novel was published in 1987, McMillan, dissatisfied with her publisher's efforts, decided to promote the novel on her own, sending over 3,000 letters to bookstores and universities and establishing her reputation as an excellent reader and speaker. Her successful debut garnered her a National Endowment for the Arts Fellowship in 1988 and was followed by *Disappearing Acts* in 1989. The novel concerns a rocky relationship between a well-educated woman and her construction-worker boyfriend, Franklin Swift. While a commercial and critical success, it resulted in a $4.75 million defamation suit against McMillan filed by Leonard Welch, a former lover and the father of McMillan's only child, Solomon Welch, who maintained that the novel and specifically the character of Franklin

Swift were created solely to denigrate his character. The New York Supreme Court ruled in McMillan's favor in April 1991.

McMillan edited an anthology, entitled *Breaking Ice: An Anthology of Contemporary African-American Fiction,* in 1990 and contributed a critical essay to *Five for Five: The Films of Spike Lee* in 1991. In 1992, she published her most popular book, the best-selling *Waiting to Exhale,* a novel about four black women who are searching for suitable mates. The novel, written out of McMillan's frustrations with her own singleness, created a sensation and led to a number of lucrative paperback, movie, and foreign rights deals.

McMillan taught at the University of Wyoming at Laramie from 1987 to 1990, then as a tenured professor at the University of Arizona from 1990 to 1992. She currently lives with her son in Danville, California, where she is working on a film adaptation of *Waiting to Exhale.*

▦ *Critical Extracts*

CAROLYN SEE   Mildred is a black woman, and this ⟨*Mama*⟩ is a "black" novel, but in the most profound sense that's not the point. In America, where one in every two marriages ends in divorce, where women earn 59 cents for every dollar men earn, something like 50% of all American families are eventually going to be involved with aspects either of matriarchy or poverty. The author's artistic question here is—how does that dynamic work? Can children raised that way *live?* ⟨. . .⟩

Freda, that oldest girl who had to give up her Christmas presents and act as a substitute mama to the younger kids whenever her own mama went under, opts for education as her way out. She moves to Los Angeles, finds a bachelor apartment with a glittery ceiling, and proceeds by fits and starts through the university system.

But there's a moment—up in Marin County, when she and some handsome gent lounge in a hot tub, buzzing on cocaine—when the reader realizes that Freda and her mama are caught in the same trap. And it's not just men, and not just white society. It's alcohol and drugs and the wish to use sex as oblivion, a way not to notice the demands of the outside world. These are the patterns that Mildred and Freda share.

The story here, then, is what happens to people when they're locked out of mainstream life. Terry McMillan only mentions in one sentence that white journalists in New York aren't exactly waiting on pins and needles for a penniless black woman to come and join their ranks. The racism, the "oppression" she's addressing comes from far, far back, and it's been completely internalized. If you didn't deserve to have electric lights in your house when you were a kid, how can you deserve freedom, happiness and love when you've grown up?

The end here should not be given away, but the author suggests, almost as a Zen exercise, that the first way for the locked-out to break from the prison of their souls is to love each other; that if all those who are "locked out" could turn to each other for comfort and love and support, then it might be the tight, white, Establishment patriarchy that might end up, in fact, locked in.

> Carolyn See, "Down-and-Out Family, Out of the Mainstream, Wants In," *Los Angeles Times*, 23 February 1987, p. V4

VALERIE SAYERS   Terry McMillan's new novel is a love story waiting to explode. The lovers of *Disappearing Acts* are both intelligent and good-looking, both possessed of dreams—but Zora Banks is an educated black woman and Franklin Swift is an unschooled black man. It's Brooklyn, it's 1982, and it's clear from page 1 that the two of them are sitting in a mine field and something's going to blow.

Ms. McMillan's first novel, *Mama*, was original in concept and style, a runaway narrative pulling a crowded cast of funny, earthy characters. *Disappearing Acts* is also full of momentum, and it's a pleasurable, often moving novel. In this intricate look at a love affair, Ms. McMillan strikes out in a whole new direction and changes her narrative footing with ease. But *Disappearing Acts* is also a far more conventional popular novel than *Mama* was. Despite its raunchy language and its narrative construction (Franklin's voice and Zora's alternate), its descriptions, its situations, even its generic minor characters are often predictable. I say this with some surprise, because it seems to me that Terry McMillan has the power to be an important contemporary novelist. ⟨. . .⟩

Zora's voice, though generally likeable, has a bland quality (Franklin's son says she "talk like white people"), and her narrative is sometimes written in a pop-magazine style that has her forever reminding her readers how handsome Franklin is. ⟨. . .⟩

⟨. . .⟩ Franklin Swift is smart, bigoted, passionate, loving, generous, mean-spirited, ignorant, intractable, forgiving, resentful. His voice is far grittier than Zora's and it's genuine. In addition, Ms. McMillan takes some real chances not only with Franklin's voice but with his life. Summarized, his history makes him sound like a loser: he's a high school dropout who's played with drugs and seen the inside of a prison; a man who despises his mother and his wife; a father who sees and supports his two children sporadically; a lover who sometimes asks for sex in a repellent, coarse whine; an expectant father so frustrated by his dealings with the white construction world that he hits a pregnant Zora—and later does worse. Much worse.

The miracle is that Ms. McMillan takes the reader so deep into this man's head—and makes what goes on there so complicated—that his story becomes not only comprehensible but affecting. The reader comes to see why Zora loves him, and why she kicks him out. Franklin is a more compelling character than Zora because he's allowed his moments of childishness and even wickedness: he's a whole person. Ms. McMillan's portrayal of this man may well be controversial (anybody looking for a successful, strong-but-gentle African-American male won't find him here), but it's undeniably alive.

Valerie Sayers, "Someone to Walk Over Me," *New York Times Book Review*, 6 August 1989, p. 8

DAVID NICHOLSON   For the past decade or more, books by black women have appeared in such numbers as to constitute almost a separate genre within an all too frequently ghettoized American literature. Surely, however, this second novel by Terry McMillan ⟨*Disappearing Acts*⟩ must be one of the few to contain rounded, sympathetic portraits of black men and to depict relationships between black men and black women as something more than the relationship between victimizer and victim, oppressor and oppressed.

For that, and for daring to create a heroine who, though disappointed in love, does not condemn all men or retreat to militant homosexuality, McMillan deserves applause. She has refused to perpetuate the well-worn conventions of black women's writing. And, in fact, she may have created a whole new category—the post-feminist black urban romance novel.

The novel concerns the two-year affair of Franklin Swift, a high-school dropout in his 30s who works intermittently doing construction, and Zora Banks (yes, she *is* named after the novelist, anthropologist and free spirit of the Harlem Renaissance), a junior high school music teacher who wants to become a singer. ⟨. . .⟩

⟨. . .⟩ Their biggest problem ⟨. . .⟩ is the difference in their backgrounds.

That last device is, of course, one of the oldest in literature, but the specifics here are of particular relevance to black Americans. Professional black women complain of an ever-shrinking pool of eligible men, citing statistics that show the number of black men in prison is increasing, while the number of black men in college is decreasing. Articles on alternatives for women, from celibacy to "man-sharing" to relationships with blue-collar workers like Franklin, have long been a staple of black general interest and women's magazines. ⟨. . .⟩

Despite the "equal time" given Franklin and the sympathetic way in which he is portrayed, this is, I think, a women's novel. I can't imagine most men liking it, in part because of the hard truths Zora and her friends have to tell (in the female equivalent of lockerroom bull sessions) about men they've known. Mostly, though, it's that there is a sweetness about *Disappearing Acts*; it is really an old-fashioned love story, albeit a sincere one. ⟨. . .⟩

For all that is good about this novel, however, I like it more for what it represents than for what it achieves, and I think McMillan deserves congratulations for what she has attempted, not for what she has accomplished.

David Nicholson, "Love's Old Sweet Song," *Washington Post Book World*, 27 August 1989, p. 6

THULANI DAVIS   Now that the '90s are at hand, it's inevitable that someone will announce a new generation of writers, folks who'll be the bridge to the next century. (WOW!) The "new generation" of African-American writers, novelist Terry McMillan said not too long ago, are "different from a generation before" because "they are not as race oriented, and they are not as protest oriented." I wondered at first who she was talking about. The novelists being published right now are, for the most part, around 40. Most of them began getting published 20 years ago, but those who were the talk of the '70s seem wildly different—and I mean wildly—from the crew McMillan is describing. The young writers back then were full of the anger, rhythms, sexuality, and wicked humor of jazz, r&b, and the '60s. I doubt if anyone would have guessed that the next generation was going to be less "race oriented." ⟨. . .⟩

If four novels published in the past few months, including one by McMillan, are any indication, there *is* a crop of African-American fiction coming in the '90s, written by 40ish folk, that's less interested in race and protest. It speaks in the practiced tongue of white mainstream literature. Melvin Dixon, Marita Golden, Tina McElroy Ansa, and McMillan show in their work a silent—in some cases maybe unconscious—struggle with assimilation. Each of their books describes some part of the lonely, self-involved journey of the middle-class African American who has access to some little piece of the Dream and is as deeply ensconced in American mass culture as in our boisterous yet closely held black world. ⟨. . .⟩

Even though Zora and Franklin ⟨of *Disappearing Acts*⟩ are last-week contemporary, they are also like classic folklore characters come to life in Brooklyn. She's the wily black woman of yore, smart-talking Eve who's always got a little something on the rail for the lizard, as we used to say. She's also a sophisticated shopper, who likes fancy cheeses and bottled water, and she says shit all the time. Zora has all the pulls and tugs of feminism versus the feminine that a modern black woman who's read Walker and Shange is supposed to have. She's not unlike Zora Neale Hurston's sassy folk women—characters *Cosmo* would never dare to pop-psychoanalyze.

Complicated as Franklin is supposed to be, he is a savvy urban John Henry—he don't take no tea fo' the fever. An intellectual Tina Turner meets a hardhat Ike. They are both bricks and though they may chip each other, they ain't never gonna blend. They live and work in New York City, but are in a very insulated world; their problems are completely personal. Their relationship is doomed by mutual expectations and ended by an outburst of gratuitous male violence. Let's just say it wasn't needed for the love affair to fall apart.

These two are as they are; like other folk heroes, they don't change much, or drag skeletons out of the closet, and they learn their lessons the hard way. They've been created by years of past mythologizing, drawn their images from popular culture, black and white. They are black, sho' nuff—the last thing I would say about McMillan's people is that they ain't black—but they're black in big, bold strokes. And that means her work will continue to raise questions among African Americans about the fuzzy line between realism and popular misconception. And at the same time, McMillan is, as she said, less race-conscious. She confines herself to the day-to-day life struggle, as told from behind the mask Claude McKay so poignantly described. McMillan uses, almost exclusively, the performance side of black character, emphasizing the most public, most familiar aspects of us. If you smell a little song and dance in the self-sufficient ribaldry, it's there.

Thulani Davis, "Don't Worry, Be Buppie: Black Novelists Head for the Mainstream," *Voice Literary Supplement* No. 85 (May 1990): 26, 29

TERRY McMILLAN   As a child, I didn't know that African-American people wrote books. I grew up in a small town in northern Michigan, where the only books I came across were the Bible and required reading for school. I did not read for pleasure, and it wasn't until I was sixteen when I got a job shelving books at the public library that I got lost in a book. It was a biography of Louisa May Alcott. I was excited because I had not really read about poor white folks before; her father was so eccentric and idealistic that at the time I just thought he was crazy. I related to Louisa because she had to help support her family at a young age, which was what I was doing at the library.

Then one day I went to put a book away, and saw James Baldwin's face staring up at me. "Who in the world is this?" I wondered. I remember feeling embarrassed and did not read his book because I was too afraid. I couldn't imagine that he'd have anything better or different to say than Thomas Mann, Henry Thoreau, Ralph Waldo Emerson, Nathaniel Hawthorne, Ernest Hemingway, William Faulkner, etc. and a horde of other mostly white male writers that I'd been introduced to in Literature 101 in high school. I mean, not only had there not been any African-American authors included in any of those textbooks, but I'd never been given a clue that if we did have anything important to say that somebody would actually publish it. Needless to say, I was not just naïve, but had not yet acquired an ounce of black pride. I never once questioned why there were no representative works by us in any of those textbooks. After all, I had never heard of any African-American writers, and no one I knew hardly read *any* books. ⟨. . .⟩

Not once, throughout my entire four years as an undergraduate, did it occur to me that I might one day *be* a writer. I mean, these folks had genuine knowledge and insight. They also had a fascination with the truth. They had something to write about. Their work was bold, not flamboyant. They learned how to exploit the language so that the readers would be affected by what they said and how they said it. And they had talent.

I never considered myself to be in possession of much of the above, and yet when I was twenty years old the first man I fell in love with broke my heart. I was so devastated and felt so helpless that my reaction manifested itself in a poem. I did not sit down and say, "I'm going to write a poem about this." It was more like magic. I didn't even know I was writing a poem until I had written it. Afterward, I felt lighter, as if something had happened to lessen the pain. And when I read this "thing" I was shocked because I didn't know where the words came from. I was scared, to say the least, about what I had just experienced, because I didn't understand what had happened. ⟨. . .⟩

⟨. . .⟩ I ended up majoring in journalism because writing was "easy" for me, but it didn't take long for me to learn that I did not like answering the "who, what, when, where, and why" of anything. I then—upon the urging of my mother and friends who had graduated and gotten "normal" jobs—decided to try something that would still allow me to "express myself" but was relatively safer, though still risky: I went to film school. Of course what was inherent in my quest to find my "spot" in the world was this whole notion of affecting people on some grand scale. Malcolm and Martin caused me to think like this. Writing for me, as it's turned out, is philanthropy. It didn't take years for me to realize the impact that other writers' work had had on me, and if I was going to write, I did not want to write inconsequential, mediocre stories that didn't conjure up or arouse much in a reader. So I had to start by exciting myself and paying special attention to what I cared about, what mattered to me.

Film school didn't work out. Besides, I never could stop writing, which ultimately forced me to stop fighting it. It took even longer to realize that writing was not something you aspired to, it was something you did because you had to.

Terry McMillan, "Introduction," *Breaking Ice: An Anthology of Contemporary African-American Fiction*, ed. Terry McMillan (New York: Viking, 1990), pp. xv–xviii

JACQUELINE TRESCOTT   As a novelist McMillan explores
black family relationships through a yeasty jumble of contemporary hardships
and blessings. As an essayist she reveals the feelings of one black woman's
questions about single parenthood, the lack of male friendships, the dissatis-
factions of wanting to be physically perfect. Once she elicited an echo of
Amens across the country's phone lines with these words on black men:
"They're like an itch we can't reach and won't be satisfied until we scratch
it."

For the last few weeks, she has been on the road, discussing *Breaking Ice:
An Anthology of Contemporary African-American Fiction*, which she edited.
⟨. . .⟩ In the wake of its praise, she has been indulging in the joy of introducing
some lesser-known writers to a wider audience. ⟨. . .⟩

Breaking Ice was born out of a need to correct the publishing industry's
neglect of black writers, to provide a handy reference book for some of the
writing of the 1970s and 1980s and to share some of the good words she
was reading. The anthology contains the works of esteemed veterans such
as John A. Williams, Paule Marshall, Alice Walker and Amiri Baraka but
also the lesser-known work of Barbara Neely, Steven Corbin, Doris Jean
Austin and Randall Kenan.

"There are very few areas where you will see our work on a continuous
basis," McMillan says. Three years ago when she was teaching at the University of Wyoming, Laramie, she was bothered by an edition of a short story
collection. "It just hit me, there are no black writers, no Third World
writers," she says. "I am like, 'hold it a minute.' " Her anger led to research
and a book proposal drawing from the 30 non-household names that "popped
into my head."

Why do black writers continue to be overlooked, except for the burst of
enthusiasm for black female writers during the last decade and the occasional
male entry?

"Lack of respect," says McMillan. "In some ways it is laced with racism
but not always. . . . Right now that doesn't happen to be the case with me
because my work is getting a lot of attention. A lot of people at readings
ask, 'Terry, how did you get to be so successful?' I haven't thought of myself
as successful until you people remind me of it. I say to be honest with you
I think the white folks chose me as the flavor of the year. Next year it
could be someone else." ⟨. . .⟩

Attention to McMillan's work enabled her to push for the anthology.
⟨. . .⟩ And she has edited a work that, like her fiction, grabs the hand and

leads to discovery. Arranged in alphabetical order, the book does not have the traditional groupings of humor, science fiction or folk tale categories.

"I wanted it to be democratic, I wanted it to reflect the diversity of our experiences. That is why it is gay, lesbian, erotic, science fiction," she says. What emerged during those two decades are stories of love, identity, family, age and transition. The themes of protest are retreating, she says. "There are no stories about anger or rage unless the character was angry. Not when the writer was angry."

> Jacqueline Trescott, "The Urban Author, Straight to the Point," *Washington Post*, 17 November 1990, pp. D1, D4

CHARLES R. LARSON   In the climactic scene of Terry McMillan's wickedly acerbic third novel, *Waiting to Exhale*, four African-American women—Gloria, Savannah, Bernadine and Robin, all between the ages of 34 and 38—celebrate the birthday of the youngest by drinking five bottles of champagne and talking about their on-going problems with men. All of them are single and/or recently divorced and "waiting to exhale"—yearning for the ideal mate who takes your breath away, although he never seems to materialize.

Furthermore, these women are all economically independent, horny and explicit in their feelings. Among other things, they conclude that the problem with black men is that they are "with white women," "gay," "ugly," "stupid," "in prison," "unemployed," "crackheads," "short," "liars," "unreliable," "irresponsible," "too possessive," "dogs," "shallow," "stuck in the sixties," "arrogant," "childish," "wimps" and too "old and set in their ways."

McMillan's dialogue is raunchy and wild, half black street speech and half one-liners. It's as if we're listening to four foul-mouth stand-up comediennes—all of them lashing out blindly at MEN. 〈. . .〉

While the dialogue sparkles throughout, the F-word appears so frequently that one has the feeling that McMillan is trying to one-up Spike Lee (whose films are alluded to a number of times). Indeed, McMillan seems to have written her novel with one eye on Hollywood and the other on the sisterhood of educated, articulate, independent black women who are very successful in their professions but frustrated and neurotic about the fact that there are so few black men they consider their equals.

This problem of mating is, however, about the only true lament of this otherwise very funny novel. Because of her biting comic tone, McMillan's work is distanced from that of a number of her contemporaries (Toni Morrison, Alice Walker, Marita Golden, for example). Although *Waiting to Exhale* is rooted in ethnicity, that ethnicity is never angry, bitter or bleak. One of McMillan's characters says, "I don't have anything against most white folks." The issue is gender, not race, and, above all, the question of sisterhood. ⟨. . .⟩

When Lorraine Hansberry wrote *A Raisin in the Sun* back in 1959, one critic accused her of writing a Jewish play about people who happened to be black. I can hear readers on the beach this summer laughing away and saying something like that about *Waiting to Exhale*.

These aren't black women; they're most women at a certain point of no return. And that may make you think about race—if not gender—in a totally different light.

> Charles R. Larson, "The Comic Unlikelihood of Finding Mr. Right," *Chicago Tribune Books*, 31 May 1992, pp. 6–7

CAROLYN SEE   It's inappropriate to compare Terry McMillan's third novel, *Waiting to Exhale*, to the works of other contemporary black women writers, like Alice Walker, Toni Morrison, Bebe Moore Campbell. This work isn't lofty, luminous or particularly "brilliant."

It also isn't right to stick McMillan in a box with elegant black *guy* writers, like charming Charles Johnson or grouchy Ishmael Reed. McMillan's new work is part of another genre entirely, so new it doesn't really have a name yet. This genre has to do with women, triumph, revenge, comradeship.

McMillan's immediate literary predecessor is, oddly enough, Olivia Goldsmith, who, last March, gave us *The First Wives Club*. There, four (white) women, having been dumped by their brutal, insolent, materialistic husbands, banded together and found justice—not by ruining their husbands, who weren't worth the effort, but by learning to live well on their own terms: to become, like that legendary lady in Chaucer's *Canterbury Tales*, their own women, well at ease.

McMillan sets up four middle-class black women, living in the highly symbolic town of Phoenix (because all of them will rise up, glorious, from the ashes of their present lives). This quartet is not oppressed greatly—or at all—by the problem of race. "White folks" wander around the periphery of this story like sad, soft, wiggly worms.

McMillan's plucky females are beleaguered, put upon, bugged, by black men—their misdeeds, their absences, their lies, their treachery. It's a tough life for a smart, pretty black woman. Maybe the only way to fight the system-as-it-exists is to unite to conquer. ⟨. . .⟩

These women help each other, cheer each other up, turn nightmare nights into daytime laughs. *Waiting to Exhale* has been marked to be a commercial success and it should be (it debuted June 7 at No. 5 on the bestseller list). Like *The First Wives Club*, it is a paean to the sisterhood of all women and should put the fear of God into any husband squirreling money away in numbered Swiss accounts against his upcoming divorce.

Carolyn See, "A Novel of Women: Triumph, Revenge and Comradeship," *Los Angeles Times*, 22 June 1992, p. E2

DANIEL MAX   Terry McMillan, at age 40, might just be as far as you can get from the traditional image of a tweedy novelist. She wears stylish clothes, lives in a plush Southwestern-style house in Danville, near Oakland, and rolls off the amounts of money made or owed to her with the ease of an agent—book advances, foreign publishing contracts, movie option money, book club money, reserves held against returns. She has a walk-in closet with rows of designer dresses and negligees. And she collects earrings, favoring ones with great dangling hoops and pyramids. Big earrings are one of her signatures. Another is her white sun-roofed BMW that still bears Arizona plates, a vestige of her last teaching assignment, in Tucson. ⟨. . .⟩

McMillan frequently draws from her own life for her fiction. Critics often object to her simple characters and dialogue-driven plots. Nonetheless, they regard her as an important chronicler of 1990's black life. ⟨. . . *Waiting to Exhale's*⟩ emphasis on brand names—BMW, Coach leather, Calvin Klein and Perrier—has earned the author the title of "the black Judith Krantz," but this is indicative more of how unfamiliar whites are with successful blacks than of the novel's content. Except for Bernadine, who is truly affluent, these women are only solidly middle class—it is their delight in their success that makes them seem richer.

McMillan's relationship with the white world is marked by such misinterpretations. A mutual fascination framed by uneasy jousting prevails. "They keep talking about my energy or something," she says, suspecting a putdown. Touring the Capitol and the Supreme Court with a group of writers last year as part of the PEN/Faulkner prize ceremonies, she wandered around the echoing marble halls with a minority phalanx, the black essayist Al Young and the novelist Charles Johnson, as well as the Asian-American novelist Amy Tan, teasing all the while that she wanted to introduce herself to the suspicious white faces in suits as the pop singer Anita Baker, playing with their inability to distinguish among black faces. ⟨. . .⟩

McMillan walks an even trickier line with black intellectuals. Despite the harsh portrait she paints of them, some black men are surprisingly supportive. Spike Lee contributed a blurb for *Waiting to Exhale*. Ishmael Reed, who elsewhere has been vociferous in opposing male-bashing by black female writers, nevertheless is a friend of McMillan's and has helped her. But McMillan has done less well with black female novelists. Alice Walker, Toni Morrison and Gloria Naylor, names often on McMillan's mind, are nowhere to be found on her book jackets. ⟨. . .⟩

What this reveals, on one level, is McMillan's search for literary respect. McMillan can remember the length of the reviews of all her books. "Am I gonna get a boxed interview this time [in *The New York Times Book Review*]?" she asked before the publication of *Waiting to Exhale*. In fact she did not, symptomatic to her of a lack of appreciation from established literary circles: "The bottom line is that at this point I've applied five or six years in a row for a Guggenheim and I can't get one. The same is true for a box in *The Times*. You can't beg for respect."

Paradoxically, the most radical and perhaps most important aspect of McMillan's success may be her very conventionality. She writes the kind of popular books white authors have long written, but which black authors were discouraged from undertaking because publishing wisdom decreed that black people didn't buy books.

Daniel Max, "McMillan's Millions," *New York Times Magazine*, 9 August 1992, pp. 20, 22–24

FRANCES STEAD SELLERS   Most black women writers are associated with a recognizable tradition of serious, ideologically inspired black

literature, written primarily for "concerned" whites and black intellectuals. McMillan, however, has little truck with ideology of any kind. She writes to entertain, by providing the type of sexy, popular novel that has been making Jilly Cooper and Danielle Steel rich for years.

Written for and about educated black women, *Waiting to Exhale* reflects the growing numbers of successful African-Americans who have fled the drugs and violence of the ghettoes for fashionable neighbourhoods, while trying to preserve a uniquely black cultural heritage. McMillan's characters believe in black solidarity. To act like a white is an act of betrayal. "White folks" hover disconcertingly on the novel's margins. ⟨. . .⟩

⟨. . .⟩ McMillan's generalized male-bashing has understandably alienated some black men. Her portrayal of women may be more sympathetic, but it is equally shallow. Her characters' preoccupation with deodorants, douches and dates soon grows wearisome. And the attention McMillan draws to male-female rifts within the African-American community seems at odds with the black solidarity she otherwise implicitly approves.

But whether her views are politically correct or not, McMillan has hit a nerve. Many African-American women identify with her heroines. Using the vibrant street-talk McMillan grew up speaking, her protagonists tackle sexual issues that most women can relate to.

It may in part be concern to avoid accusations of racism that has prevented some critics putting this book firmly where it belongs—among the glitzy, commercial women's novels. Its one true importance is that it appeals to a market that American publishers have previously overlooked—the new black middle class. But its literary merits are modest.

> Frances Stead Sellers, [Review of *Waiting to Exhale*], *Times Literary Supplement*, 6 November 1992, p. 20

▣ *Bibliography*

Mama. 1987.

Disappearing Acts. 1989.

Breaking Ice: An Anthology of Contemporary African-American Fiction (editor). 1990.

Waiting to Exhale. 1992.

⊗ ⊗ ⊗

Clarence Major
b. 1936

CLARENCE MAJOR was born in Atlanta, Georgia, on December 31, 1936. After his parents' divorce he moved to Chicago with his mother, although retaining connections with the South by frequent visits with his father and other relatives. Major began writing at the age of twelve, and continued to experiment in both fiction and poetry throughout high school while reading voraciously in American, English, and foreign literature. He developed a passion for the visual arts and in 1953 studied briefly at the Art Institute at Chicago, but he felt he lacked technical skill and abandoned his art studies. At this time he published a small pamphlet of poetry, *The Fires That Burn in Heaven* (1954).

In 1955 Major joined the air force, concurrently studying at the Armed Forces Institute. After his discharge in 1957 he worked in a steel factory in Omaha. During this same period he also began editing and publishing the *Coercion Review*, launching his fruitful literary career. In 1966, after issuing two mimeographed volumes of poetry, he moved to New York and became associated with the Harlem Education Program at the New Lincoln School. Major has subsequently been a lecturer at Sarah Lawrence College (1972–75) and a professor of English at Howard University (1974–76) and, since 1977, the University of Colorado at Boulder.

Although he has continued to write poetry, Major is best known for his seven novels. The first, *All-Night Visitors* (1969), was published by the Olympia Press and was extensively edited so as to emphasize the sex scenes and downplay the portrayal of character. Major's next novel, *NO* (1973), is the first to introduce his characteristic postmodernist or "experimental" techniques, including rapid shifts of point of view, authorial interruptions of the narrative, and unusual typographical devices. These techniques are particularly evident in *Reflex and Bone Structure* (1975), which won wide acclaim from critics and reviewers, and *Emergency Exit* (1979). Major's more recent novels are *My Amputations* (1986; winner of the Western States Book Award for fiction), *Such Was the Season* (1987), and *Painted Turtle:*

Woman with Guitar (1988). A collection of short stories, *Fun & Games*, was issued in 1989.

Major was a columnist for the *American Poetry Review*, has been a reviewer for *Essence* and *Library Journal*, and has edited several anthologies of black literature. He is also an accomplished lexicographer, responsible for *The Dictionary of Afro-American Slang* (1970). His earlier essays have been collected in *The Dark and Feeling: Black American Writers and Their Work* (1974) and feature many of his provocative opinions on black literature and culture. He has been the recipient of many awards and grants and has been a guest lecturer at universities around the world.

Major has been married three times and lives with his current wife, Pamela, in Boulder, Colorado.

▒ *Critical Extracts*

RON WELBURN   A sure thing about Clarence Major's first novel, *All-Night Visitors*, is that a lot of us, particularly the soul sisters, do or will not like it, and will not think too highly of Clarence Major for writing it. This will be because Eli Bolton, the central character in *All-Night Visitors*, is an aimless cockhound whose scores are mostly with white chicks and he describes all of his sex-based relationships with vivid detail in the first 60 pages. Understandably, the novel might not be finished by some who pick it up. Still, I believe there are reasons why Major, editor of *The New Black Poetry*, has offered us what appears to be a stud novel; I believe his reasons are literary and social. ⟨. . .⟩

Despite the fact that lengthy sex scenes seem a standard or a necessity for the "acceptable" contemporary American novel, the success or failure of *All-Night Visitors* will ultimately lie with what it represents as a novel by a Black American writer. Most of us agree that white America's current psycho-sexual fixation represents part of its demise. The fact to consider is Major's intent in starting out on this rubbish heap with his first novel. If we give *All-Night Visitors* an absolute condemnation it would contradict a casually accepted image (both in and outside art) of the walking Black phallus, an image Eli doesn't mind fulfilling; this image has been assumed at times because it is what white America thinks of the Black man in the first place. But in Major's novel we do watch an apathetic Black man take his first steps toward maturity—social (community) responsibility. Eli Bolton is a numbed individual; sex is his only meaningful outlet. Eli, too, is not by himself. *All-Night Visitors* depicts a libidinous urge. But its character is headed in a worthwhile direction; he begins to live up to his honorable name when he *acts* in a manner that will attest to his selfless responsibility to reach out for others.

Clarence Major has the novelist's talent; but since he is contributing to contemporary Afro-American literature, his craft should be high-lighted by a central character who is able to carry the aesthetic motion of the story on a more active social level. Major already shows signs of being able to handle the psychological drama. The Afro novel today must project meaningful social concepts and spiritual values into the bloodstream of Black America, and this can be done and done well, with all the possibilities of style and message taken into account. In order to tell his story, in order to get the message across, Major gives us both what we want and don't want—his decision to do so is the artist's prerogative and his energy/vision is involved in the telling of truths. (What would have been the significance of John Coltrane, for example, if he had given the people the music they would have preferred to hear?) It is my guess that Clarence Major sees beyond this novel to the real needs of the Black community as those needs can be expressed and illustrated through fiction. Soul Brother Eli Bolton represents the living problem of apathy, and as both a wanderer of the psyche and a sexual waystation, his initial steps toward self-transformation were inevitable and justify his honesty.

Ron Welburn, [Review of *All-Night Visitors*], *Negro Digest* 19, No. 2 (December 1969): 85, 87

JEROME KLINKOWITZ   Major's genius is his ability to lyricize the physical, to work his imagination upon the bedrock world not usually indulged by poetry. His first novel, *All-Night Visitors* (New York: Olympia Press, 1969), uses sexuality as the vehicle, courting the danger that such an approach tends so easily toward the pornographic (the volume was published in Maurice Girodias's Olympia Press series, and was in fact heavily cut to fit that format, at the publisher's insistence). The argument begins, "This thing that I am, this body—it is me. *I* am it. I am not a concept in your mind, whoever you are! I am *here*, right here, myself, MYSELF, fucking or being driven to the ends of my ability to contain myself in the ecstasy her little red mouth inspires as it works at the knobby head of my weapon, or if I am eating this goat's cheese, the pumpernickel, drinking beer I have just bought, or whatever I happen to be doing." The lyrical is too often reserved for the subjective or ideal, things already lyrical in themselves. Major roots his work in the deeply physical. As his character in *All-Night Visitors* insists, "I am not *your* idea of anything."

More simply, in *No* (New York: Emerson Hall, 1973) the protagonist announced, "Another thing I'm fast discovering to be mine and mine alone. It's my dick. Though there isn't very much I can do, I can do whatever I want with it." Sexuality is the means of self-definition. Major has commented on the difficulties black authors have in incorporating sex in their works, and how *All-Night Visitors* is a fundamentally "un-Christian" book. An earlier variant of this experience was crime, as he indicates in his collected essays, *The Dark and Feeling* (New York: Third Press, 1974): in Richard Wright's *Native Son*, Bigger Thomas finds that "The crime liberates him (whereas in a white novel, *Sister Carrie* by Theodore Dreiser, the hero's crime ultimately leads him to destruction, inwardly as well as outwardly)." In *All-Night Visitors* Eli Bolton is distraught when his girlfriend leaves; "I'm seriously considering killing Cathy," he admits, "to keep her body here, if nothing else." When it comes, the murder is symbolically accomplished by rape. In *No*, Moses Westby actually kills four children, and then himself, rather than see them suffer more. But murder is hardly preferable—even beyond these deaths, the spokesman of the novel must kill these people "in his head" before he can be free; Moses's actual murder had made little difference. Imaginative action, lyricizing the physical rather than destroying it, is a better option. Against the social realism of a Richard Wright, Major takes an imaginative journey toward the discovery of self, and the scene— instead of the slums of Chicago—is the bed where he's fellated by his girlfriend. "I want to stay right here, with her, focused on every protrusion, every cord, abstract circle of myself, of her every 'feeling,' every hurling, every fleshy spit-rich convexity, mentally centered in all the invisible 'constructs' of myself, right here, where she and I now form, perform an orchestra she is constructing in juicy floodtides." Language takes over beyond the action, as he "is percolating, oozing, dribbling at the dick like a river, but a slow river, being tapped by the mysterious rainfalls of Mother, voids, secrets, wet holes of the fleshy world, carried on an expedition to the ends

of my psychophysical reality; at the floodgates of emergency, my dark fleshy
Anita, love, a gateway into which I exist, and erupt, enter."

> Jerome Klinkowitz, "Clarence Major," *The Life of Fiction* (Urbana: University of
> Illinois Press, 1977), p. 97

DOUG BOLLING   When he is at his best Major helps us to see
that fiction created within an aesthetic of fluidity and denial of "closure"
and verbal freedom can generate an excitement and awareness of great
value; that the rigidities of plot, characterization, and illusioned depth can
be softened and, finally, dropped in favor of new and valid rhythms. Spaces
and times need no longer conform to the abstract demands either of plot
or symbolic urgency, for example, but can be free to float in their own
energies. Similarly what the textbooks sometimes still call "authorial intrusion" need not be construed as a felony or even a misdemeanor but rather
as another manifestation of verbal energy and in fact as no "intrusion" at
all. If some of his stories seem difficult or even incoherent to readers, it is
because they are attempting to read by means of categories applicable to
older fictional contexts but inadequate to the highly elliptical and at times
improvisational way of Major's fiction. His way and that of all other postmod-
ern writers can help us realize all over again that the activity of "reading"
is a highly conditioned one, too often a matter of the learned response
rather than an engagement of the free and open mind. Thus, time spent
with the fictions can be both a trip into the richness and surprise of words
and their relationships and a way of redefining the self. In place of the
hermetic quality with its correlative webbing of internally sustained ironies
and symbols that one associates with modernist writing, the reader of Major's
fiction finds that he must himself take part in the creation of the work and
that in doing so he experiences a pleasurable liberation quite removed from
the kind of response elicited by older fiction. In place of the glimpse into
archetypal profundities often claimed—and justly so—for the latter, the
reader of the new fiction experiences the relatively "informal" release of
the creative and perhaps a sense of collaboration—communion even—with
the writer. Because these are affirming and positive responses they may
suggest, at least to whatever remains of the New Critical rear guard, that
Major's work is shallow and lacking in seriousness. Such a view deserves
no reply although it is worth saying that we desperately *need* the affirmative

in the arts and the culture generally. And in any case Major shows us the grimness and horror of modern civilization to the point that he is hardly an escapist.

> Doug Bolling, "A Reading of Clarence Major's Short Fiction," *Black American Literature Forum* 13, No. 1 (Summer 1979 [Special Clarence Major Issue]): 52

PETER QUARTERMAIN   The storyline of *Emergency Exit,* about the Ingram family ("rich niggers from Inlet, Connecticut") and their friends, lovers, mistresses, consists of a series of more or less self-contained, straight-forward narrative fragments interrupted by clusters of one-paragraph "takes" culled from dreams, real or imaginary cures for disease or against witchcraft, incidents in the life of Clarence Major, bits of conversation, new reports, city- and landscapes, and so on. There are also monotone reproductions of paintings, a photograph of Clarence Major and about a dozen cows (the text tells us there were thirty of them), quotations from literary (and other) sources, bits of telegrams, conference programs, bibliographies, phone books—and even, on page 174, a represention of a tennis match ("WA CK OCK"). It's all great fun, and when, about a dozen pages before the end, a whole page asks "Well, dear reader, how do you feel about?", the sheer energetic gusto of the book has carried us along and we have been, well, entertained. And even, indeed, charmed. All through the book there is the author himself (or so he claims), who takes up more of our attention in the second half, until the distinctions between the fictive world of the story line and the (presumably) "real" world of the fragments breaks down completely and Deborah Ingram, "my favorite character in this whole book," says the author, "has become my lover." There are savage little asides about Hollywood, politics, religion; there are juxtapositions of dreams and "reality"; there are comic and/or grotesque fantasies. There are some fine sequences and fragments—notable conversations, for example, between Julie Ingram (the daughter) and her lover/boyfriend Al; descriptive vignettes of people crying, playing, swimming, dreaming; brilliant images drawn (or so it seems) from Hieronymous Bosch. These have somewhat the effect of set-pieces in the novel, and they manage both to remind us that what we are doing is reading a novel and, at the same time, that we are looking at the world. One effect of traditional narrative and novelistic conventions, after all (and especially in self-styled "experimental" writing), is to remind us that the novel does refer to a world "out there" as well as it does to the one "in here." They remind us, that is to say, of the novel as a representation. As we read the book, we find that the two kinds of writing—the story line and the interruptions—become increasingly interdependent, so that what occurs in one generates something in the other. In the story, the town of Inlet has recently passed the Threshold Law, which forbids all women over the age of eighteen from walking through or touching any doorway (they must be carried by men), and we follow the domestic fortunes of the Ingrams against this background. In the fragments, we perceive a wider and wider range of diversity in the world of man and the world of nature, in the external world of matter and the inner world of dream and thought (*and in the writing*), and as the novel gets cumulatively richer the two merge and we cease to question (if we ever did) the accuracy of the representation, and take the world of *Emergency Exit*, which is also the world of Clarence Major, on trust. The book thus teaches us how to read, is its own instructional manual. ⟨. . .⟩

Thus the main thrust of the book's dynamic is in the play between the world as thing and the world as not-thing (invention, word), and when Major lets his book act out this interplay by itself, without commentary, then it is a fine and at times passionate celebration of the world of things, of people in that world, and at the same time a plea for language uncluttered by overlays of artifice and thus of falsehood. It is equally an excellent diagnosis of the traps people fall into, the ones they themselves build as well as those others build, out of words, out of desire, out of expectation, and out of hope, and of how they put their trust in women, or in sex, or in violence, or in position, or in myth, as a means of escape (Emergency Exit).

Peter Quartermain, "Trusting the Reader," Chicago Review 32, No. 2 (Autumn 1980):
66–69

LARRY D. BRADFIELD   In *Reflex and Bone Structure*, ⟨Major⟩ disrupts the continuity of story and character (so that no illusion of an external reality can be maintained) and adds the author's responses to the characters and situations his imagination creates. He presents the novel in two sections, "A Bad Connection" and "Body Heat," because his aesthetic demands a bad connection with the external world so that the audience must focus on the body heat of the imaginer. In Romantic literature, the body heat, passion, of the imaginer had been focused on; but the Romantic artist required a good connection between his imagination and the external world to generate passionate responses. In modern literature, Jean-Paul Sartre, Albert Camus, and other existential absurdists have focused on the bad connection; but this focus was achieved at the expense of body heat, of emotional participation by the imaginer. By bringing the bad connection with the external world and the body heat of the imaginer together, Major avoids the dishonesty of mimesis and creates an honest fiction.

Generating this fiction not from the world *of* his imagination, Major presents *Reflex and Bone Structure* as an account of an author's sustained imaginative interaction with a set of characters and a story. The characters and story, as deliberately imaginative creations rather than imitations of people and life, initiate intellectual, emotional, and physical reactions in the author, whose narrative reality of his imagination resembles the fragmentary entries in a journal or logbook. The novel, then, avoids the illusory dishonesty of imitating a world outside an author's mind, with the requirements for selection, invented causality, invented consequence, and imposition of order. *Reflex and Bone Structure*, as the title implies, allows Major to set down the workings of his imagination, as it conjures up characters and incidents, and to complement this material with his reactions to what his imagination puts forth. By simple, spontaneous reflex action, his imagination can create characters who have sufficient reality, or bone structure, to generate responses, or further reflexes to be recorded. ⟨ . . .⟩

⟨. . .⟩ What is fictive and what is real are one and the same. No character will walk out of the story, because wherever the character goes in the universe of the imagination, the story goes, too. ⟨Frank⟩ Kermode's implication that contingency—the world of chance and unforeseen possibilities—is inappropriate in fiction has been sidestepped: Imitating contingency might be unacceptable, but the imaginative creation of contingency is wholly consistent with a world of fiction located wholly in the imagination.

However, the universe of the imagination is also limited, and Major reacts to its limitations as he has reacted to its creations: "I know I'm in my mind. What I really want, though, is to be out of it. I would like nothing better, at the moment, than to wander around outside myself. See what the world is from another angle." Later, he responds to the same problem: "I'm way back in my mind and I have no room to move around. It is crowded back here. Faces and hands and movements. I try to see how far I can see and I find only the inside surface of my brain. Cora is hiding behind the skin." Denying the mimetic illusion of a world outside the imagination may be honest, but it is not without frustrations. So, for his character Cora, Major creates a background such as that which characters in mimetic fiction have. He sends her "South to Atlanta, her birthplace, to march, demonstrate." He comments, "She had to become a non-combustible person. Build an inner framework that could easily absorb not only pain but also endless shock . . ." He puts her, at twelve, in Atlanta to witness her father stepping aside for a white man, and to be told by her mother to believe it did not happen, " 'Repeat after me: My father is a brave and strong man and nobody pushes him around.' " At fifteen, Cora asks her father, " 'Am I more than Black?' " and he responds, " 'Tomorrow I will teach you how to do calculus.' " Cora, as a young girl, visits her grandparents outside Atlanta, sees her mother scrubbing and singing, and is warned by her father to remember that what he says is right. Cora is the only character created for the novel by Major's imagination who so completely engrosses him that he creates for her a past pertinent to her present. She is given a past wherein it was necessary to accept illusions, and she takes part in an action to overthrow the world of these illusions. In Cora, Major tests the limits of the non-mimetic, imaginatively generated character. "There's no doubt about it: everything Cora does happens first in my mind." With Cora, Major shows that imagined characters of non-mimetic fiction can achieve the wholeness of mimetic characters, but that the truth of their origin in the imagination must be maintained.

Larry D. Bradfield, "Beyond Mimetic Exhaustion: The *Reflex and Bone Structure* Experiment," *Black American Literature Forum* 17, No. 3 (Fall 1983): 120–22

STUART KLAWANS   At the end of this review, I will do the unforgivable and reveal the punch line of Clarence Major's new novel, since that may be the only way to convince you to read the book. Mere description cannot convey the wild humor and audacity to be found here, nor the anxiety and cunning. The virtues of My *Amputations* are all active ones, best summarized, perhaps, as jumpiness. Only a demonstration of them will do.

Major—the author of *Reflex and Bone Structure* and *Emergency Exit*—has produced as his fifth novel a fantasy of the black writer as con artist, kept on the run over three continents. Part travelogue and part imaginary self-portrait, the book begins with its protagonist huddled in a closet in New York and ends with him in a hut in Liberia, having by that point met the Devil and worse. He has, in fact, met himself. Mason Ellis, the character on the run, is a half-mad ex-convict who imagines himself to be, of all people, Clarence Major—or perhaps Clarence Major, huddled in the closet, fears he's really Mason Ellis. ⟨. . .⟩

It is not enough for Mason to capture CM. He must also claim, or perhaps reclaim, his identity. For that, he needs money. In the company of petty crooks, Mason undertakes a series of crimes that might well have been planned by Laurel and Hardy. The narrator, it seems, takes a malicious pleasure in subjecting Mason Elliot to slapstick; perhaps this is the only revenge CM can exact for being represented by such a lowdown ME. Mason is just capable enough to buy a fake passport from the Mob. With that in hand, he diverts $50,000 from the Magnan-Rockford Foundation, signs up with a speakers' bureau and sets off on a lecture tour.

Perhaps the summary I've given so far seems crammed with incident. Forget it. That was merely the setup—an artful setup, granted, but ultimately just so much machinery. My *Amputations* begins in earnest when Mason hits the road, and the riddle of his identity becomes secondary to the puzzle of what the hell is going on in the world. ⟨. . .⟩

⟨. . . Major⟩ has fashioned a novel that is simultaneously a deception and one great, roaring self-revelation. It has the accent of a black American— or precisely *one* black American, in fact—but its tone should be recognizable to anybody who's ever gotten nervous looking in the mirror. Mason is not the first character to venture into the world playing a role, only to be mistaken for someone playing still other roles. Nor is he the first to try to go home, wearing a mask as self-protection. It is interesting, though, that in his case the mask is a real one, of carved wood, and the home is a hut outside Monrovia.

He has sought first money and fame, then wholeness, then wisdom, and as a result everything that could be amputated from him has been lopped off. Now he has come to the end of his world. Though he should know better, he tamely produces the Magnan-Rockford letter for Chief Q. Tee. He is about to receive the punch line; read it, if you need further demonstration.

"The old man spoke: 'The envelope, please.' Mason pulled it from his pocket and handed it over. The old man ripped it open and read aloud: '*Keep* this nigger!' "

Stuart Klawans, "All of Me," *Nation*, 24 January 1987, pp. 90–92

GREG TATE　　In *My Amputations*, Clarence Major goes Ralph Ellison one better, proclaiming invisibility—these days we call it misrepresentation—as not just the black American everyman's fate, but the black American writer's private hell. His protagonist, Mason Ellis, is an extremely literate black ex-con who kidnaps a famous Afro-American writer (Clarence McKay), accuses him of plagiarism, steals his identity, then finances a literary tour of America, Europe, and Africa with the fat grant McKay received from a prestigious foundation. That hardly anyone notices the switch is Major's blunt way of saying all black writers look alike to an indifferent world.

In this picaresque parody of the literary hustle, Ellis is expected to play a triple role: the black writer as militant activist, cosmopolitan cocksman, and colored plaything. Wherever he turns up, Ellis finds his identity circumscribed by the racial politics of his hosts. White students at Brooklyn College care no more about his opinions on liberation movements than his poetry; those at Howard want to know who he writes for, black or white people. In Greece he's invited to an antebellum costume ball; just off the plane in London, he's hustled onto a bill with punk-rock poets; in Berlin, neo-Nazis threaten him with a leadership role in the Fifth Reich; in Ghana, he's interrogated by academics about his love for the Motherland and African literature, then mistaken for a political subversive by government police.

Give or take a wild ballyhoo, such myopic misinterpretations have been Clarence Major's bane since he published *All-Night Visitors*, black literature's answer to *Tropic of Cancer*. But *My Amputations* is no self-pitying exercise in racial farce as the best revenge. Major writes with one of black letters' most experimental fictive voices (as well as its most lyrically unhinged), and the pleasures of this novel come more from the fluid sophistication of the text than from its venting of authorial ire. Although the surface theme of *My Amputations* is the black writer in flight from himself and his public, its true subject is Major's singing and stammering prose. The liberties he takes with narrative suggest his belief that language is the only prison house a writer should ever allow himself to be boxed up in.

Greg Tate, [Review of *My Amputations*], *Voice Literary Supplement* No. 52 (February 1987): 3

AL YOUNG　　In the antique parlance of its narrator, a widowed Atlanta matriarch whose name is Annie Eliza Hicks, this latest novel of

Clarence Major's is a killer-diller. Unlike his previous fiction, which was unstintingly experimental, *Such Was the Season* is an old-fashioned, straight-ahead narrative crammed with action. But it's the widow Annie Eliza's melodic voice, by turns lilting and gruff, that salts and peppers and sweetens this story, enriching its flavor and meaning.

While elaborating on what took place last week, when her divorced nephew Juneboy surprised Annie Eliza and the rest of his relatives by coming to Atlanta to lecture at Spelman College, she also reveals a great deal about herself and the Georgia she grew up in—to say nothing of what's been cooking lately around Atlanta and the Georgia that spawned her. And what a stew she serves up! Mayors and ministers, hoi polloi and the ragtag, cops and crooks, scholars and blue-collar scufflers and drunks—Annie Eliza, through either kinship or friendship, has been tight with four generations of them. ⟨. . .⟩

Clarence Major has created a delightfully lifelike, storytelling woman whose candor is matched only by her devotion to truth and her down-to-earth yea-saying to life. When Annie Eliza talks about watching television, not even a commercial goes undescribed: "I changed the channel. A pretty woman was spreading lipstick across her lips. She winked her eye at me. No, maybe she was winking at Juneboy." And, from time to time, Annie Eliza Hicks gives the listening reader a slow wink or two for good measure. It is as if Clarence Major, the avid *avant-gardiste*, has himself come home to touch base with the blues and spirituals that continue to nourish and express the lives of those people he writes about so knowingly, and with contagious affection.

Al Young, "God Never Drove Those Cadillacs," *New York Times Book Review*, 13 December 1987, p. 19

NANCY MAIRS   In the prologue to Clarence Major's lyrical short novel, *Painted Turtle: Woman with Guitar*, the narrator, Baldwin Saiyataca, says that he met the gifted Zuñi singer Painted Turtle on the "grimy cantina circuit" of the Southwest when their agent asked him to persuade her to switch from acoustic to electric guitar in order to increase her commercial appeal. From the outset of his own career, however, he has known that the electric guitar "wasn't me, that the real me was somewhere else, in a quieter place," and Painted Turtle opens the way to that place, where "love turned me into the flesh of a song itself." By the epilogue, he has traded in his guitar for a "pearl-inlaid Epiphone Deluxe" model, and he has set out with Painted Turtle on the road with "not only a love relationship we liked and wanted to keep but a musical one that was probably going to work equally well." The transformer has been transformed. ⟨. . .⟩

An older Painted Turtle, "moody, depressed, at the end of much failure, a helpless singer without a song," appears in a prior novel, My Amputations, for which Mr. Major won the 1986 Western States Book Award. But there she, like the other characters, is almost wholly rubbed out by the relentless language play that writers seem still to believe a necessary and sufficient condition of "experimental" fiction. By and large, however, My Amputations takes few risks. Behind a screen of verbal tricks, Mr. Major has erected a picaresque structure of wearisome, if not quite benumbing, conventionality. Despite its plain surfaces, Painted Turtle is actually the riskier venture: a fresh tale of the spiritually transforming power of love told without sanctimony or sentimentality.

> Nancy Mairs, "Where a Zuñi's Soul Dies," New York Times Book Review, 30 October 1988, p. 37

CLARENCE MAJOR   My first novel, written at the age of twelve, was twenty pages long. It was the story of a wild, free-spirited horse, leading a herd. Influenced by movies, I thought it would make a terrific movie, so I sent it to Hollywood. A man named William Self read it and sent it back with a letter of encouragement. I never forgot his kindness. It was the beginning of a long, long process of learning to live with rejection—not just rejection slips. And that experience too was necessary as a correlation to the writing process, necessary because one of the most *important* things I was going to have to learn was *how* to detect my own failures and be the first to reject them.

Was there, then, a particular point when I said: *Hey! I'm going to become a writer!* I think there *was*, but it now seems irrelevant because I must have been evolving toward that conscious moment long, long before I had any idea what was going on. (I was going to have to find my way—with more imperfection than not—through *many* disciplines—such as painting, music, anthropology, history, philosophy, psychology, sociology—before such a consciousness would begin to emerge.)

I think I was in the fifth grade when a girl who sat behind me snuck a copy of Raymond Radiguet's *Devil in the Flesh* to me. This was *adult fiction!* And judging from the cover, the book was going to have some *good* parts. But as it turned out the *single* good part was *the writing itself.* I was reading that book one day at home, and about halfway through, I stood up and went crazy with an important discovery: *Writing had a life of its own!* And I soon fell in love with the *life* of writing, by way of this book—Kay Boyle's translation of Radiguet.

From that moment on, up to about the age of twenty, I set out to discover other books that might change my perception—forever. Hawthorne's *Scarlet Letter* showed me how *gracefully* a story could be told and how *terrifying* human affairs—and self-deception within those affairs—can be. Conrad's *Heart of Darkness* caught me in an aesthetic network of *magic* so powerful I never untangled myself. I then went on to read other nineteenth-century— and even earlier—works by Melville, Baudelaire, Emerson, Dostoyevsky, and the like.

But I always hung on—with more comfort—to the twentieth century. I read J. D. Salinger's *The Catcher in the Rye* early enough for it to have spoken profoundly and directly to me about what I was *feeling* and *thinking* about the adult world at the time that its agony affirmed my faith in life. Richard Wright's *Native Son* was an overwhelming experience, and so was Rimbaud's poetry. But the important thing about these discoveries is that each of them led to Cocteau and other French writers, going back to the nineteenth century; Salinger led me to a discovery of modern and contemporary American fiction—Hemingway, Faulkner, Sherwood Anderson, and on and on. Wright led to Dos Passos, to James T. Farrell, to Jean Toomer, to Chester Himes, to William Gardner Smith, to Ann Petry, to Nella Larsen and other Afro-American writers; and Rimbaud led to the discovery of *American poetry*—which was not so much of a leap as it sounds— to Williams, to Marianne Moore, to Eliot, to cummings. This activity began roughly during the last year of grade school and took on full, focused direction in high school. Now, none of these writers was being taught in school. I was reading them *on my own*. In school we had to read O. Henry and Joyce Kilmer. ⟨. . .⟩

Although I was learning to appreciate good writing, I had no command of the language myself. I had the *need* to write well, but that was about all. Only the most sensitive teacher—and there were two or three along the way—was able to detect some talent and imagination in my efforts. Every time I gathered enough courage to dream of writing seriously, the notion ended in frustration or, sometimes, despair. Not only did I not have command of the language, I didn't have the *necessary distance* on experience to have anything important to say about even the things I knew something about.

I daydreamed about a solution to these problems: I could *learn* to write and I could go out and *live it up* in order to have experience. But this solution would take time. I was not willing to *wait* for time. In my sense of urgency, I didn't have that much time.

Clarence Major, "Necessary Distance: Afterthoughts on Becoming a Writer," Black American Literature Forum 23, No. 2 (Summer 1989): 199–201

PAUL KAPLAN   Clarence Major's *Fun & Games: Short Fictions* takes a look at the world in a new and fresh way. The story of "My Mother & Mitch," one of the longest and ablest in the book, is told through the eyes of a wise black child living with his single mother who is both proud and lonesome. One day she receives a misdialed phone call and enjoys an interesting conversation with a stranger. The child is puzzled by his mother's behavior as she continues the phone relationship with the caller, a slow-talking white man. Although the time frame is the early 1950s, the couple are not affected by their color difference. The mother-child relationship is nicely portrayed, and the boy learns that just as he is growing and learning the angles in life, so is his mother. Readers who enjoy the intensity of John Edgar Wideman will appreciate Major.

Paul Kaplan, [Review of Fun & Games], Library Journal 117, No. 1 (January 1992): 216

Bibliography

The Fires That Burn in Heaven. 1954.
#2. 1959.
Love Poems of a Black Man. 1965.
Human Juices. 1966.
Writers Workshop Anthology (editor). 1967.

Man Is Like a Child: An Anthology of Creative Writing by Students (editor).
　　1968.

The New Black Poetry (editor). 1969.

All-Night Visitors. 1969.

Dictionary of Afro-American Slang (editor). 1970, 1994 (as *Juba to Jive: A*
　　Dictionary of African-American Slang).

Swallow the Lake. 1970.

Symptoms & Madness. 1971.

Private Line. 1971.

The Cotton Club: New Poems. 1972.

NO. 1973.

The Dark and Feeling: Black American Writers and Their Work. 1974.

The Syncopated Cakewalk. 1974.

Reflex and Bone Structure. 1975.

Emergency Exit. 1979.

Inside Diameter: The France Poems. 1985.

My Amputations. 1986.

Such Was the Season. 1987.

Surfaces and Masks. 1988.

Painted Turtle: Woman with Guitar. 1988.

Fun & Games. 1989.

Some Observations of a Stranger at Zuñi in the Latter Part of the Century. 1989.

Parking Lots. 1992.

Calling the Wind: Twentieth Century African-American Short Stories (editor).
　　1993.

Toni Morrison
b. 1931

TONI MORRISON was born Chloe Anthony Wofford in Lorain, Ohio, on February 18, 1931, the second of four children of George Wofford, a shipyard welder, and his wife Ramah Willis Wofford. After attending Lorain High School, she went to Howard University, where she earned a B.A. in 1953, with a major in English and a minor in classics. She joined the Howard University Players and in the summer toured the South with a student-faculty repertory troupe.

After securing an M.A. at Cornell in 1955, Morrison taught for two years at Texas Southern University, then in 1957 returned to Howard, where she became an instructor of English and married Harold Morrison, a Jamaican architect. In 1964 she divorced Morrison and returned with her two sons to Lorain; a year and a half later she became an editor for a textbook subsidiary of Random House in Syracuse. By 1970 she had moved to an editorial position at Random House in New York, where she eventually became senior editor. In this capacity she anonymously edited *The Black Book* (1974), a collection of documents relating to the history of black Americans. Morrison has taught black American literature and creative writing at two branches of the State University of New York (Purchase and Albany), as well as at Yale University, Bard College, and Trinity College, Cambridge. She is currently Robert F. Goheen Professor in the Council of the Humanities at Princeton University.

Toni Morrison began to write when she returned to Howard in 1957, and since then she has published several novels in which the problems of black women in the Midwest are a major theme. Her first novel, *The Bluest Eye* (1970), draws upon her childhood in Lorain by depicting the lives of several young women, one of whom, Pecola, comes to believe that blue eyes are a symbol of whiteness and, therefore, of superiority. *Sula* (1973), set in the mythical town of Medallion, Ohio, has an even tougher edge, addressing issues of both racial and gender equality in its portrayal of the contrasting lives of two young women, one of whom settles down to middle-class conformity and the other of whom, Sula, attempts to achieve freedom by flaunting these conventions.

Morrison's third novel, *Song of Solomon* (1977), is a rich evocation of history in its chronicle of a black family over nearly a century; it was both a popular and critical success, winning the National Book Critics Circle Award and the American Academy and Institute of Arts and Letters Award. *Tar Baby* (1981), set on an imaginary Caribbean island, was less well received. But with her fifth novel, *Beloved* (1987), Morrison came to be recognized as perhaps the leading black American writer of her generation. This dense historical novel about a fugitive slave, Sethe, and her descendents not only achieved best-seller status but won the Pulitzer Prize for fiction. *Jazz* (1992) is a less ambitious work but is nonetheless a poignant depiction of the lives of black Americans in a mythical "City" in the 1920s.

Morrison has also written a small body of nonfiction. In the 1970s she wrote several pieces on black American women for the *New York Times Magazine*. Simultaneously with the release of *Jazz* appeared a challenging monograph, *Playing in the Dark: Whiteness and the Literary Imagination* (1992), probing the role of black Americans as symbols of the "other" in white American literature. In 1993 Morrison was awarded the Nobel Prize for literature. She is currently at work on a revision of *The Bluest Eye* and a new novel, tentatively entitled *Paradise*.

▨ *Critical Extracts*

L. E. SISSMAN   *The Bluest Eye* is not flawless. Miss Morrison's touching and disturbing picture of the doomed youth of her race is marred by an occasional error of fact or judgment. She places the story in a frame of the bland white words of a conventional school "reader"—surely an unnecessary and unsubtle irony. She writes an occasional false or bombastic line: "They were through with lust and lactation, beyond tears and terror." She permits herself some inconsistencies: the real name of Soaphead Church is given as both Elihue Micah Whitcomb and Micah Elihue Whitcomb. None of this matters, though, beside her real and greatly promising achievement: to write truly (and sometimes very beautifully) of every generation of blacks—the young, their parents, their rural grandparents—in this country thirty years ago, and, I'm afraid, today.

L. E. Sissman, "Beginner's Luck," *New Yorker*, 23 January 1971, p. 94

JERRY H. BRYANT   Sula, Ms. Morrison's protagonist, has qualities I have seen in a fictional black female only recently. When she is 11 years old, she cuts off the tip of her finger to demonstrate to a gang of threatening boys what she can do to them if she can do that to herself. She swings a child around by the wrists and half intentionally lets him slip out of her grasp into the river, where he drowns. In the shadows of her porch, she watches in an "interested" way while her mother burns to death.

Most of us have been conditioned to expect something else in black characters—guiltless victims of brutal white men, yearning for a respectable life of middle-class security; whores driven to their profession by impossible conditions; housekeepers exhausted by their work for lazy white women. We do not expect to see a fierceness bordering on the demonic. ⟨. . .⟩

⟨. . .⟩ Morrison at first seems to combine the aims of the Black Freedom Movement and women's liberation. Sula and Nel discover when they are 11 years old "that they were neither white nor male, and that all freedom and triumph was forbidden to them." When they grow up, Nel slips on the collar of convention. She marries, has two children, becomes tied to her "nest," a slave to racism and sexism. Sula goes to the big city, gets herself an education, and returns a "liberated" woman with a strange mixture of cynicism and innocence: "She lived out her days exploring her own thoughts and emotions, giving them full rein, feeling no obligation to please anybody unless their pleasure pleased her . . . hers was an experimental life." ⟨. . .⟩

Morrison does not accept—nor does she expect us to accept—the unqualified tenets of either of the two current freedom movements. There is more to both society and the individual, and she subjects each of these to a merciless analysis. The result is that neither lends itself to a clear moral judgment. For all her selfishness and cruelty, Sula's presence elicits the best in people, diluting their usual meanness and small-spiritedness. Indeed, with Sula's death the "Bottom" dies, its black people rushing headlessly in a comi-tragedy of communal suicide.

Jerry H. Bryant, "Something Ominous Here," *Nation*, 6 July 1974, pp. 23–24

JOAN BISCHOFF   Henry James delineated one of the earliest and most memorable precocious female protagonists in depicting the title character in *What Maisie Knew*. The extent of little Maisie's understanding of the adult world has remained tantalizingly elusive for several generations of readers, while her innocent suffering has shone with terrible poignance. Now, it seems, a new American novelist is offering some contemporary twists of the Jamesian type. With the publication of *The Bluest Eye* in 1970 and *Sula* in 1974, Toni Morrison has laid claim to modern portrayal of the preternaturally sensitive but rudely thwarted black girl in today's society. *Sula* is more fully dominated by the title character, and Sula's characterization is the more complex; in both novels, however, the protagonist is forced into premature adulthood by the *donnée* of her life. Pecola's comprehension of her world is never articulated for either the other characters or the reader; Sula, too, remains a partial enigma both in and out of her narrative. But the pain that each experiences is made vivid and plain. Taken together, the two novels can—and I think must—be read as offering different answers to a single question: What is to become of a finely attuned child who is offered no healthy outlet for her aspirations and yearnings? Pecola escapes in madness; Sula rejects society for amoral self-reliance. For both, sensitivity is a curse rather than a blessing. Morrison's second novel, though richer in many ways, is essentially a reworking of the material of the first with an alternative ending. Though her characters' problems are conditioned by the black milieu of which she writes, her concerns are broader, universal ones. Her fiction is a study of thwarted sensitivity. ⟨. . .⟩

Both Morrison's novels find beauty in sensitive response and show its inevitable doom in a world in which only the hard, the cagey, and the self-interested can triumph. Although both Pecola and Sula fill essential roles in their communities, it is not the admirable in their characters that has an influence. Pecola serves as the bottom-most societal rung whose lowliness raises the self-esteem of everyone else, while Sula's acknowledged "evil" encourages others' righteous sense of comparative superiority. Sensitivity is lovely, but impractical, says Morrison. It is a pragmatic outlook, if not a particularly happy one.

Joan Bischoff, "The Novels of Toni Morrison: Studies in Thwarted Sensitivity," *Studies in Black Literature* 6, No. 3 (Fall 1975): 21, 23

REYNOLDS PRICE   Toni Morrison's first two books—*The Bluest Eye* with the purity of its terrors and *Sula* with its dense poetry and the depth of its probing into a small circle of lives—were strong novels. Yet, firm as they both were in achievement and promise, they didn't fully forecast her new book, *Song of Solomon*. Here the depths of the younger work are still evident, but now they thrust outward, into wider fields, for longer intervals, encompassing many more lives. The result is a long prose tale that surveys nearly a century of American history as it impinges upon a single family. In short, this is a full novel—rich, slow enough to impress itself upon us like a love affair or a sickness—not the two-hour penny dreadful which is again in vogue nor one of the airless cat's cradles custom-woven for the delight and job-assistance of graduate students of all ages.

Song of Solomon isn't, however, cast in the basically realistic mode of most family novels. In fact, its negotiations with fantasy, fable, song and allegory are so organic, continuous and unpredictable as to make any summary of its plot sound absurd; but absurdity is neither Morrison's strategy nor purpose. The purpose seems to be communication of painfully discovered and powerfully held convictions about the possibility of transcendence within human life, on the time-scale of a single life.

  Reynolds Price, "Black Family Chronicle," *New York Times Book Review*, 11 September 1977, p. 1

SUSAN L. BLAKE   The "Song of Solomon" that provides the title of Toni Morrison's third novel is a variant of a well-known Gullah folktale about a group of African-born slaves who rose up one day from the field where they were working and flew back to Africa. In the novel, this tale becomes both the end of, and a metaphor for, the protagonist's identity quest: Macon Dead III, known as Milkman, finds himself when he learns the story of his great-granddaddy Solomon who could fly. From this story he himself learns to fly, metaphorically: "For now he knew what Shalimar [Solomon] knew: if you surrendered to the air, you could *ride* it."

  In basing Milkman's identity quest on a folktale, Morrison calls attention to one of the central themes in all her fiction, the relationship between individual identity and community, for folklore is by definition the expression of community—of the common experiences, beliefs, and values that identify a folk as a group. The use of the folktale of the flying Africans in this quest seems to establish equivalence between Milkman's discovery of community and his achievement of identity, but paradoxes in the use of the folktale suggest a more complex relationship and help to define just what Morrison means by the concept of community, a concept which she vigorously endorses.

The flight of the transplanted Africans dramatizes the communal identity of Afro-Americans in several ways. It establishes "home" as the place of common origin and dissociates the Africans from the American plantation where their identity is violated. It dissociates them as well from American-born slaves, for only the African-born have the power to fly. At the same time, as the ability to fly distinguishes the Africans from their descendants, it represents an identity that the African-descended tellers of the tale believe they would have if they had not had another identity forced upon them by slavery. The tale thus represents a common dream, a common disappointment, and a group identity. As the object of Milkman's quest, it suggests a multi-leveled equivalence between individual identity and community. Simply as folktale, it is an artifact of Afro-American history; its content links Afro-American to pan-African history; it is localized to represent Milkman's family history. His discovery of the tale thus represents Milkman's discovery of his membership in ever more inclusive communities; his family, Afro-Americans, all blacks. ⟨. . .⟩

The multiple ways of seeing Milkman's discovery as a discovery of community suggest that *Song of Solomon* is an elaborate, and entertaining, expansion of the equation between identity and community. In fact, however, the end of Milkman's quest is not the discovery of community, but a solitary leap into the void. And its mythical foundation is not the typical tale of the Africans flying as a group to their common home, but a highly individualistic variant. Milkman's discovery does not result in any of the conventional indications of community. Although Milkman is reconciled with Pilate and the two of them return to Shalimar to bury the bones of her father, Pilate dies (as she has lived, protecting Milkman's life) as soon as the burial is accomplished.

Susan L. Blake, "Folklore and Community in *Song of Solomon*," *MELUS* 7, No. 3 (Fall 1980): 77–79

DARRYL PINCKNEY   The setting ⟨of *Tar Baby*⟩ is exotic—an imagined tropical island called Isle des Chevaliers, privately owned, found off Dominique. But, like the small towns in ⟨Morrison's⟩ previous books, it also has its allegorical lore. ⟨. . .⟩

The story is not entirely confined to this mysterious island. The characters in *Tar Baby* recall the mansions of Philadelphia, trailers in Maine, the cream-colored streets of Paris of their past lives. There are heated moments in Manhattan. A hamlet in northern Florida, an all black town called Eloe, turns out to be very much like Eatonville, Zora Neale Hurston's celebrated birthplace in the same region. Travel, in Morrison's earlier novels, tended to mean crossing the country. Here, there are frequent and anxious escapes to the reservations counter at Air France.

Something else has changed. The laboring poor of *The Bluest Eye*, the self-sufficient women and drifting men of *Sula*, the avaricious middle class and defiantly marginal citizens of *Song of Solomon*—they are gone, replaced, in *Tar Baby*, by the rich, their servants, their dependents, and the sans culottes who threaten their security. Though much is made of money, fashion, commodities as consciousness, and the experiences open to the privileged, the cultured, and those clever enough to hustle a piece of the action, the people living on Isle des Chevaliers, voluntary exiles all, seem to inhabit a world that is oppressively parochial and provincial. ⟨. . .⟩

Many of Morrison's previous concerns are here—having to do with the inner life of black women and especially the offhand, domestic violence and conjugal brutality that burn out daily life. Much of the recent fiction by Afro-American women contains these themes. Their message is new and arresting, as if, in the past, the worries of the kitchen or the bedroom were not sufficiently large to encompass the intense lives of black people in a racist society. But *Tar Baby*'s sense of such experience is inchoate, muffled. One wishes for the fierce concentration, the radical economy of the novels of Gayl Jones as they describe the inner world of black women in language that is harsh, disturbing, and utterly unsentimental.

Darryl Pinckney, "Every Which Way," New York Review of Books, 30 April 1981, pp. 24–25

GLORIA NAYLOR and TONI MORRISON   TM: ⟨. . .⟩ I

remember after *The Bluest Eye* having an extremely sad six or eight months. And I didn't know what it was because that was the first time I had ever written a novel. And I wasn't thinking about being a novelist then. I just wrote *that* and I thought that would be *that* and that would be the end of *that* 'cause I liked to read it and that was enough. But then I moved from one town to another, for one thing, and I was feeling, for this very sustained period, what can only be described now as missing something, missing the company I had been keeping all those years when I wrote *The Bluest Eye*, and I couldn't just write because I was able to write. I had to write with the same feeling that I had when I did *The Bluest Eye*, which was that there was this exciting collection of people that only I knew about. I had the direct line and I was the receiver of all this information. And then when I began to think about *Sula*, everything changed, I mean, all the colors of the world changed, the sounds and so on. I recognized what that period was when I finished *Sula*, and I had another idea which was *Song of Solomon*. When I finished *Song of Solomon*, I didn't have another idea for *Tar Baby* but then I knew that it arrives or it doesn't arrive and I'm not terrified of a block, of what people call a block. I think when you hit a place where you can't write, you probably should be still for a while because it's not there yet.

GN: Even a block with an idea itself? That doesn't frighten you?

TM: It doesn't bother me. And that brings me to the book that I'm writing now called *Beloved*. I had an idea that I didn't know was a book idea, but I do remember being obsessed by two or three little fragments of stories that I heard from different places. One was a newspaper clipping about a woman named Margaret Garner in 1851. It said that the Abolitionists made a great deal out of her case because she had escaped from Kentucky, I think, with her four children. She lived in a little neighborhood just outside of Cincinnati and she had killed her children. She succeeded in killing one; she tried to kill two others. She hit them in the head with a shovel and they were wounded but they didn't die. And there was a smaller one that she had at her breast. The interesting thing, in addition to that, was the interviews that she gave. She was a young woman. In the inked pictures of her she seemed a very quiet, very serene-looking woman and everyone who interviewed her remarked about her serenity and tranquility. She said, "I will not let those children live how I have lived." She had run off into a little woodshed right outside her house to kill them because she had been caught as a fugitive. And she had made up her mind that they would not suffer the way that she had and it was better for them to die. And her mother-in-law was in the house at the same time and she said, "I watched her and I neither encouraged her nor discouraged her." They put her in jail for a little while and I'm not even sure what the denouement is of her story. But that moment, that decision was a piece, a tail of something that was always around ⟨. . .⟩

Gloria Naylor and Toni Morrison, "Gloria Naylor and Toni Morrison: A Conversation," *Southern Review* 21, No. 3 (July 1985): 583–84

STANLEY CROUCH   *Beloved* ⟨. . .⟩ explains black behavior in terms of social conditioning, as if listing atrocities solves the mystery of human motive and behavior. It is designed to placate sentimental feminist ideology, and to make sure that the vision of black woman as the most scorned and rebuked of the victims doesn't weaken. Yet perhaps it is best understood by its italicized inscription: *"Sixty Million and more."* Morrison recently told *Newsweek* that the reference was to all the captured Africans, who died coming across the Atlantic. But sixty is ten times six, of course. That is very important to remember. For *Beloved*, above all else, is a blackface holocaust novel. It seems to have been written in order to enter American slavery into the big-time martyr contest, a contest usually won by references to, and works about, the experience of Jews at the hands of Nazis. As a holocaust novel, it includes disfranchisement, brutal transport, sadistic guards, failed and successful escapes, murder, liberals among the oppressors, a big war, underground cells, separation of family members, losses of loved ones to the violence of the mad order, and characters who, like the Jew in *The Pawnbroker*, have been made emotionally catatonic by the past.

That Morrison chose to set the Afro-American experience in the framework of collective tragedy is fine, of course. But she lacks a true sense of the tragic. Such a sense is stark, but it is never simpleminded. For all the memory within this book, including recollections of the trip across the Atlantic and the slave trading in the Caribbean, no one ever recalls how the Africans were captured. That would complicate matters. It would have demanded that the Africans who raided the villages of their enemies to sell them for guns, drink, and trinkets be included in the equation of injustice, something far too many Afro-Americans are loath to do—including Toni Morrison. In *Beloved* Morrison only asks that her readers tally up the sins committed against the darker people and feel sorry for them, not experience the horrors of slavery as they do. ⟨. . .⟩

But Morrison ⟨. . .⟩ can't resist the temptation of the trite or the sentimental. There is the usual scene in which the black woman is assaulted by white men while her man looks on; Halle, Sethe's husband, goes mad at the sight. Sixo, a slave who is captured trying to escape, is burned alive but doesn't scream: he sings "Seven-o" over and over, because his woman has escaped and is pregnant. But nothing is more contrived than the figure of Beloved herself, who is the reincarnated force of the malevolent ghost that was chased from the house. Beloved's revenge—she takes over the house, turns her mother into a servant manipulated by guilt, and becomes more and more vicious—unfolds as portentous melodrama. Whan Beloved finally threatens to kill Sethe, 30 black women come to the rescue. At the fence of the haunted property, one of them shouts, and we are given this: "Instantly the kneelers and the standers joined her. They stopped praying and took a step back to the beginning. In the beginning there were no words. In the beginning was the sound, and they all knew what that sound sounded like."

Too many such attempts at biblical grandeur, run through by Negro folk rhythms, stymie a book that might have been important. Had Morrison higher intentions when she appropriated the conventions of a holocaust tale, *Beloved* might stand next to, or outdistance, Ernest Gaines's *The Autobiography of Miss Jane Pittman* and Charles Johnson's *Oxherding Tale*, neither of which submits to the contrived, post-Baldwin vision of Afro-American experience. Clearly the subject is far from exhausted, the epic intricacies apparently unlimited. Yet to render slavery with aesthetic authority demands not only talent, but the courage to face the ambiguities of the human soul, which transcend the race. Had Toni Morrison that kind of courage, had she the passion necessary to liberate her work from the failure of feeling that is sentimentality, there is much that she could achieve. But why should she try to achieve anything? The position of literary conjure woman has paid off quite well. At last year's PEN Congress she announced that she had never considered herself American, but with *Beloved* she proves that she is as American as P. T. Barnum.

Stanley Crouch, "Aunt Medea," *New Republic*, 19 October 1987, pp. 41–43

SUSAN WILLIS   There is a sense of urgency in Morrison's writing, produced by the realization that a great deal is at stake. The novels may focus on individual characters like Milkman and Jadine, but the salvation of individuals is not the point. Rather, these individuals, struggling to reclaim or redefine themselves, are portrayed as epiphenomenal to community and culture, and it is the strength and continuity of the black cultural heritage as a whole that is at stake and being tested.

As Morrison sees it, the most serious threat to black culture is the obliterating influence of social change. The opening line from *Sula* might well have been the novel's conclusion, so complete is the destruction it records: "In that place, where they tore the night shade and blackberry patches from their roots to make room for the Medallion City Golf Course, there was once a neighborhood." This is the community Morrison is writing to reclaim. Its history, terminated and dramatically obliterated, is condensed into a single sentence whose content spans from rural South to urban development. Here, as throughout Morrison's writing, natural imagery refers to the past, the rural South, the reservoir of culture that has been uprooted— like the blackberry bushes—to make way for modernization. In contrast, the future is perceived of as an amorphous, institutionalized power embodied in the notion of "Medallion City," which suggests neither nature nor a people. Joining the past to the future is the neighborhood, which occupies a very different temporal moment (which history has shown to be transitional), and defines a very different social mode, as distinct from its rural origins as it is from the amorphous urban future.

It is impossible to read Morrison's four novels without coming to see the neighborhood as a concept crucial to her understanding of history. The neighborhood defines a Northern social mode rather than a Southern one, for it describes the relationship of an economic satellite, contiguous to a larger metropolis rather than separate subsistence economics like the Southern rural towns of Shalimar and Eloe. It is a Midwestern phenomenon rather than a Northeastern big-city category, because it defines the birth of principally first-generation, Northern, working-class black communities. It is a mode of the forties rather than the sixties or the eighties, and it evokes the many locally specific black populations in the North before these became assimilated to a larger, more generalized, and less regionally specific sense of black culture that we today refer to as the "black community."

Susan Willis, "Eruptions of Funk: Historicizing Toni Morrison," *Specifying: Black Women Writing the American Experience* (Madison: University of Wisconsin Press, 1987), pp. 93–95

TERRY OTTEN   In Toni Morrison's fiction characters one way or another enact the historical plight of blacks in American society. She offers no apology for her black female perspective. Though the black experience frames and informs her fictional narratives, it in no way reduces their universality. For all their complexity and diversity, the novels are woven together by common themes: the passage from innocence to experience, the quest for identity, the ambiguity of good and evil, the nature of the divided self, and especially, the concept of a fortunate fall. Morrison works the gray areas, avoiding simpleminded absolutes. Guitar tells Milkman at one point that "there are no innocent white people," but Milkman knows that there are no innocent blacks, either, least of all himself. Blacks as frequently as whites inflict extreme physical and psychological violence on blacks: the Breedloves torment each other, and Cholly rapes his daughter; Eva Peace burns her son, and Nel and Sula betray the other self; Milkman callously rejects Hagar, and Guitar kills Pilate; Son takes revenge on the childlike Cheyenne, and Jadine abandons Son; Sethe murders her daughter, and Beloved demands uncompromising payment—and of course much more. There is no doubt, though, that underlying all these manifestations of cruelty is the pernicious racism of American culture which wields its power to pervert and distort the moral center. Clearly, Morrison wants us to see the most insidious form of evil in the malevolent ability of racism to misshape the human spirit.

Terry Otten, *The Crime of Innocence in the Fiction of Toni Morrison* (Columbia: University of Missouri Press, 1989), p. 95

HAROLD BLOOM   Morrison, like any potentially strong novelist, battles against being subsumed by the traditions of narrative fiction. As a leader of African-American literary culture, Morrison is particularly intense in resisting critical characterizations that she believes misrepresent her own loyalties, her social and political fealties to the complex cause of her people. If one is a student of literary influence as such, and I am, then one's own allegiances as a critic are aesthetic, as I insist mine are. One is aware that the aesthetic has been a mask for those who would deny vital differences in gender, race, social class, and yet it need not be an instrument for the prolongation of exploiting forces. The aesthetic stance, as taught by Ruskin, Pater, and Wilde, enhances a reader's apprehension of perception and sensation. Such a mode of knowing literature seems to me inescapable, despite times like our own, in which societal and historical resentments, all with their own validity, tend to crowd out aesthetic considerations. Yet, as an artist, Morrison has few affinities with Zora Neale Hurston or Ralph Ellison, or with other masters of African-American fiction. Her curious resemblance to certain aspects of D. H. Lawrence does not ensue from the actual influence of Lawrence, but comes out of the two dominant precursors who have shaped her narrative sensibility, William Faulkner and Virginia Woolf. Faulkner and Woolf have little in common, but if you mixed them potently enough you might get Lawrence, or Toni Morrison.

Lest this seem a remote matter to a passionate reader of Morrison, I would observe mildly that one function of literary study is to help us make choices, because choice is inescapable, this late in Western cultural history. I do not believe that Morrison writes fiction of a kind I am not yet competent to read and judge, because I attend to her work with pleasure and enlighten-ment, amply rewarded by the perception and sensation that her art generates. Reading Alice Walker or Ishmael Reed, I cannot trust my own aesthetic reactions, and decide that their mode of writing must be left to critics more responsive than myself. But then I reflect that every reader must choose for herself or himself. Does one read and reread the novels of Alice Walker, or of Toni Morrison? I reread Morrison because her imagination, whatever her social purposes, transcends ideology and polemics, and enters again into the literary space occupied only by fantasy and romance of authentic aes-thetic dignity. Extraliterary purposes, however valid or momentous they may be for a time, ebb away, and we are left with story, characters, and style, that is to say, with literature or the lack of literature. Morrison's five novels to date leave us with literature, and not with a manifesto for social change, however necessary and admirable such change would be in our America of Chairman Atwater, Senator Helms, President Bush, and the other luminaries of what we ought to go on calling the Willie Horton election of 1988.

Harold Bloom, "Introduction," *Toni Morrison*, ed. Harold Bloom (New York: Chelsea House, 1990), pp. 1–2

WILFRED D. SAMUELS and CLENORA HUDSON-WEEMS
⟨. . .⟩ Morrison writes to and for blacks. She has no problems stating

this fact. "When I view the world, perceive it and write it, it is the world of black people. It is not that I won't write about white people. I just know that when I'm trying to develop the various themes I write about, the people who best manifest these for me are the black people whom I invent. It is not deliberate or calculated or self-consciously black, because I recognize and despise the artificial black writing some writers do." As Morrison told Walter Clemons, however, this does not mean that whites cannot adequately respond to her works. "When I write, I don't try to translate for white readers . . . Dostoevski wrote for a Russian audience, but we're able to read him. If I'm specific, and I don't overexplain, then anybody can overhear me."

It is clear, then, that Morrison sees her work as speaking to a specific audience but as reaching beyond the bounds of that audience to the rest of humankind. ⟨. . .⟩ Morrison uses the black slave experience in America as a metaphor for the human condition, which is necessarily all-inclusive.

Wilfred D. Samuels and Clenora Hudson-Weems, *Toni Morrison* (Boston: Twayne, 1990), p. 140

DOROTHEA DRUMMOND MBALIA   *Tar Baby* is an assimilation and advancement of the primary theme of her three earlier novels. For the first time, Morrison frees her work from the narrow geographical boundaries of American society. Recognizing that people of African descent, no matter where they live, share a common identity, a common history, and a common oppression, she uses an island in the Caribbean as the dominant and pivotal setting for her novel. In doing so, Morrison reflects her own maturing consciousness of the fact that African people must seek a common solution to their plight. She herself states that "Black culture survives everywhere pretty much the same" and that "Black people take their culture wherever they go."

Furthermore, in *Tar Baby* Morrison creates a revolutionary protagonist, Son, who realizes that he cannot run away and leave a body. Having discovered first the importance of knowing one's history and one's relationship to his people, Son commits himself to sharing this knowledge with other Africans. Thus, by struggling to politically educate Therese, Gideon, Sydney, Ondine, and, in particular, Jadine—symbols of the larger Pan-African society—Son becomes a disciple for African people, a modern-day revolutionary. ⟨. . . But⟩ what Son fails to realize is that there are some Africans, like Jadine, who—because they share the aspirations of the ruling class and receive handouts from it—will refuse to struggle against capitalism even though they are conscious of the fact that it is the primary enemy of African people.

Despite its weaknesses, the novel's theme and narrative structure reflect Morrison's heightened class consciousness. Structurally, she has embraced the traditional African concept of collectivism, for each of the major characters, as well as the omniscient narrator, contributes to the organic world of the novel. The story is told, in effect, by taking individual threads and sewing them into a whole, a wholeness that she so ardently wishes for African people.

Dorothea Drummond Mbalia, Toni Morrison's Developing Class Consciousness (Selinsgrove, PA: Susquehanna University Press, 1991), pp. 26–27

JANE MILLER   Within the first half-page of Toni Morrison's novel ⟨*Jazz*⟩, an 18-year-old girl has been shot dead by her middle-aged lover, and his wife has been manhandled from the funeral after attempting to cut the dead girl's face with a knife. Both events are witnessed and kept secret by a community which has reason to distrust the police and to look kindly upon a hitherto gentle, childless couple, whose sudden, violent sorrows they recognise and are able to forgive. And as the spring of that year, 1926, bursts a month or two later upon the 'City' of this extraordinary novel, its all-seeing gossip of a narrator is moved to declare—if only provisionally— that 'history is over, you all, and everything's ahead at last.'

The novel's theme tune is spun out from these contrasts and whirled through a series of playful improvisations by a storyteller who admits to being—and, as it turns out, expects the reader to be—'curious, inventive and well-informed'. It is impossible to resist the seductions of this particular narrative voice as it announces its own fallibilities, mourns its distance from some of the events it will therefore need to invent, boldly revises its own speculations, even as it recalls, replays, retrieves them for us before our very eyes and with our assumed complicity. For, of course, this voice also undertakes to guarantee both tale and telling as truth, history, music known and shared by all who have roots in the black urban communities of America in the Twenties. And for readers with quite other roots? Well, the voice is no more prepared than Morrison is herself to 'footnote the black experience for white readers'. As she put it in a recent interview: 'I wouldn't try to explain what a reader like me already knew.' ⟨. . .⟩

Jazz is a love story, indeed a romance. And romance and its high-risk seductions for young women come with special health warnings when it is poor young black women who might succumb to it. For romance has always been white, popular, capitalistic in its account of love as transactions voluntarily undertaken between class and beauty and money. But the romance which is a snare and a delusion has also spelled out a future for young women, a destiny, significance and pleasure—and particularly when there was little enough of those possibilities for them or for the men they knew. The older women of Morrison's novels know that sex can be a woman's undoing, that men, 'ridiculous and delicious and terrible', are always trouble. The narrator in *Jazz* is generous with warnings: 'The girls have red lips and their legs whisper to each other through silk stockings. The red lips and the silk flash power. A power they will exchange for the right to be overcome, penetrated.'

Morrison's writing of a black romance pays its debt to blues music, the rhythms and the melancholy pleasures of which she has so magically transformed into a novel. More than that, she has claimed new sources and new kinds of reading as the inspiration for a thriving literature.

Jane Miller, "New Romance," *London Review of Books*, 14 May 1992, p. 12

DENISE HEINZE   As an artist, Morrison negotiates a very complex matrix of reality in which she is both despised and revered, absent and present, ignored and sought after. The result is a double-visionary canon, a symbiosis of novel-writing in which Morrison has complete mastery over the fictive reality she creates. And by her creative mediation between the real and fictive worlds, she generates possibilities rather than records continued frustration and oppression. Morrison may not write from a stance of art as life, but she may be a psychological and spiritual Wizard of Oz for life as art. ⟨. . .⟩

By combining political consciousness with aesthetic sensibility, Morrison achieves a very delicate balance: without directly denouncing white society, she illustrates the demise of blacks who have adopted the corrupting influence of the white community. By indirection Morrison avoids the polarization of black and white humanity—one as inherently good, the other irrevocably corrupt—and thus allows all people to vicariously experience a rebirth through the black community. While her intent may be to valorize the black community and ignite both blacks and whites into political action, what she also wishes is to elevate through art the beautiful—and hence reclaimable—in the human condition.

Perhaps therein lies her appeal, for in denouncing the dominant culture she presents to an aging America alternatives that have always existed and are now emerging, but which have long been suppressed by the rhetoric of an entrenched ideology. Morrison's success as a great American writer is perhaps a function of two factors: (1) her ability to manipulate her insider/outsider status, for she both subverts and maintains, is exploited by and exploits the literary establishment, and (2) her recognition that her double-consciousness can never be, perhaps never should be, integrated into a single vision. Indeed, she is in the truly remarkable position of being able to articulate with near impunity two cultures—one black, the other white American. By orchestrating this sense of connectedness between cultures rather than attempting to dissolve the differences, Morrison's successful career appears to have transcended the "permanent condition" of double-consciousness that afflicts her fictional characters.

Denise Heinze, <i>The Dilemma of "Double Consciousness": Toni Morrison's Novels</i> (Athens: University of Georgia Press, 1993), pp. 8–10

🔲 *Bibliography*

The Bluest Eye. 1970.

Sula. 1973.

The Black Book (editor). 1974.

Song of Solomon. 1977.

Tar Baby. 1981.

Beloved. 1987.

Race-ing Justice, En-gendering Power: Essays on Anita Hill, Clarence Thomas, and the Construction of Social Reality (editor). 1992.

Jazz. 1992.

Playing in the Dark: Whiteness and the Literary Imagination. 1992.

Lecture and Speech of Acceptance, upon the Award of the Nobel Prize for Literature.
    1994.
Conversations with Toni Morrison. Ed. Danille Taylor-Guthrie. 1994.

Gloria Naylor
b. 1950

GLORIA NAYLOR was born on January 25, 1950, in New York City to Roosevelt Naylor, a transit worker, and Alberta McAlpin Naylor, a telephone operator. Her interest in writing dates from grade school, but upon graduating from high school in 1968 she decided not to continue her education, instead becoming a missionary for the Jehovah's Witnesses. Naylor spent the next seven years proselytizing in New York, North Carolina, and Florida before becoming disenchanted with the movement and returning to New York in 1975.

Naylor worked as a telephone operator in various hospitals in New York City to support herself as she continued her education. After a brief attempt to study nursing at Medgar Evers College, Naylor enrolled in the English program at Brooklyn College, where she received her B.A. in 1981. The next year she published *The Women of Brewster Place*, a "Novel in Seven Stories" that describes the lives of a group of women living in a slum neighborhood. The book was a critical success, and in 1983 Naylor won the American Book Award for best first novel and a Distinguished Writer Award from the Mid-Atlantic Writers Association. The book was also turned into a successful television special (and an unsuccessful series) on ABC in 1989.

In 1985 Naylor published *Linden Hills*, a novel that is set in an upscale black neighborhood within sight of Brewster Place. *Linden Hills* was inspired by Dante's *Inferno*; in Naylor's novel middle- and upper-class blacks sacrifice some part of their soul to attain upward mobility. *Linden Hills* was followed by *Mama Day* (1988), a novel about a community on a small, isolated island off the coasts of Georgia and South Carolina that was orginally settled by an African-born fugitive slave. Most recently, Naylor published *Bailey's Cafe* (1992), a magical realist novel that takes place in a mysterious post–World War II cafe.

Since the publication of *The Women of Brewster Place*, Naylor has held a variety of academic positions at various universities, including Princeton

122

University, the University of Pennsylvania, Brandeis University, and Cornell University. In addition, she received a fellowship from the National Endowment for the Arts in 1985 and a Guggenheim Fellowship in 1988. She recently completed a play adaptation of *Bailey's Cafe*, which opened in April 1994 at the Hartford Stage in Hartford, Conneticut, to good reviews. Naylor currently resides in the Washington Heights area of Manhattan.

Critical Extracts

DOROTHY WICKENDEN   Like any ghetto, Brewster Place has its horrors and its desperate charms. A dead-end street, cut off from the city's main arteries by a brick wall, this neighborhood is inhabited by decaying apartment buildings, children who "bloom in colorful shorts and tops plastered against gold, ebony, and nut-brown arms and legs," and women who "pin their dreams to wet laundry hung out to dry." There are men who live here too, of course. They visit their women like nightmares, leaving behind them babies and bile. But Gloria Naylor's women, much like those of Toni Morrison and Alice Walker, are daunting even in desolation. Most of them find that through laughter and companionship they can make themselves virtually impregnable. ⟨. . .⟩

It won't come as a surprise to readers of contemporary fiction by black women that Gloria Naylor has few kind words to waste on members of the other sex: Yet *The Women of Brewster Place*, like Alice Walker's extraordinary *The Color Purple* ⟨. . .⟩—and unlike much current fiction by privileged white feminists—is not simply a self-indulgent celebration of female solidarity. Naylor and Walker write with equal lucidity about the cruelty that poverty breeds and the ways in which people achieve redemption. Nor is there a wariness about traditional women's roles. *The Women of Brewster Place* is a novel about motherhood, a concept embraced by Naylor's women, each of whom is a surrogate child or mother to the next.

Despite the simple elegance of Naylor's prose, there is a risk that the accumulation of horrific experiences may deaden some readers' senses before the novel builds to its devastating climax. Yet the spirit with which these women cope is, finally, more powerful than the circumstances of their lives.

Dorothy Wickenden, [Review of *The Women of Brewster Place*], *New Republic*, 6 September 1982, pp. 37–38

GLORIA NAYLOR and TONI MORRISON   GN: You know,

it takes a lot to finally say that. That "Yes, I write. No, Mama, I'll never have a regular job for more than a year. This is what I do."

You know, there are moments with my work when I can achieve the type of atmosphere that's permeating this house and our conversation now. It's as if I've arrived in a place where it's all spirit and no body—an overwhelming sense of calm. But those moments are rare. Usually, I vacillate between an intense love of my work and "What in the hell am I doing this for?" There has to be an easier way to get the type of pain that I'm inflicting upon myself at this desk. But I guess I keep at it because of those times when I can reach that spiritual center. It's like floating in the middle of that river, and waves are all around you . . . I actually begin to feel blessed.

TM: It is a blessing. Any art form that can do that for you is a special thing. People have to have that sense of having moved something from one place to another and made out of nothing something. Having added something to something and having seen a mess and made it orderly or seen rigidity and given it fluidity. You know, something. And writing encompasses for me all there isn't.

GN: Do you even think that you've been chosen, knowing that you're always going to do this? Because I really feel as if it's sort of like a calling. Not a calling meaning anything special or different, because the men who come up there to clean your road perform a service to this planet just like an artist performs a service. But I really feel that for me it goes beyond just a gift to handle words, but that it was *meant* for me to be writing as opposed to other things that I'm talented enough to do and can do well when I put my mind to it. For example, I do teach and I enjoy it. But there's not the same type of pull—I think I would self-destruct if I didn't write. I wouldn't self-destruct if I didn't teach.

TM: You *would* self-destruct if you didn't write. You know, I wanted to ask you whether or not, when you finished *The Women ⟨of Brewster Place⟩*, did you know what the next book was? ⟨. . .⟩ When you finished *The Women of Brewster Place*, what was the time period and the emotional trek to *Linden Hills*?

GN: Well, two things were going on, Toni. One was that I wanted there to be a *Linden Hills*.

TM: Even before you finished . . .

GN: Yes, because I had a character in *Brewster Place* named Kiswana Browne who lived in Linden Hills. And my next dream—you know, the daydreams about what you want to do, the easy part of writing any book—was that I would love to do a whole treatment of her neighborhood. And at about that time, I was taking this course at Brooklyn College, "Great Works of Literature." And we had read *The Inferno* and I was overwhelmed by the philosophical underpinnings of the poem as well as the characters that Dante created. Then the idea came to me that I could try to sketch out this neighborhood along the lines of *The Inferno*. But it was a while before I could actually sit down and work on the book because there was fear, a little, because this was going to be a *real* novel. *Brewster Place* was really interconnected short stories and that type of work demands a shorter time span, a different emotional involvement. So it was in the summer of 1981 when I began to seriously sketch out what I might like to do with *Linden Hills* and it was a year later when I literally sat down and said, "Here is the emotional involvement. I have the idea and I'm going to go for it."

Gloria Naylor and Toni Morrison, "Gloria Naylor and Toni Morrison: A Conversation," *Southern Review* 21, No. 3 (July 1985): 581–82

CATHERINE C. WARD   Gloria Naylor's second novel, *Linden Hills,* is a modern version of Dante's *Inferno* in which souls are damned not because they have offended God or have violated a religious system but because they have offended themselves. In their single-minded pursuit of upward mobility, the inhabitants of Linden Hills, a black, middle-class suburb, have turned away from their past and from their deepest sense of who they are. Naylor feels that the subject of who-we-are and what we are willing to give up of who-we-are to get where-we-want-to-go is a question of the highest seriousness—as serious as a Christian's concern over his salvation. ⟨. . .⟩

Naylor's tale is an allegory based on the physical and moral topography of Dante's *Inferno*. It covers four days in the life of a twenty-year-old black poet, Willie Mason, who lives in a poor neighborhood called Putney Wayne that lies above Linden Hills. Working temporarily as a handyman to earn money to buy Christmas presents, Willie passes through Linden Hills and, like Dante, analyzes the moral failures of the lost souls he encounters. By the time Willie escapes from the frozen lake at the bottom of Linden Hills and crosses to the safety of a nearby apple orchard, he has experienced a spiritual awakening. The "new" Willie has decided to give up his aimless drifting and to take charge of his life. He becomes, as his name implies, a decisive builder. He accepts responsibility for his life, he refuses to blame his problems on others or on fate, and he realizes that he can choose a middle way between the poverty of the ghetto and the depravity of Linden Hills.

Eight concentric drives cross Linden Hills. First Crescent Drive through Fifth Crescent Drive correspond to Circles One through Five in Dante's upper Hell. Below upper Linden Hills lies a more exclusive section, the Tupelo Drive area, which corresponds to the City of Dis. At the center of Linden Hills is the house of Luther Nedeed, surrounded by a frozen lake. Luther Nedeed is the fifth of his line; the original Luther Nedeed came from Tupelo, Mississippi, and founded the area in 1820. The Luther Nedeeds are the Satans or anti-Christs of Linden Hills. Each one has been both an undertaker and a real estate developer and thus has been able to control the residents in death as well as in life. ⟨. . .⟩

In Linden Hills up is down; the most prestigious lots are those lower down the hill. To gain one of those lots, which are never sold but are leased for 1001 years, each of the residents must give up something—a part of his soul, ties with his past, ties with his community, his spiritual values, even his sense of who he is. Like Dante's lost souls, the people of Linden Hills live on a circle that is appropriate to their "sins." Here most residents stay for the rest of their lives, locked in their wrong choices.

> Catherine C. Ward, "Gloria Naylor's *Linden Hills*: A Modern *Inferno*," *Contemporary Literature* 28, No. 1 (Spring 1987): 67, 69–70

RITA MAE BROWN   God created the universe in six days. It took her longer, but Gloria Naylor has created her own universe in *Mama Day*.

The novel's title is the pet name of the most powerful figure in Willow Springs, a fictional Southern island. Miranda Day, born in 1895, is the great-aunt of Cocoa Day, a young, too-smart woman who moves to New York City.

Just why Cocoa would want to live among both the cold and the Yankees mystifies the residents of Willow Springs. Mama Day figures, observing the male inhabitants of the island, that there have to be better men in New York, even if they do talk funny. ⟨. . .⟩

Into this upside-down world ⟨of Willow Springs⟩ comes George Andrews, Cocoa's new husband. George's power comes from his logical Western mind. He is an engineer and values precision. He is also an orphan cut off from his roots, and therefore beguiled by Willow Springs where bloodlines can be traced through the centuries. ⟨. . .⟩

George is the linchpin of *Mama Day*. His rational mind allows the reader to experience the island as George experiences it. Mama Day and Cocoa are of the island and therefore less immediately accessible to the reader.

The turning point of the book comes when George is asked not only to believe in Mama Day's power but to act on it. Cocoa is desperately ill. A hurricane has washed out the bridge so that no mainland doctor can be summoned. Only Mama Day can show George the way to save his wife. He is told to go into the chicken coop and search in the northwest corner for the nest of an old red hen. He is to bring back to Mama Day what he finds there. He tries to do as he is told, but George needs a quantifiable result. He misses the symbolism of the eggs, of the old hen, and of the objects he must carry into the hen house. And so he "fails," but his action allows his wife to live even though the result of this task is horrible for him.

The formula for heterosexual salvation in conventional novels is for the man and woman either to understand one another and live happily ever after or to understand each other and realize they can't live together. The key is thinking, not necessarily feeling. Not so here. George must let go of his rigidity, his "male" mind. When he can't do that, he sacrifices himself on the altar of love. Success is a form of surrender: the opposite of the desire to control.

> Rita Mae Brown, "Black Laughter in an Offshore Showoff Novel," *Los Angeles Times Book Review*, 6 March 1988, p. 2

LARRY R. ANDREWS   Female power and wisdom are vividly incarnated in Miranda, the title character ⟨of *Mama Day*. . . .⟩ Forced prematurely into a nurturing role in her family after her mother's suicide, Miranda eventually becomes not only a mother to her grandniece Ophelia but a "Mama" to the whole island community of Willow Springs. For decades she is not only the community's midwife but also its guardian of tradition and its central authority figure: "Mama Day say no, everybody say no." She is a powerful conjure woman with special gifts derived, in the community's view, from "being a direct descendant of Sapphira Wade, piled on the fact of springing from the seventh son of a seventh son." She feels the burdensome responsibility of her intuitive powers and her knowledge of nature and uses them only to advance the cause of life (making Bernice fertile or calling down lightning to punish the murderous Ruby).

Miranda's womanpower is thus presented as an expression of natural forces (note her gardening ability) and as an inheritance from the legendary ur-mother of the community. When Sapphira Wade liberated herself from her white husband and master, Bascombe Wade, in 1823, she initiated a tradition of female power as well as a religious tradition (Candle Walk) and strengthened the myth of the great conjure woman on hand at God's creation of the island. She was also legendary for bringing into the open the unresolved tensions between men and women. Miranda feels largely an unconscious sisterhood with Sapphira through various intuitive experiences of knowledge and power. For example, when she handles Sapphira's fabric while making a quilt for Ophelia, she has a sudden premonition that George will not be coming, and when she finds Bascombe's undecipherable ledger and Sapphira's bill of sale, she has vague dreams that lead to a way to save Ophelia's life. On the other hand, Miranda feels a more *conscious* bond of sisterhood with her mother. And her mother's madness and suicide, described partly as an escape from her husband, connect her mother and hence Miranda to Sapphira again.

Thus female power is *there* in the legendary past for the females of Willow Springs to learn, to accept, and to draw strength from in their own lives. As ⟨Susan⟩ Willis says, "For black women history is a bridge defined along motherlines." Sisterhood here is not a relationship that arises for the nonce as a *response to* a particular condition, such as oppression. It is a force that transcends particulars and is allied to nature itself. Miranda is the role model for the full acceptance and living of this power.

> Larry R. Andrews, "Black Sisterhood in Gloria Naylor's Novels," CLA Journal 33,
> No. 1 (September 1989): 18–19

MICHAEL AWKWARD   The unity of form and content in Gloria Naylor's *The Women of Brewster Place* is, like that of its female-authored precursors, essentially related to its exploration of the redemptive possibilities of female coalescence. But because it is a work that consists of the narratively *disconnected* stories of individual women, such coalescence does not involve simply an individual protagonist's inside and outside as it does in *Their Eyes Were Watching God* and *The Bluest Eye*. Rather, it involves demonstrating— both by exhibiting essential psychological and circumstantial affinities between the women and by offering significant evidence of these women's recognition of such affinities—that the protagonists of the individual texts actually form, at the novel's conclusion, a community of women. As is the case in both of the texts on which this study has concentrated to this point, textual explorations of female unity in Naylor's novel are unmistakably related to the work's narrative strategies, strategies whose ends are under-scored by the novel's subtitle, "A Novel in Seven Stories": to demonstrate that the narratively disconnected texts of individual protagonists can be forged into a unified whole.

Naylor's narrative tasks are seemingly complicated by the means she chooses to demonstrate an achieved Afro-American's woman's community. In a novel in which unrealistic dreams are the source of much of the female characters' pain, the author's depiction of the scene of female coalescence— the women's unified efforts to tear down the wall that separates Brewster Place from the rest of the city—as the grief-inspired dream of one of these characters prevents a reading of Naylor's portrait of female nexus as either an actual narrative event or a realistic possibility. *The Women of Brewster Place*'s totalizing gesture, then, evidences the work's textual disjunctions. If Naylor's novel displays a unity of form and content, it is a unity based on a common *disunity*, on a shared failure to achieve wholeness.

> Michael Awkward, "Authorial Dreams of Wholeness: (Dis)Unity, (Literary) Parent-
> age, and *The Women of Brewster Place*," *Inspiriting Influences: Tradition, Revision, and
> Afro-American Women's Novels* (New York: Columbia University Press, 1989), p. 98

JILL L. MATUS   The inconclusive last chapter ⟨of *The Women of Brewster Place*⟩ opens into an epilogue that ⟨. . .⟩ teases the reader with the sense of an ending by appearing to be talking about the death of the street, Brewster Place. The epilogue itself is not unexpected, since the novel opens with a prologue describing the birth of the street. So why not a last word on how it dies? Again, expectations are subverted and closure is subtly deferred. Although the epilogue begins with a meditation on how a street dies and tells us that Brewster Place is waiting to die, *waiting* is a present participle that never becomes past. "Dawn" (the prologue) is coupled neither with death nor darkness, but with "dusk," a condition whose half-light underscores the half-life of the street. Despite the fact that in the epilogue Brewster Place is abandoned, its daughters still get up elsewhere and go about their daily activities. In a reiteration of the domestic routines that are always carefully attended to in the novel—the making of soup, the hanging of laundry, the diapering of babies—, Brewster's death is forestalled and postponed. More importantly, the narrator emphasizes that the dreams of Brewster's inhabitants are what keep them alive. *"They get up and pin those dreams to wet laundry hung out to dry, they're mixed with a pinch of salt and thrown into pots of soup, and they're diapered around babies. They ebb and flow, ebb and flow, but never disappear." They* refers initially to the "colored daughters" but thereafter repeatedly to the dreams. The end of the novel raises questions about the relation of dreams to the persistence of life, since the capacity of Brewster's women to dream on is identified as their capacity to live on. The street continues to exist marginally, on the edge of death; it is the "end of the line" for most of its inhabitants. Like the street, the novel hovers, moving toward the end of its line, but deferring. What prolongs both the text and the lives of Brewster's inhabitants is dream; in the same way that Mattie's dream of destruction postpones the end of the novel, the narrator's last words identify dream as that which affirms and perpetuates the life of the street.

Jill L. Matus, "Dream, Deferral, and Closure in *The Women of Brewster Place*," *Black American Literature Forum* 24, No. 1 (Spring 1990): 49–50

BARBARA CHRISTIAN   It is precisely the fact that Naylor's two neighborhoods ⟨Brewster Place and Linden Hills⟩ *are* black that causes them to perceive so clearly their difference. Importantly, Naylor locates their similarities and differences in a historical process. Both Brewster Place and Linden Hills have been created by racism, or more precisely, as a result of the effects of racism on their founders. Linden Hills is literally carved out of a seemingly worthless soil by an ex-slave, Luther Nedeed, who in the 1820s had the secret dream of developing "an ebony jewel," a community of successful blacks who could stave off the racism of America and exhibit through their fine houses that members of the race can be powerful. In contrast, Brewster Place is "the bastard child of clandestine meetings" between local white politicians, at first to satisfy expected protests from the Irish community over the undeserved dismissal of their too-honest police chief. Later, Brewster Place becomes the neighborhood of successive waves of European immigrants, unwanted Americans who finally become, over time, the black poor.

The origin of communities and their historical development are as critical to the structure of Naylor's novels as they are to ⟨Paule⟩ Marshall's and ⟨Toni⟩ Morrison's. These two writers—Marshall particularly in *Brown Girl, Brownstones*, Morrison particularly in *Sula*—begin their narrative not with the introduction of their characters but with the history of their characters' natal communities. ⟨. . .⟩ The differences between these authors' respective treatments, however, is instructive, for Marshall's West Indian immigrants see their brownstones as places they can eventually own, as a step up, while Naylor's blacks of Brewster Place are at a dead end. Morrison's ex-slave earns his "bottom" as payment from his ex-master and is cheated in the process, for he is given the worst land in the area. But Naylor's Nedeed carefully *chooses* his site, outwitting everyone who sees his plateau as having no value.

Although Naylor characterizes one neighborhood as held together by women and the other as controlled by a family, she stresses that both are started by men for the purpose of consolidating power. The intentions of these men are evident in the geographical choices they make. Nedeed's choice of "a V-shaped section of land," "the northern face of a worthless plateau" indicates his direction. Not only is his site so clearly visible; even more important, its V-shape allows his land to be self-enclosed yet situated in the world. And since Nedeed lives on the lowest level of "the hills," he stands as a sentry to his private development. The shape of Brewster Place too is self-enclosed, for a wall is put up, separating it from other neighborhoods and making it a dead end. Ironically, what is positive in one context is negative in another, depending on who has power. For black Nedeed uses his enclosed V-shape to select those who will be allowed to live near him, while the people of Brewster Place have a wall imposed on them by white city officials who want them separated from more "respectable" folk.

Barbara Christian, "Gloria Naylor's Geography: Community, Class, and Patriarchy in *The Women of Brewster Place* and *Linden Hills*," *Reading Black, Reading Feminist: A Critical Anthology*, ed. Henry Louis Gates, Jr. (New York: Meridian, 1990), pp. 351–52

BARBARA SMITH   In "The Two" ⟨in *The Women of Brewster Place* . . .⟩, Naylor sets up the women's response to their ⟨lesbian⟩ identity as an either/or dichotomy. Lorraine's desire for acceptance, although completely comprehensible, is based upon assimilation and denial, while Naylor depicts Theresa's healthier defiance as an individual stance. In the clearest statement of resistance in the story, Theresa thinks: "If they practiced that way with each other, then they could turn back to back and beat the hell out of the world for trying to invade their territory. But she had found no such sparring partner in Lorraine, and the strain of fighting alone was beginning to show on her." A mediating position between complete assimilation or alienation might well evolve from some sense of connection to a Lesbian/gay community. Involvement with other Lesbians and gay men could provide a reference point and support that would help diffuse some of the straight world's power. Naylor mentions that Theresa socializes with gay men and perhaps Lesbians at a bar, but her interactions with them occur outside the action of the story. The author's decision not to portray other Lesbians and gay men, but only to allude to them, is a significant one. The reader is never given an opportunity to view Theresa or Lorraine in a context in which they are the norm. Naylor instead presents them as "the two" exceptions in an entirely heterosexual world. Both women are extremely isolated and although their relationship is loving, it also feels claustrophobic. ⟨. . .⟩ Lorraine's rejection of other Lesbians and gay men is excruciating, as is the self-hatred that obviously prompts it. It is painfully ironic that she considers herself in the same boat with Black people in the story, who are heterosexual, most of whom ostracize her, but not with black people who are Lesbian and gay. The one time that Lorraine actually decides to go to the club by herself, ignoring Theresa's warning that she won't have a good time without her, is the night that she is literally destroyed. ⟨. . .⟩

Whatever their opinions, it is not the women of the neighborhood who are directly responsible for Lorraine's destruction, but six actively homophobic and woman-hating teenage boys. Earlier that day Lorraine and Kiswana Browne had encountered the toughs who unleashed their sexist and homophobic violence on the two young women. Kiswana verbally bests their leader, C. C. Baker, but he is dissuaded from physically retaliating because one of the other boys reminds him: " 'That's Abshu's woman, and that big dude don't mind kickin' ass.' " As a Lesbian, Lorraine does not have any kind of "dude" to stand between her and the violence of other men. Although she is completely silent during the encounter, C. C.'s parting words to her are, "I'm gonna remember this, Butch!" That night when Lorraine returns from the bar alone, she walks into the alley which is the boy's turf. They are waiting for her and gang-rape her in one of the most devastating scenes in literature. ⟨. . .⟩

⟨. . .⟩ Although the Lesbian characters in "The Two" lack authenticity, the story possesses a certain level of verisimilitude. The generalized homophobia that the women face, which culminates in retaliatory rape and near murderous decimation, is quite true to life. Gay and Lesbian newspapers provide weekly accounts, which sometimes surface in the mainstream media, of the constant violence leveled at members of our communities. What feels disturbing and inauthentic to me is how utterly hopeless Naylor's view of Lesbian existence is. Lorraine and Theresa are classically unhappy homosexuals of the type who populated white literature during a much earlier era, when the only options for the "deviant" were isolation, loneliness, mental illness, suicide, or death.

Barbara Smith, "The Truth That Never Hurts: Black Lesbians in Fiction in the 1980s," *Wild Women in the Whirlwind: Afra-American Culture and the Contemporary Literary Renaissance*, ed. Joanne M. Braxton and Andrée Nicola McLaughlin (New Brunswick, NJ: Rutgers University Press, 1990), pp. 227–30

JACQUELINE BOBO and ELLEN SEITER   ⟨The television special⟩ *The Women of Brewster Place* runs close to the codes of the television melodrama (especially of soap operas and made-for-television movies), but at the same time is very different. There are three notable features appearing in the television adaptation that the novel *The Women of Brewster Place* shares with other works by black women writers ⟨. . .⟩: an exploration of the sense of community among black women, an indictment of sexism, and an emphasis on the importance of black women supporting each other. In *The Women of Brewster Place*, the black community is used for survival rather than individual advancement and upward mobility. Although the programme tells the story of seven women, the first and longest story establishes Mattie Michael (the Oprah Winfrey character) as a pivotal figure—functioning much as the 'tentpole character' does in soap opera. Mattie's story covers about eighteen years, beginning with her first and only pregnancy. Through good fortune, hard work and the friendship of an older woman, Mattie achieves one of her dreams of success: she becomes a home owner. Miss Eva's and Mattie's house is represented neither as a cold and alienating bourgeois prison in the tradition of family melodrama on film (and of avant-garde feminist films such as *Jeanne Dielmann*), nor as the flimsy, obviously artificial, temporary set of American soap operas. Rather, the characters' aspirations to the comforts and the aesthetics of cosy domestic space are dignified with many lingering takes of interiors in which an absence of dialogue focuses attention on the sounds and the rhythms of life within the home. These images contrast sharply with the cramped rooms without views on Brewster Place. At the end of the first episode, Mattie loses the house when her son, on a murder charge, skips bail and disappears. The rest of the story traces Mattie's descent, her fall from economic grace and her arrival at Brewster Place. By the end of the programme, we realize that Mattie's personal fall has permitted her move into a nexus of women friends and neighbours, and thus the beginning of the community—troubled though it may be—of Brewster Place.

This is a strikingly different structure from that of most Hollywood film narratives, in which images of community are for the most part entirely lacking, and narrative conventions are typically based on the autonomous, unconnected individual. *The Women of Brewster Place*, though, does not offer a utopian image of community: poverty, violence, and bigotry are permanent features, and these are shown to deform personal relationships and threaten women. Yet it contains striking instances of deeply held values that are starkly opposed to the values of the mainstream white culture and economy. For example, after Mattie has left her rat-infested apartment and searched futilely for another place to live, she and her infant son are taken in by Miss Eva to share her home. Miss Eva rejects the money that Mattie offers her for board, refusing to translate into market relations her gesture of help to a woman in need. Mattie, bewildered by this generosity, puts money in the cookie jar every week, but Miss Eva never takes it. Miss Eva shares all her material wealth and comfort with Mattie—literally a stranger off the street—without hesitation. It is almost impossible to conceive of this kind of act towards a person unrelated by blood in the universe of the white family melodrama.

Jacqueline Bobo and Ellen Seiter, "Black Feminism and Media Criticism: *The Women of Brewster Place*," *Screen* 32, No. 3 (Autumn 1991): 294–95

RICHARD EDER   Gloria Naylor's new novel ⟨*Bailey's Cafe*⟩ is devotional at heart, though it is told in contrasting shades of harsh, comic and magic realism. Its stories of ravaged urban blacks, most of them women, are savage and sardonic, but they float in a mystical lyricism. They are the stories of the regulars who frequent Bailey's, and they are told by the proprietor, doorkeeper and gritty good shepherd who both runs it and expounds it, along with his laconically nurturing wife, Nadine. It stands "on the margin between the edge of the world and infinite possibility," he tells us.

Naylor writes consummately well of the real world's edge. Her infinite possibility is shakier. It is cloudy or downright sentimental at times, though it can also be moving. Magic is a tricky proposition; when it doesn't transport you, it strands you. The seedy watering-place as a place of dreams—Saroyan's saloon in "The Time of Your Life," the End of the Line Cafe in *The Iceman Cometh*, Lanford Wilson's Hot L Baltimore and Bailey's place need a vigilant bouncer to keep bathos out. Bailey, like some of his predecessors, can grow distracted. ⟨. . .⟩

The horrors of our time—at war, and for blacks in the cities—defy practical remedy. And so, Bailey and Nadine ⟨. . .⟩ move into the partly grounded, partly floating Cafe. It is a place of kindness but it is more than a refuge. It is a place for stories and for healing—not healing as a cure but as a power to endure—by primal power. Much of this power, which suggests female shamanic traditions from Africa and the Caribbean, is lodged in Eve. She runs a boarding house—as real and supernatural as the Cafe— that is a brothel too, and a convent. Many of the brutalized women, whose story Bailey tells, live there. Their "gentleman callers" cannot buy them. They must, however, buy flowers from Eve to present to them; and each woman has her own totemic flower.

The Eve figure, her flowers and ancient female mysteries, impart a certain forced wonder, and over-dosed and over-sweet exhortation; though Naylor gives her fierceness and resourcefulness as well. Some of the women's stories, such as that of the Ethiopian child, Mariam, who gives birth at the Cafe although she is a virgin; and disappears in a wall of water that her parched longings have summoned up, show similar indulgence.

In others, the sheer strength and color of the story more than make up for a spot of undigested uplift here and there. "Josie" tells of a righteous woman who is both undone and transfigured by abuse. ⟨. . .⟩

When she sits in the cafe, her dream of a just and gracious life shines so strongly that she imparts grace to her shaking coffee mug. And when a kind and comic iceman recognizes her light and wants to marry her, she imagines making a perfect home with him. And in an impressive twist, Naylor suddenly suggests imagination as a kingdom more powerful than reality.

> Richard Eder, "Grounds for the City," *Los Angeles Times Book Review*, 30 August 1992, p. 3

◈ *Bibliography*

The Women of Brewster Place: A Novel in Seven Stories. 1982.
Linden Hills. 1985.
Mama Day. 1988.
He's a Russian Jew. 1992.
Bailey's Cafe. 1992.

Ishmael Reed
b. 1938

ISHMAEL REED was born on February 22, 1938, in Chattanooga, Tennessee, the son of Henry Lenoir, a fundraiser for the YMCA, and Thelma Coleman; he took his name from his stepfather, Bennie Stephen Reed, an autoworker. The family moved to Buffalo in 1942, where Reed spent a few years at Buffalo Technical High School before graduating from East High School in 1956. He then attended the State University of New York at Buffalo, but had to withdraw in 1960 for lack of funds. At this time he married Priscilla Rose, with whom he would have two children before separating in 1963; they divorced in 1970.

Reed began working at the Talbert Mall Project, a black housing project in Buffalo. This experience led to a period of social activism, which included work on a newspaper, the *Empire Star Weekly*, and a controversial radio station, WVFO. In 1962 Reed moved to New York City, where he edited an underground magazine, the *Advance*, in Newark, New Jersey; he also participated in the Umbra Workshop, a black writers' group, and, in 1965, organized the American Festival of Negro Art.

Reed had begun writing satirical sketches in college. In 1967, the year he moved to Berkeley, California, his first novel, *The Free-Lance Pallbearers*, was published. This wide-ranging satire set the tone for Reed's other novels, whose only unifying themes are outrageousness and a refusal to toe a party line: *Yellow Back Radio Broke-Down* (1969), a vicious attack on Christianity; *Mumbo Jumbo* (1972) and *The Last Days of Louisiana Red* (1974), parodies of the detective novel in which a black detective uses HooDoo to probe African-American cultural history; *Flight to Canada* (1976), an ironic imitation of the slave narrative; *The Terrible Twos* (1982) and its sequel, *The Terrible Threes* (1989), satires on conservative politics and religion; *Reckless Eyeballing* (1986), a send-up of black feminism; and *Japanese by Spring* (1993), an attack on academic life.

Reed has also distinguished himself as a poet. His first volume of poetry was *catechism of d neoamerican hoodoo church* (1970), and it was followed by

Conjure: Selected Poems 1963–1970 (1972; nominated for the National Book Award and the Pulitzer Prize in poetry), *Chattanooga* (1973), *A Secretary to the Spirits* (1978), and *New and Collected Poems* (1988).

In 1970 Reed married Carla Blank, a dancer, with whom he had one child. The next year, with Steve Cannon and Al Young, he founded the Yardbird Publishing Company, which published an annual *Yardbird Reader* from 1972 to 1976; Reed has also won acclaim for his anthologies, *19 Necromancers from Now* (1970) and *Calafia: The California Poetry* (1979). In 1976 he formed the Before Columbus Foundation to promote the work of ethnic writers.

As an essayist Reed is as outspoken as he is as a novelist and poet. Four collections of his essays have appeared: *Shrovetide in Old New Orleans* (1978), *God Made Alaska for the Indians* (1982), *Writin' Is Fightin'* (1988), and *Airing Dirty Laundry* (1993). In much of his work, especially his novels and essays, Reed has faced accusations of misogyny and of being more successful at attacking his perceived enemies than advocating his own beliefs. But Reed was a pioneer of multiculturalism as opposed to the "monoculturalism" that he sees as still dominant in the United States.

In spite of his hostility to the academy, Reed has been a guest lecturer at many universities, including Yale, Harvard, Columbia, and Dartmouth. He has been the recipient of many awards, including a Guggenheim award for fiction, an American Civil Liberties Award, and a Pushcart Prize.

▦ *Critical Extracts*

KENETH KINNAMON   Ishmael Reed is a man both amused and outraged by the absurdities and obscenities of the state of the nation as the last third of the century begins. In his first novel, *The Free-Lance Pallbearers,* an extravagantly satirical allegory of the journey of Bukka Doopeyduk from innocence to experience in a mad, mad, mad, mad country called Harry Sam, Mr. Reed is more successful in conveying his amusement than his outrage.

Dropping out of college, where he had aspired to become "the first bacteriological warfare expert of the colored race," Bukka marries a sloppy shrew named Fannie Mae, moves into a housing project in Soulsville (Harlem), and works as a hospital orderly efficiently enough to be awarded a golden bedpan engraved with his initials. Originally right thinking, anti-subversive, and religiously orthodox, the protagonist is hoodooed and dehoodooed, henpecked and insulted, patronized and exploited, duped and deceived until dictator Sam, "a self-made Pole and former used-car salesman," appoints him to replace Eclair Porkchop as Nazarene Bishop of Soulsville. But the disillusioned Bukka recoils at last from his Tomism to lead an assault against Sam, part of an apocalyptic world revolution. He manages to do Sam in before meeting his own death at the hands of counterrevolutionaries.

In this kaleidoscopic narrative, Mr. Reed aims his satire at a bewildering variety of targets. Academicians, anti-busing racists, Uncle Toms, the anti-communist paranoia, white liberals and radicals, the Roman Catholic hierarchy, the Black Muslims, *Studies on the Left* and *The Village Voice*, medical ethics, Ralph Ellison, the W. E. B. Du Bois Clubs, Richard Nixon and Checkers, down-home types in New York, hippies, Cardinal Spellman, Edgar Allan Poe and T. S. Eliot, conservative civil rights leaders, organized labor, petition signers, veterans' organizations, *Ebony* magazine, Jewish slumlords and their Negro flunkies, homosexuality, American judicial processes, black writers' conferences, anti-Semitism, Bostonian gentility, happenings, the anti-poverty program, the East Village scene, the *Playboy* cult, J. Robert Oppenheimer, television interviews, the United Nations, militarism, Rutherford Birchard Hayes and Lyndon Baines Johnson—the list is by no means exhaustive. Mr. Reed's basic difficulty is simple enough. His scattergun technique disperses rather than concentrates his satiric energy.

Keneth Kinnamon, [Review of *The Free-Lance Pallbearers*], *Negro American Literature Forum* 1, No. 2 (Winter 1967): 18

NEIL SCHMITZ   In the "Neo-HooDoo Manifesto," which first appeared in the Los Angeles *Free Press* (September 18–24, 1970), Reed devises a myth that divides history into a war between two churches, two communities of consciousness: the "Cop Religion" of Christianity and the transformed Osirian rite, Voodoo. Sounding at once like ⟨William⟩ Burroughs and Davy Crockett, he then declares the contest: "Neo-HooDoos are detectives of the metaphysical about to make a pinch. We have issued warrants for a god arrest." ⟨. . .⟩

If only in theory, then, Neo-HooDoo represents a new direction (so Reed argues) for the Black writer, an escape from the decadence of Anglo-American literature that reverses the path historically taken by Black writers and intellectuals in the United States. In *The Narrative of the Life of Frederick Douglass*, just before Douglass' epical fight with the "nigger-breaker," Edward Covey, another slave gives Douglass "a certain *root*, which if I would take some of it with me, *carrying it always on my right side*, would render it impossible for Mr. Covey, or any other white man, to whip me." Douglass keeps this *"root"* italicised in his discussion of the event—it is Black magic—and what Douglass is striving to assert in his narrative is his possession of White magic, the word. Neo-HooDoo in effect stresses the power of that *"root"* and contends that the word is without value unless suffused and transformed by its occult force. It is this piece of Africa given to Douglass, and then forgotten by Douglass, that Reed strives to redeem.

But where are the "original folk tales" and native idioms in Reed's fiction? How far indeed does Neo-HooDoo (both as myth and mode) take him from established literary canons? His discourse in *Yellow Back Radio* and *Mumbo Jumbo* curves in and around colloquial Black English, which serves him as a stylistic device, not as a language. It is withal a learned and allusive discourse as mixed in its diction as Mark Twain's. His forms are not narrative legends taken from an oral tradition, but rather the popular forms of the Western and the Gangster Novel. As A. B. Spellman observes in *Black Fire*, this frustrated search for indigenous forms "is not the exclusive predicament of the Afro-American artist—the exponents of negritude in Africa and the Indies have spent years dealing with it. Novelist Edouard Glissant of Martinique had an extremely difficult time reorienting his style to develop a fictional form that conformed more to the oral folk tale than to the French novel. Glissant's compatriot, Aimé Césaire, feeling trapped in a European language, went back into Surrealism to find an anti-French, which would, in a sense, punish the colonialists for forcing him to write in a European language." Césaire's fate, writing anti-French, resembles Reed's in *Yellow Back Radio* and *Mumbo Jumbo*. Reed is driven to Burroughs for an anti-English as Césaire was to André Breton. *Yellow Back Radio* is a Black version of the Western Burroughs has been writing in fragments and promising in full since the fifties. Not only is the content of the fiction eclectic in its composition, but Loop's performance as a *houngan* in it has a good deal of Burroughs' "Honest Bill." For the core of his narrative, Reed borrows almost intact the sociological drama Norman Mailer describes in *The White Negro*—

that migration of White middle-class youth in revolt against the values of their own culture toward the counter-culture of Black America—and then weaves into this phenomenon a barely disguised account of the student uprisings at Berkeley and other campuses. The shooting at Kent State comes after the publication of *Yellow Back Radio*, but it is accurately prefigured in the book.

Neil Schmitz, "Neo-HooDoo: The Experimental Fiction of Ishmael Reed," *Twentieth Century Literature* 20, No. 2 (April 1974): 132–33

ISHMAEL REED   ⟨. . .⟩ I think, probably, my material is more within the classical Afro-American tradition than some critics who accuse my characters of being pathological—like this person, Addison Gayle, Jr., whom the liberal establishment has made the black aesthetic czar. You see, there was a fight there in the sixties where somebody said that he didn't feel he was qualified to judge Eldridge Cleaver's work. I don't feel that I'm qualified to listen to Duke Ellington, you know—it's just absurd. They had been intimidated by these fascist types, you know. ⟨. . .⟩ And they felt that they wanted to bow out. So then these black opportunists in the English departments, who really didn't care that much about Afro-American culture—as a matter of fact, had contempt for it—people like Houston Baker, Jr. and Addison Gayle, Jr.—both juniors, incidentally—were the ones that they set up to arbitrate taste. Not Gayle as much as Baker. Baker and I had an exchange where it got really personal. It's always been that kind of attack which people have made.

There was a nonaggression pact signed where liberal whites said, "Well, you guys do it. You be the guardians of the Afro-American experience. Check them, you know." They had a lot in common. They both were against any kind of experimentation in form or content. So they wanted to keep Afro-American writers in their place. To the novel of nightmare and pain that Roger Rosenblatt and Irving Howe. . . . They are all together; they all publish in the same magazines. I was naughty enough to call Harold Courlander a tourist for the *Washington Post*, because his material on Afro-American culture was not substantial. For example, he did a book on the Afro-American culture, Afro-American folklore, in which he didn't use many of the writings of the Afro-Americans and natives, not many Haitian writers, not any writers from the country. They used white nineteenth-century tourists to describe the kind of dances that the Africans were doing in New Orleans, which is not very accurate when there were a lot of other sources they could have used. So I said that. So the next thing I know, they're jumping on *Flight to Canada*. It's predictable.

Rosenblatt and Irving Howe, I understand they have some kind of relationship with *The New Republic*. I had *The New Republic* in the book, you know. And then McPherson is connected with *The New Republic*. I guess white writers have the same problem, but it just seems like some kind of assassination thing: "You don't fit in." If you're not giving them some kind of decorative prose—what they call elegance and eloquence—then you're a bad boy; you're a heathen, you know. When it comes between heathens and the kind of writers they promote—the tokens they got back East, dependent upon them—I'd rather be on the side of the heathens. That's why I've been more around Alaska among Eskimos and the Indians in the Southwest. I get along with people like that; I'm influenced by their cultures. But this is a transition. I think some of the people I'm working with and I have to take credit for this, we have changed the whole way of Afro-American writing in that there's been a revolt. We came to the West Coast instead of going to Europe, as was the practice in the forties and fifties, and others went South and to the Midwest. And so this machine that they tried to create has crumbled.

> Ishmael Reed, cited in Cameron Northouse, "Ishmael Reed," *Conversations with Writers II* (Detroit: Gale Research Co., 1978), pp. 219–20

JOE WEIXLMANN   Even the most casual reader of Ishmael Reed's novels is aware that Reed is a formal gamesman. His prose is pun-packed and grooves to a variety of jazz rhythms; exuberant parody abounds in his fiction; the cinema informs his scene changes, which occur in quick-splice fashion; a metafictional impulse plays through his tales; and purposeful anachronism penetrates his reader's defenses. Published between 1967 and 1976, Reed's five novels—*The Free-Lance Pallbearers, Yellow Back Radio Broke-Down, Mumbo Jumbo, The Last Days of Louisiana Red,* and *Flight to Canada*—shatter the mold of traditional Black American fiction in a manner anticipated by Ralph Ellison in his 1952 novel *Invisible Man:* Realism, seriousness, and the *engagé* give way to surrealism and pointed, often hyperbolic comedy and satire. ⟨. . .⟩

Set during the Civil War, *Flight to Canada* is narrated by Raven Quickskill, a slave-poet who, having escaped from the Swille plantation in Virginia and crossed America's northern border, discovers that freedom does not reside in a place but is "*a state of mind.*" Also pursuing his freedom, though he never leaves the Swille estate, is Uncle Robin, whom Arthur Swille perceives to be a faithful retainer, comparable to Harriet Beecher Stowe's Uncle Tom. Unlike Raven, who is "always on the move," Robin uses his obsequious demeanor to trick his master into willing him the plantation, Swine'rd, which Robin and his wife Judy occupy at the novel's end.

For the Black man in the nineteenth century, the road to freedom was a thorny one—fraught with hardship and successfully traveled only by those capable of great self-sacrifice. And that brambles still dot the trail today Reed forces us to acknowledge through his allusions to jumbo jets, the electronic media, leisure suits, and the like, which compel the reader to project the tale out of its Civil War setting and into the present. But before readers can fully understand the novel's contemporary relevance, it is necessary that their consciousness return in time to the America of the last century, an era that seemed to have special significance for Ishmael Reed. ⟨. . .⟩

Reed, of course, is concerned with culture. If fact, he regards one's culture as his most valuable possession. " 'Words built the world,' " Quickskill tells 40s, a fellow fugitive slave, " 'and words can destroy the world . . .' " And since Reed places such importance on culture, he firmly opposes all those who, like Mrs. Stowe, would attempt to pillage it. A key subplot in Reed's 1972 novel *Mumbo Jumbo* dramatizes the attempt of a multi-ethnic group, the *Mu'tafikah*, to recover those Black-American, Asian-American, Chicano, and Native American artifacts which Biff Musclewhite holds in the Center of Art Detention. And in *Flight to Canada*, in addition to Reed's assailing the larcenous Mrs. Stowe, he paints a harsh picture of Yankee Jack, an alleged supporter of minority cultures in America who, in actuality, loots those cultures in order to fill his own coffers.

Joe Weixlmann, "Politics, Piracy, and Other Games: Slavery and Liberation in *Flight to Canada*," MELUS 6, No. 3 (Fall 1979): 41–42, 45–46

STANLEY CROUCH   The trouble with *The Terrible Twos* is that he's said it all before and said it much better. This time out, he's picked another genre to tear apart with his imposition of varied forms and combinations of perspective. Just as he used *Antigone* in *The Last Days of Louisiana Red* to create a brilliant satire that collapsed under the strain of its near-misogyny, and just as he used the western for *Yellow Back Radio Broke-Down*, the detective story for *Mumbo Jumbo*, the slave narrative and *Uncle Tom's Cabin* for *Flight to Canada*, Reed weaves Rastafarianism and a reverse of the Todd Clifton dummy sequence from *Invisible Man* together with Dickens's *A Christmas Carol* in *The Terrible Twos*. Again we get the self-obsessed harpies, the mission Indians, the black hero who takes over the white form (unlike Todd Clifton, Black Peter is not controlled by whites who speak through his mouth—he speaks through theirs), the dumb black street hustlers who get into a game too complicated for them to understand, the corruption of Christianity, the secret society of powerful white bosses, the argument that preliterate custom and belief are just as good as modern civilization (if not better) and the beleaguered black hero who has woman problems (Reed touches on the sexual provincialism of black women, which didn't begin to change until the late 1960s when they had to compete with liberated and liberal white women for the affections of black men, but he doesn't do anything with that proverbial hot potato).

I'm not saying that Reed should abandon his concerns, but I am saying that for all the literary appropriations in *The Terrible Twos*, it hasn't the level of invention that made his best work succeed. There is too much predictability, too much dependence on revelation through conversation and interior monologue. Most of the mysteries must be explained by the characters, and what we do discover through their narratives isn't very interesting. ⟨. . .⟩ There are some funny passages along the way, however. There is even an attempt to infuse his surreal puppet show with realistic relationships, especially on an erotic level, and this brings what freshness there is to the novel. It also suggests that Reed may soon examine the range of sexual and social attractions that a multiracial society makes so possible, especially since the passage from Europe to the Third World can sometimes take place within only a few city blocks. If that is what he intends for his sequels—*The Terrible Threes* and *The Terrible Fours*—then the world he has developed, one quilted with endless allusions, mythology, improvisation and concentric circles of time and culture, could give birth to the potential so basic to the social contract and to the diversity of this country—Ishmael Reed's All-American Novel. *The Terrible Twos*, unfortunately, is mostly a shadow of his former work, and a shadow that tells us little we don't already know.

Stanley Crouch, "Kinships and Aginships," *Nation*, 22 May 1982, pp. 618–19

JEROME KLINKOWITZ   Those dour guardians of official culture Ishmael Reed calls "high-ass Anglo critics" have always had trouble with his work, especially when they try to segregate facts from fiction. Even his partisans have rough going from time to time as they try to pigeonhole this writer who's built much of his career on the flamboyant eclipse of stereotypes. Take a friend who's been wondering if he should zap poor Ishmael for being a "grant-hoarder" (the term is Reed's and he isn't one). This investigator's crowning argument is that among the contributors' notes to *Yardbird Lives!* (coedited with Al Young for Grove Press in 1978), Reed simply lists himself as "a businessman," as if admitting he's in league with the folks who run America's acronymic corporations and grants establishments.

"Hey wait," I beg my friend and cite Reed's disclaimer from the first page of his funniest novel, *The Last Days of Louisiana Red* (Random House, 1974), a note which warns that "in order to avoid detection by powerful enemies and industrial spies, nineteenth-century HooDoo people referred to their Work as 'The Business.' " The inspired grant-getting hustle my friend rightly condemns is hardly The Business our novelist describes, for if you read into *Louisiana Red* you'll find the HooDoo Businessmen have their own name for such shenanigans every decent person would deplore: Moochism, as in Cab Calloway's "Minnie the Moocher." But for the victims of a monocultural education, artists like Calloway don't exist. ⟨. . .⟩

Syncretism is one of the few formally abstract words in Reed's critical vocabulary, and he feels it is the key to a true national American literature reflecting the uniquely multicultural art which has evolved here. "Anglo" culture, as he calls it, then becomes one element among many, and the only loss is that of a dominant intellectual academy sworn to upholding the beliefs of a long-dead order. Gabriel García Márquez says much the same about his own multicultural, coastal Caribbean background where, as opposed to the rigidly colonial Spanish cultural of the highlands capital in Bogotá, history and fiction were allowed to blend, making truth "one more illusion, just one more version of many possible vantage points" where "people change their reality by changing their perception of it." Within this aesthetic, fact and imagination become one. And as our present age has been shaped by this union, so Reed creates a common method for writing novels and essays by using the best of it while warning of its dangers when abused.

Jerome Klinkowitz, "Ishmael Reed's Multicultural Aesthetic," *Literary Subversions* (Carbondale: Southern Illinois University Press, 1985), pp. 18–19, 21

ROBERT ELLIOT FOX   *Mumbo Jumbo* is an historico-aesthetic textbook, complete with illustrations, bibliography, and footnotes. It is Reed's dissertation on the metaphysics of consciousness and, simultaneously, a filmscript: though taking place primarily in New York, it opens with a prologue in New Orleans, following which Reed "rolls" the title and credits before plunging back into the story. The cinematic aspect is played up from the beginning: the first reference to Jew Grew as "a Creeping Thing" immediately brings to mind a Hollywood horror film, and the people dancing on hospital carts while the doctor is "slipping dipping gliding" is like a Marx Brothers comedy. (In fact, monster movies, slapstick, and detective films—*Mumbo Jumbo*, after all, is a "mystery"—all are significant influences on Reed's fiction which await more detailed analysis.)

The "heterophany of elements" found in Reed's work, which *Mumbo Junbo* exploits with particular brilliance, derives not only from modernist collage and postmodernist bricolage techniques, it is found as well in jazz, which, it is important to recognize, was the first mode of both black American modernism and postmodernism. This "heterophany of elements" is also a feature of Jew Grew and is analogous to the syncretization of the worship of African and other deities in Voodoo, the many varieties of gumbo, and such, which are found in Afro-American experience. Impromptu variations, based on individual refinement of collective knowledge, are crucial. There is a common saying among Yoruba masqueraders: "There is no house where supper is not prepared / But one stew tastes better than another." This is a form of artistic criticism used to distinguish one oral performer from another in terms of excellence, employing the same idea of recipe as Reed's poem "The Neo-Hoodoo Aesthetic," where everything depends upon the "cook."

However, the polyglot quality of *Mumbo Jumbo* may have another source: the slave narratives. Citing their "extremely mixed nature," James Olney offers the following description of what might be included:

an engraved portrait or photograph of the subject of the narrative; authenticity testimonials, prefixed or postfixed; poetic epigraphs, snatches of poetry in the text, poems appended; illustrations . . .; interruptions of the narrative by way of declamatory addresses to the reader . . .; a bewildering variety of documents—letters to and from the narrator, bills of sale, newspaper clippings, notices of slave auctions and of escaped slaves . . .; and sermons and anti-slavery speeches and essays tacked on at the end to demonstrate the post-narrative activities of the narrative.

Many of these elements are to be found in *Mumbo Jumbo* and in *Flight to Canada* (Reed's fifth novel, a deliberate parody of slave narratives). It is further proof of the correctness of Reed's position when he denies that his work is derived from white models. Black literature and black art have their own lineage, their own heritage of experimentation and innovation. The uprooted (Africans in the Diaspora) have proven to be masters of rootwork, and, indeed, the concern with roots is a form of spiritual ecology, the preservation of the signs and symbols of a culture.

Robert Elliot Fox, "Ishmael Reed: Gathering the Limbs of Osiris," *Conscientious Sorcerers: The Black Postmodernist Fiction of LeRoi Jones/Amiri Baraka, Ishmael Reed, and Samuel R. Delany* (New York: Greenwood Press, 1987), pp. 50–51

DARRYL PINCKNEY   Ishmael Reed's most recent novel, *Reckless Eyeballing*, is in part a comic rebuttal to ⟨the⟩ work by black women since the Seventies, like Ntozake Shange's *For Colored Girls Who Have Considered Suicide When the Rainbow Is Enuf* (1977), as well as Alice Walker's novels. These feminist works shared a mood in which black women began to question "myths," like whether freedom was to come first for the black man, or whether black women felt guilty because of the "emasculation" of the black male. *Reckless Eyeballing* is a satirical narrative that mocks racial and American sexual taboos in the manner of George Schuyler's *Black No More* (1931) or Chester Himes's *Pinktoes* (1961). It is the story of Ian Ball, a black playwright who has been "sex-listed," and who is trying to get back into favor with theatrical power brokers by writing a militant play for women. Ball may also be the "Flower Phantom," an intruder who shaves the heads of black women who, in his opinion, have collaborated with the enemies of black men.

The premise is a little nasty, even for Reed, but his gift is for the outrageous, for giving vivid expression to cultural controversies very much in the air. When one young black detective complains of a black woman playwright, "She makes out like we're all wife beaters and child molesters," an older black (male) playwright says:

> It's these white women who are carrying on the attack against black men today, because they struck a deal with white men who run the country. *You give us women the jobs, the opportunities, and we'll take the heat off you and put it on Mose*, is the deal they struck. They have maneuvered these white boys who run the country, but they have to keep the persecution thing up in order to win new followers, and so they jump on po' Mose.

The question is whether Reed has uncovered a rift or a rivalry between black men and black women. ⟨. . .⟩

Interestingly, *Reckless Eyeballing* is one of Reed's most accessible, even realistic, works. Perhaps this has something to do with the constraints imposed by the subject matter. But it is also very different from other fictions that approach the subject of sexuality and black life, works in the naturalistic tradition like Richard Wright's *Uncle Tom's Children* (1938), Chester Himes's *If He Hollers Let Him Go* (1945), or James Baldwin's *Another Country* (1962). In these books every psychological brutality could be described so long as it conformed to the sense that even as a fiction, it was part of a documentary truth that reached back to the slave narratives. It is this high ground that Alice Walker herself attempts to claim. But it must be said that she is playing a safe hand, given the acceptability of feminism and the historical conditioning that has the country afraid of black men. Reed's subtext might be that the rape of black women and the lynching of black men are part of the same historical tragedy.

Darryl Pinckney, "Black Victims, Black Villains," *New York Review of Books*, 29 January 1987, pp. 18–20

REGINALD MARTIN   What is the position of Ishmael Reed within and external to the new black aesthetic? It is my assertion that Reed's work fails to meet the demanded criteria from the major aestheticians such as Addison Gayle, Houston Baker, and Amiri Baraka on these points:

(1) Reed uses humour, especially satire (in all his works, but especially *Mumbo Jumbo*) in dealing with subjects only entertained with seriousness before. Humour was an early insertion in the tenets of the original black aesthetic, but the tenor of the times in the 1960s, when the new black aesthetic was solidifying, demanded a direct confronting of social issues, and this was most often done in serious prose. For example, critics still have a difficult time handling Reed's *The Freelance Pallbearers* (1967), which was extreme satire containing negative black characterizations. Some critics have seen Reed's use of humour as a shirking of responsibility on his part; that is, he should be responsible (read serious) toward the serious problems which face black Americans.

(2) On the surface, Reed's protagonists are good role models only in that they are extremely intelligent and witty. Unlike the often totally serious and unflippant characters of other writers, Reed's main characters use wit and humour when faced with an oppressive society, as in *The Freelance Pallbearers* and *Yellow Back Radio Broke-Down* (1969), and not weapons, steadfastness, or religious dedication. Though his characters must be examined closely to see the positiveness they really convey, critics such as Baker and Baraka have denigrated Reed's humorous characterizations with the labels 'spurious' and 'unfocused'.

(3) Reed's work is often surreal. He opposes hate with humour, often synchronically presented, as in *Yellow Back Radio Broke-Down* and *The Terrible Twos* (1982), to achieve a textual structure that is not easily identifiable on the 'plain surface'. Critics have said that this is an attempt to escape discussing critical social issues.

(4) Reed's microcosms, being surreal, do not easily lend themselves to an identifiable social macrocosm; it is sometimes difficult for the reader to find a common experience to which to relate. Thus, that part of the new black aesthetic which insists on its own version of 'universality' is disappointed and repelled by Reed.

(5) Reed refuses to accommodate the demands of the adherents and leading aestheticians of the new black aesthetic, and confronts them, by name, in print; further, he refuses to accommodate the tastes of the general public, black or white, which has limited expectations and boundaries for the American writer who is black, as in *The Last Days of Louisiana Red* (1974) and *Flight to Canada* (1976).

Reed's battle with the new black aesthetic critics began early in his career. From the very start, he has disliked being categorized and seems to find it impossible to play the literary game by the rules of others.

Reginald Martin, *Ishmael Reed and the New Black Aesthetic Critics* (New York: St. Martin's Press, 1988), pp. 41–43

MERLE RUBIN   His new novel, *Japanese by Spring,* offers a guided tour of the groves—more aptly, the jungles—of contemporary academe, seen through the eyes of one hapless black junior professor struggling to achieve tenure. ⟨. . .⟩

Summarized briefly, the targets of Reed's satire include out-and-out racists, xenophobes, Japan-bashers, and neoconservative defenders of Western Civilization courses, as well as tenured radicals, feminists, and other groups trying, as it were, to steal the thunder of the black civil rights movement by claiming to be equally, if not more, victimized. Nationalism in any form is identified as the chief foe, and cultural diversity the internationalist antidote to any one culture's attempt to dominate others.

All of which raises some questions: Is everyone who favors teaching Western Civilization merely, as this novel seems to suggest, a racist in disguise? Is "cultural diversity" a panacea for nationalism or a potential hothouse for new outgrowths of ethnic chauvinism?

And, while it's easy to make fun of well-heeled feminists claiming to be as victimized as blacks trapped by systemic discrimination and poverty, Reed's seeming inability to comprehend the pervasive oppression of women in almost every culture is a blind spot that undermines the force of an otherwise shrewd, funny, and instructive satire.

Merle Rubin, "Clever Satire, Inspired Nonsense," *Christian Science Monitor,* 9 March 1993, p. 14

RICHARD WALSH   The direct source for Reed's aesthetic is actually HooDoo, the Afro-American version of the Haitian original. The importation of Voodoo into America not only provided it with the Afro-American pedigree that allows Reed to advance it in the name of both his own culture *and* the principle of multiculturalism; it also involved a process of distillation and accommodation to the existing cultural conditions, which accentuated exactly the qualities Reed values and makes the foundation of his aesthetic. ⟨. . .⟩

By way of Neo-HooDooism, then, Reed is able to return in *Flight to Canada* to the slave narrative he had earlier disowned. The fundamental condition of this return is a transformation of style: he defies the norms of the genre in almost every aspect of his novel. The objectives of the slave narrative were primarily to bear witness to the realities of slavery and to affirm the humanity of the slave against the brutal conditions that enslaved him. The realization of these priorities depended upon the accumulation of detail to give force to the testimony. Reed, however, proclaims himself a cartoonist. The slave narrative is constrained by its moral seriousness, while Reed cultivates irreverent humour: the slave-owner Swille tells Lincoln to "stop putting your fingers in your lapels like that. You ought to at least try to polish yourself, man. Go to the theatre. Get some culture." This disrespect for Lincoln in particular and his nonfictional characters generally is symptomatic of another of Reed's heresies, his abuse of historical veracity. His manipulation of these characters is not an intellectual exploitation of lacunae in the historical record, as it might be in the hands of E. L. Doctorow, but a flagrantly unhistorical farce. His abuses are always grounded to some degree in an assumed familiarity with the received text of history, and feed satirically or humorously upon it: their main function is to effect a transformation of the reverent tone handed down in this text by subverting the dignity of its icons.

Implicit in all this is Reed's complete lack of concern with the criterion of realism upon which the slave narratives depended. His artistic concerns place a lower value on the surface coherence of his narrative than on imperatives of his fictional argument, or the opportunistic satirical points to which he continually sacrifices narrative continuity. As a result of these priorities, the novel unselfconsciously displays its inconsistencies of character and motivation, illogical narrative developments, loose ends and mismatched plotlines. There is little point in objecting that Reed does not reconcile his perspectives on Lincoln as player and fool, nor provide adequately for the swings in the relationship between Quickskill and the pirate Yankee Jack; that he refers back to Quickskill's dream as an event, and has Yankee Jack and his wife Quaw Quaw united at the opening of the novel, chronologically *after* her discovery that he uses her father's skull as an ashtray. The rationale for these aberrations lies on another plane: Reed refuses to be a slave to his narrative.

Reed's aesthetic decisions are motivated by his concern to affirm the multiculture in the *form* of his novel, a function for which the form of the original slave narratives is inadequate because of their appropriation as documents for the Abolitionist cause: "The political use to which the abolitionists put black literacy demanded a painstaking verisimilitude—a concern with even the most minute concrete detail" ⟨Henry Louis Gates, Jr.⟩. As such the slave narratives were denied the freedom of form through which their authors could have expressed *their* culture. And Reed insists that this co-opting of black literature by white liberals is a contemporary problem: "In fact, our worst enemies are radical liberals because they have so much influence on how we look in the media and in American culture. . . . They are only interested in the social realist, the 'experience' of black people. And this treatment limits and enslaves us."

Reed's revisionary interest in the slave narrative arises from his belief that the forms of slavery still exist in modern America, under the guise of the monoculture's institutionalized subordination of all other cultures: the institutional structure of slavery remains in sublimated form, as the machinery of a state of oppression he regards as *cultural* slavery. The material of the slave narrative therefore allows Reed to practise his necromancy, exploring the analogies it generates in the relative positions taken by the various factions of contemporary culture. But, more than just providing a metaphorical map of the system of cultural slavery he sees in modern America, he is also arguing for a direct continuity between the two levels, for an evolutionary transformation of actual into cultural slavery. In doing so, he is also engaging in the struggle "to get to our aesthetic Canada" by asserting in the novel's form his emancipation from the dictates of the dominant monoculture.

> Richard Walsh, " 'A Man's Story Is His Gris-Gris': Cultural Slavery, Literary Emancipation and Ishmael Reed's *Flight to Canada*," *Journal of American Studies* 27, No. 1 (April 1993): 61–63.

▦ Bibliography

The Free-Lance Pallbearers. 1967.
Yellow Back Radio Broke-Down. 1969.

19 Necromancers from Now (editor). 1970.

catechism of d neoamerican hoodoo church. 1970.

Yardbird Reader (editor; with Al Young). 1972–76. 5 vols.

Mumbo Jumbo. 1972.

Conjure: Selected Poems 1963–1970. 1972.

Chattanooga. 1973.

The Last Days of Louisiana Red. 1974.

Flight to Canada. 1976.

Poetry Makes Rhythm in Philosophy. 1976.

Shrovetide in Old New Orleans. 1978.

Yardbird Lives! (editor; with Al Young). 1978.

A Secretary to the Spirits. 1978.

Calafia: The California Poetry (editor). 1979.

The Terrible Twos. 1982.

God Made Alaska for the Indians: Selected Essays. 1982.

Reckless Eyeballing. 1986.

Cab Calloway Stands In for the Moon. 1986.

New and Collected Poems. 1988.

Writin' Is Fightin': Thirty-seven Years of Boxing on Paper. 1988.

The Terrible Threes. 1989.

The Before Columbus Foundation Fiction Anthology: Selections from the American Book Awards 1980–1990 (editor; with Kathryn Trueblood and Shawn Wong). 1992.

Airing Dirty Laundry. 1993.

Ishmael Reed: An Interview (with Cameron Northouse). 1993.

Japanese by Spring. 1993.

Alice Walker
b. 1944

ALICE MALSENIOR WALKER was born on February 9, 1944, in Eatonton, Georgia, the eighth child of sharecroppers Willie Lee and Minnie Tallulah (Grant) Walker. When she was eight she was blinded in her right eye after being accidentally shot with a BB gun by one of her brothers. She attended Spelman College from 1961 to 1963, then left to travel in Africa. She transferred to Sarah Lawrence College, where she received a B.A. in 1965. About this time she underwent a severe trauma in which she aborted a pregnancy and came close to suicide. In response to these events she took to writing, producing her first published short story, "To Hell with Dying," and the poems that would form her first collection of poetry. She married civil rights lawyer Melvyn Rosenman Leventhal in 1967; they had one child before their divorce in 1976.

During the late 1960s Walker participated in the civil rights movement in Mississippi. She wrote an essay, "The Civil Rights Movement: What Good Was It?," that won an *American Scholar* essay contest. She worked with Head Start programs in Mississippi and later served as writer in residence at Tougaloo College and Jackson State University.

Alice Walker has written several volumes of poetry, including *Once* (1968), *Revolutionary Petunias and Other Poems* (1973), *Good Night, Willie Lee, I'll See You in the Morning* (1979), *Horses Make a Landscape More Beautiful* (1984), and, most recently, *Her Blue Body Everything We Know: Earthling Poems 1965–1990 Complete* (1991). They have received considerable praise, particularly from the black and feminist communities.

Walker is, however, primarily known as a novelist. Her first novel, *The Third Life of Grange Copeland* (1970), depicts three generations in the life of a poor farm family. It was praised for the sensitivity with which the characters were drawn, but it received little attention from either popular or academic circles. In 1970 Walker discovered the work of Zora Neale Hurston, whom she would be instrumental in raising to the status of a major American author. Hurston's influence can be seen in many of the short stories Walker was writing in this period. Her second novel, *Meridian* (1976), is considered by many to be the best novel of the civil rights era. *The Color Purple* (1982), an epistolary novel concerning the growth to maturity of a poor black woman in an oppressive, brutish society, launched Walker to mainstream critical success and best-seller popularity. It received the 1983 Pulitzer Prize and the American Book Award, and was made into an Academy Award–nominated film by Steven Spielberg.

In 1989 Alice Walker published her fourth novel, *The Temple of My Familiar*, a work that resurrects some characters from *The Color Purple* but whose major action takes place in Africa. This novel was on the whole poorly received for its implausibility (a goddess informs the characters of the origin of women) and the stridency of its ideological message. Her fifth novel, *Possessing the Secret of Joy* (1992), however, fared better with reviewers. It deals with female circumcision and genital mutilation, the subject of a nonfiction book Walker published the next year in collaboration with Pratibha Parmar, *Warrior Masks*.

In addition to poetry and novels, Walker has written two volumes of short stories, *In Love and Trouble: Stories of Black Women* (1973) and *You Can't Keep a Good Woman Down* (1981); a biography of Langston Hughes for children; and a book of criticism and social commentary, *In Search of Our Mothers' Gardens: Womanist Prose* (1983). A selection of her essays, *Living by the Word*, appeared in 1988.

Walker has been a lecturer at Wellesley College and the University of Massachusetts, a writer in residence at the University of California at Berkeley, and the Fannie Hurst Professor of Literature at Brandeis University. She has also served as a contributing editor of *Ms.* magazine. Since 1978 she has lived in San Francisco.

▩ *Critical Extracts*

ALICE WALKER   Perhaps my Northern brothers will not believe me when I say there is a great deal of positive material I can draw from my "underprivileged" background. But they have never lived, as I have, at the end of a long road in a house that was faced by the edge of the world on one side and nobody for miles on the other. They have never experienced the magnificent quiet of a summer day when the heat is intense and one is so very thirsty, as one moves across the dusty cotton fields, that one learns forever that water is the essence of all life. In the cities it cannot be so clear to one that he is a creature of the earth, feeling the soil between the toes, smelling the dust thrown up by the rain, loving the earth so much that one longs to taste it and sometimes does.

Nor do I intend to romanticize the Southern black country life. I can recall that I hated it, generally. The hard work in the fields, the shabby houses, the evil greedy men who worked my father to death and almost broke the courage of that strong woman, my mother. No, I am simply saying that Southern black writers, like most writers, have a heritage of love and hate, but that they also have enormous richness and beauty to draw from. And, having been placed, as Camus says, "halfway between misery and the sun," they, too, know that "though all is not well under the sun, history is not everything."

No one could wish for a more advantageous heritage than that bequeathed to the black writer in the South: a compassion for the earth, a trust in humanity beyond our knowledge of evil, and an abiding love of justice. We inherit a great responsibility as well, for we must give voice to centuries not only of silent bitterness and hate but also of neighborly kindness and sustaining love.

> Alice Walker, "The Black Writer and the Southern Experience" (1970), *In Search of Our Mothers' Gardens: Womanist Prose* (San Diego: Harcourt Brace Jovanovich, 1983), pp. 20–21

MARK SCHORER   She is not a finished novelist. She has much to learn. Fortunately, what she has to learn are the unimportant lessons, that is, those that *can* be learned: some economy, formal shaping, stylistic tightening, deletion of points too repetitiously insisted upon, the handling of time, above all development rather than mere reversal of character. The important fictional qualities that she commands, those that she was born with, she has supremely.

> Mark Schorer, "Novels and Nothingness," *American Scholar* 40, No. 1 (Winter 1970–71): 172

JERRY H. BRYANT   My initial reaction to the first several stories of *In Love & Trouble* was negative. Miss Walker's search for ways to be new and different struck me as too willful and strained. I felt the same way about her earlier novel, *The Third Life of Grange Copeland,* whose style seemed too fine for the rough subject—the way two black men, a son and a father, try to degrade and destroy each other. But as I read on through these thirteen stories, I was soon absorbed by the density of reality they convey. They contain the familiar themes and situations of conventional black political and sociological fiction. There are black revolutionaries who read books and meet in small study groups, radical lady poets who read before black student audiences shouting "Right on!," and sharecroppers victimized by white landlords. But we see all these from genuinely new angles, from the point of view of the black woman or man totally absorbed in the pains of their inner life rather than the point of view of the protester or the newspaper headline. ⟨. . .⟩

But what I like most about these stories is what Miss Walker seems to like most about her people, the ones who are themselves, naturally and unself-consciously, and live by putting what they have to "everyday use," the title of one of her stories. She is best, therefore, not when she is depicting revolutionary consciousness or sophisticated awareness of the most recent rules of race relations, but when she is getting inside the minds of the confused, the ignorant, the inward-turning character, when she lets stand the mysterious and the ambiguous, and gives up explaining by doctrine the nature of her characters' lives. She can put a lump in the reader's throat even when she is a little sentimental. But what she can do most powerfully is make me feel the heat of her characters' lives, smell their singed bodies going up in literal and figurative flames of their own making. That is when I lose touch with myself as critic and interpreter and enter Miss Walker's created world of love and trouble.

Jerry H. Bryant, "The Outskirts of a New City," *Nation,* 12 November 1973, pp. 501–2

GREIL MARCUS   At its best, ⟨. . .⟩ the tone of ⟨*Meridian* is⟩ flat, direct, measured, deliberate, with a distinct lack of drama. ⟨. . .⟩ And the tone is right; it's not the plot that carries the novel forward but Meridian's attempt to resolve, or preserve the reality of, the questions of knowledge, history, and murder that Miss Walker introduces early on. The astonishing dramatic intensity that Walker brought to *The Third Life of Grange Copeland* would in *Meridian* blow those questions apart.

But such questions lead all too easily to high-flown language and to pretensions that fictional characters cannot support, which is why most "philosophical" novels are impossible to reread. Miss Walker does not always avoid this trap; though her tendency is to insist on the prosaic, to bring philosophy down to earth, Meridian at times seems to be floating straight to Heaven. The book tries to make itself a parable—more than a mere novel—or trades the prosaic for an inert symbolism that would seem to be intended to elevate the story but instead collapses it. In an early chapter, Meridian, age seven, finds a gold bar and rushes with it to her parents; they ignore her. She buries the gold (her unrecognized gifts) and finally forgets about it (and it will be years until she finds her gifts again). In college, as Meridian lies sick in bed, a halo forms around her head. Back in the South after the meeting in New York, she works alone persuading people, one at a time, to register to vote, organizing neighborhoods around local issues, and staging symbolic protests, which she calls, wonderfully, her "performances." This is beautifully presented and utterly convincing; each incident is memorable, shaped as a story in itself. But after every "performance" Meridian falls to the ground, paralyzed, and must be carried like a corpse back to wherever she is living. A hundred years ago, an author would simply have made Meridian an epileptic if we were meant to guess that she was sainted. ⟨. . .⟩

Meridian is interesting enough without all this—without symbolism and "higher meanings" that are one-dimensional and fixed. There is no mystery in these symbols—as there is in Meridian's ability to get through to Southern blacks, or in the questions of the rebel, murder, and limits—and a symbol without mystery, without suggestive power, is not really a symbol at all. But most of the book's scenes have the power its symbols lack, and its last chapters rescue Meridian's questions from a holy oblivion.

Greil Marcus, "Limits," *New Yorker*, 7 June 1976, p. 135

TRUDIER HARRIS   Walker's use of folk material is less prominent in her novel *The Third Life of Grange Copeland* (1970), but it is apparent. Folk material becomes significant in defining the relationship between

Grange and Ruth, his granddaughter. It is a way to seal the bond between them and to identify their unity against a hostile and un-understanding world. Even Josie, Grange's wife, is shut out of the bantering between Ruth and Grange, as she will later be physically excluded from their presence. Grange tells Ruth tales and generally entertains her on the nights when they sit around peeling oranges and shredding coconut in their Georgia farmhouse.

Although Grange knows "all the Uncle Remus stories by heart" and can produce even more exciting ones about John the trickster, he is not a mindless teller of tales solely for the sake of entertainment. Walker attributes to him the analytical ability that is often only implied in historical storytellers. Grange does not accept the benign Uncle Remus as historically accurate or even as having common sense. He criticizes Uncle Remus's stance and re-interprets it with political connotations and renewed emphasis on social awareness, especially black social awareness. ⟨. . .⟩ It is obvious from Grange's attitude that Walker does not view the folk culture as something separate from life, but as an integral part of one's existence. The change Grange would impose on Uncle Remus is synonymous with the changes that take place in the novel. From sharecropping with its shuffling, head-bowing, acquiescing days, Walker moves Grange and his family into the Sixties and the days of Martin Luther King. Marching, voting, and statesmanship do indeed replace the tendency to minstrelize.

Grange also tells Ruth stories about "two-heads and conjurers; strange men and women more sensitive than the average spook," but he laments that "folks what can look at things in more than one way is done got rare." Grange's feelings are again commensurate with the theme of change that Walker explores in the novel. ⟨. . .⟩

Alice Walker is assuredly in the literary and historical traditions of the recording and creative use of black folk materials. Like ⟨Charles W.⟩ Chesnutt, she uses such material for social commentary. But her environment allows more freedom of usage than did Chesnutt's; where he had to embed his statements about slavery in an elaborate framing device and filtered them through the eyes of a white Northerner, Walker can be obvious, blatant, and direct about social injustices. Like ⟨Zora Neale⟩ Hurston, Walker reflects a keen insight into the folk mind. As Hurston reflected the nuances of relationships between men and women in *Their Eyes Were Watching God* (1937) through the use of the folk culture, so too does Walker use this culture to reflect relationships between the characters in *The Third Life of Grange Copeland*.

Trudier Harris, "Folklore in the Fiction of Alice Walker: A Perpetuation of Historical and Literary Traditions," *Black American Literature Forum* 11, No. 1 (Spring 1977): 7–8

ROBERT TOWERS   In *The Color Purple* Alice Walker moves backward in time, setting her story roughly (the chronology is kept vague) between 1916 and 1942—a period during which the post-Reconstruction settlement of black status remained almost unaltered in the Deep South. Drawing upon what must be maternal and grandmaternal accounts as well as upon her own memory and observation, Miss Walker, who is herself under forty, exposes us to a way of life that for the most part existed beyond or below the reach of fiction, and that has hitherto been made available to us chiefly through tape-recorded reminiscences: the life of poor, rural Southern blacks as it was experienced by their womenfolk. Faulkner, to be sure, touches upon it in his rendering of the terrified Nancy in "That Evening Sun," but her situation, poignant though it is, comes to us largely through the eyes and ears of the white Compson children; similarly, the majestic figure of Dilsey in *The Sound and the Fury* is, for all its insight, sympathy, and closeness of observation, a white man's portrait of a house servant, idealized and, one imagines, subtly distorted by the omission of those moments of sickening rage (as distinct from exasperation) which must have been an ingredient in Dilsey's complex attitude toward the feckless and demanding family that employs her. The suffering, submissive women in Wright's *Native Son* are no doubt authentically portrayed—but again from a man's point of view; furthermore, they are city dwellers, poor but still different from the dirt-poor countryfolk. ⟨. . .⟩

I cannot gauge the general accuracy of Miss Walker's account or the degree to which it may be colored by current male-female antagonisms within the black community—controversial reports of which from time to time appear in print. I did note certain improbabilities: it seems unlikely that a woman of Celie's education would have applied the word "amazons" to a group of feisty sisters or that Celie, in the 1930s, would have found fulfillment in designing and making pants for women. In any case, *The Color Purple* has more serious faults than its possible feminist bias. Alice Walker

still has a lot to learn about plotting and structuring what is clearly intended
to be a realistic novel. The revelations involving the fate of Celie's lost
babies and the identity of her real father seem crudely contrived—the stuff
of melodrama or fairy tales. 〈. . .〉

Fortunately, inadequacies which might tell heavily against another novel
seem relatively insignificant in view of the one great challenge which Alice
Walker has triumphantly met: the conversion, in Celie's letters, of a subliter-
ate dialect into a medium of remarkable expressiveness, color, and poignancy.
I find it impossible to imagine Celie apart from her language; through it,
not only a memorable and infinitely touching character but a whole sub-
merged world is vividly called into being. Miss Walker knows how to avoid
the excesses of literal transcription while remaining faithful to the spirit
and rhythms of Black English. I can think of no other novelist who has so
successfully tapped the poetic resources of the idiom.

Robert Towers, "Good Men Are Hard to Find," *New York Review of Books*, 12 August
1982, pp. 35–36

GERALD EARLY   〈. . .〉 *The Color Purple* remains an inferior novel
not because it seems so self-consciously a "woman's novel" and not because
it may be playing down to its mass audience, guilty of being nothing more
than a blatant "feel-good" novel, just the sort of book that is promoted
among the nonliterary. *The Color Purple* is a poor novel because it ultimately
fails the ideology that it purports to serve. It fails to be subversive enough
in substance; it only *appears* to be subversive. Indeed, far from being a
radically feminist novel, it is not even, in the end, as good a bourgeois
feminist novel as *Uncle Tom's Cabin*, written 130 years earlier. Its largest
failure lies in the novel's inability to use (ironically, subversively, or even
interestingly) the elements that constitute it. Take, for instance, these
various Victorianisms that abound in the work: the ultimate aim of the
restoration of a gynocentric, not patriarchal family; the reunion of lost
sisters; the reunion of mother and children; the glorification of cottage
industry in the establishment of the pants business; bequests of money and
land to the heroine at novel's end; Celie's discovery that her father/rapist
is really a cruel stepfather; the change of heart or moral conversion of Mr.
Albert, who becomes a feminized man at the end; the friendship between
Shug Avery and Celie, which, despite its overlay of lesbianism (a tribute
to James Baldwin's untenable thesis that nonstandard sex is the indication

of a free, holy, thoroughly unsquare heterosexual heart), is nothing more than the typical relationship between a shy ugly duckling and her more aggressive, beautiful counterpart, a relationship not unlike that between Topsy and Little Eva. Shug convinces Celie that she is not black and ugly, that somebody loves her, which is precisely what Eva does for Topsy. For Walker, these clichés are not simply those of the Victorian novel but of the *woman's* Victorian novel. This indicates recognition of and paying homage to a tradition; but the use of these clichés in *The Color Purple* is a great deal more sterile and undemanding than their use in, say, *Uncle Tom's Cabin*. Together, for Walker, these clichés take on a greater attractiveness and power than for the female Victorian, since they are meant to represent a series of values that free the individual from the power of the environment, the whim of the state, and the orthodoxy of the institution. The individual still has the power to change, and that power supersedes all others, means more than any other. Human virtue is a reality that is not only distinct from all collective arrangements except family; in the end, it can be understood only as being opposed to all collective arrangements. But all of this is only the bourgeois fascination with individualism and with the ambiguity of Western family life, in which bliss is togetherness while having a room of one's own. ⟨. . .⟩

What Walker does in her novel is allow its social protest to become the foundation for its utopia. Not surprisingly, the book lacks any real intellectual or theological rigor or coherence, and the fusing of social protest and utopia is really nothing more than confounding and blundering, each seeming to subvert the reader's attention from the other. One is left thinking that Walker wishes to thwart her own ideological ends or that she simply does not know how to write novels. In essence, the book attempts to be revisionist salvation history and fails because of its inability to use or really understand history.

> Gerald Early, "*The Color Purple* as Everybody's Protest Art," *Antioch Review* 44, No. 3 (Summer 1986): 271–73

LAUREN BERLANT   *The Color Purple's* strategy of inversion, represented in its elevation of female experience over great patriarchal events, had indeed aimed to critique the unjust practices of racism and sexism that violate the subject's complexity, reducing her to a generic biological sign.

But the model of personal and national identity with which the novel leaves us uses fairy-tale explanations of social relations to represent itself: this fairy tale embraces America for providing the Afro-American nation with the right and the opportunity to own land, to participate in the free market, and to profit from it. In the novel's own terms, American capitalism thus has contradictory effects. On one hand, capitalism veils its operations by employing racism, using the pseudonatural discourse of race to reduce the economic competitor to a subhuman object. In Celie's parental history, *The Color Purple* portrays the system of representation characteristic of capital relations that *creates* the situation of nationlessness for Afro-Americans.

But the novel also represents the mythic spirit of American capitalism as the vehicle for the production of an Afro-American utopia. Folkpants, Unlimited is an industry dedicated to the reproduction and consumption of a certain system of representation central to the version of Afro-American "cultural nationalism" enacted by *The Color Purple*. But Folkpants, Unlimited also participates in the profit motive: the image of the commodity as the subject's most perfect self-expression is the classic fantasy bribe of capitalism. The illogic of a textual system in which the very force that disenfranchises Afro-Americans provides the material for their national reconstruction is neither "solved" by the novel nor raised as a paradox. The system simply stands suspended in the heat of the family reunion on Independence Day.

What saves Celie and Nettie from disenfranchisement is their lifelong determination to learn, to become literate: Nettie's sense that knowledge was the only route to freedom from the repressive family scene gave her the confidence to escape, to seek "employment" with Samuel's family, to record the alternative and positive truth of Pan-African identity, to face the truth about her own history, to write it down, and to send it to Celie, against all odds. Writing was not only the repository of personal and national hope; it became a record of lies and violences that ultimately produced truth.

Lauren Berlant, "Race, Gender, and Nation in *The Color Purple*," *Critical Inquiry* 14, No. 4 (Summer 1988): 857–58

J. M. COETZEE   Readers of *The Color Purple* will remember that part of the book—the less convincing part—consists of letters from Miss Celie's missionary sister about her life in Africa.

The Temple of My Familiar again bears a message from Africa, but this time in a far more determined manner. The message reaches us via Miss Lissie, an ancient goddess who has been incarnated hundreds of times, usually as a woman, sometimes as a man, once even as a lion. Less a character than a narrative device, Lissie enables Alice Walker to range back in time to the beginnings of (wo)man.

Here are just three of the ages in human evolution that Lissie lives through:

First, an age just after the invention of fire, when humanfolk live in separate male and female tribes, at peace with their animal "familiars." Here Lissie is incarnated as the first white-skinned creature, a man with insufficient melanin, who flees the heat of Africa for Europe. Hating the sun, he [invents] an alternative god in his own image, cold and filled with rage.

Next, an age of pygmies, when the man tribe and the woman tribe visit back and forth with each other and with the apes. This peaceful, happy age ends when men invent warfare, attack the apes and impose themselves on women as their sole familiars. Thus, says Ms. Walker (rewriting Rousseau and others), do patriarchy and the notion of private property come into being.

Third, the time of the war waged by Europe and monotheistic Islam against the Great Goddess of Africa. The instrument of the warfare is the slave trade (Lissie lives several slave lives). Its emblem is the Gorgon's head, the head of the Goddess, still crowned with the serpents of wisdom, cut off by the white hero-warrior Perseus.

These episodes from the past of (wo)mankind give some idea of the sweep of the myth Alice Walker recounts, a myth that inverts the places assigned to man and woman, Europe and Africa, in the male-invented myth called history. In Ms. Walker's counter-myth, Africa is the cradle of true religions and civilization, and man a funny, misbegotten creature with no breasts and an elongated clitoris. ⟨. . .⟩

History is certainly written by people in positions of power, and therefore principally by men. The history of the world—including Africa—is by and large a story made up by white males. Nevertheless, history is not just storytelling. There are certain brute realities that cannot be ignored. Africa has a past that neither the white male historian nor Ms. Walker can simply invent. No doubt the world would be a better place if, like Fanny and Suwelo, we could live in bird-shaped houses and devote ourselves to bread making and massage, and generally adopt Fanny's mother's gospel: "We are

all of us in heaven already!" Furthermore, I readily concede that inventing
a better world between the covers of a book is as much as even the most
gifted of us can hope to do to bring about a better real world. But whatever
new worlds and new histories we invent must carry conviction: they must
be possible worlds, possible histories, not untethered fantasies; and they
must be born of creative energy, not dreamy fads.

> J. M. Coetzee, "The Beginnings of (Wo)man in Africa," *New York Times Book Review*,
> 30 April 1989, p. 7

ALICE HALL PETRY   Walker's disinclination for exposition, and
the concomitant impression that many of her stories are outlines or fragments
of longer works, is particularly evident in a technique which mars even her
strongest efforts: a marked preference for "telling" over "showing." This
often takes the form of summaries littered with adjectives. In "Advancing
Luna," for example, the narrator waxes nostalgic over her life with Luna
in New York: "our relationship, always marked by mutual respect, evolved
into a warm and comfortable friendship which provided a stability and
comfort we both needed at that time." But since ⟨. . .⟩ the narrator comes
across as vapid and self-absorbed, and since the only impressions she provides
of Luna are rife with contempt for this greasy-haired, Clearasil-daubed, poor-
little-rich-white-girl from Cleveland, the narrator's paean to their mutual
warmth and friendship sounds ridiculous. No wonder critic Katha Pollitt
stated outright that she "never believed for a minute" that the narrator and
Luna were close friends. Even more unfortunate is Walker's habit of telling
the reader what the story is about, of making sure that he doesn't overlook
a single theme. For example, in "The Abortion," the heroine Imani, who
is just getting over a traumatic abortion, attends the memorial service of a
local girl, Holly Monroe, who had been shot to death while returning home
from her high school graduation. Lest we miss the point, Walker spells it
out for us: "every black girl of a certain vulnerable age *was* Holly Monroe.
And an even deeper truth was that Holly Monroe was herself [i.e., Imani].
Herself shot down, aborted on the eve of becoming herself." Similarly
transparent, here is one of the last remarks in the story "Source." It is
spoken by Irene, the former teacher in a federally-funded adult education
program, to her ex-hippie friend, Anastasia/Tranquility: " 'I was looking
toward "government" for help; you were looking to Source [a California

guru]. In both cases, it was the wrong direction—*any* direction that is away from ourselves is the wrong direction.' " The irony of their parallel situation is quite clear without having Irene articulate her epiphany in an Anchorage bar. Even at the level of charactonyms, Walker "tells" things to her reader. We've already noted the over-used "he"/"she" device for underscoring sex roles, but even personal names are pressed into service. For example, any reasonably perceptive reader of the vignette "The Flowers" will quickly understand the story's theme: that one first experiences reality in all its harshness while far from home, physically and/or experientially; one's immediate surroundings are comparatively "innocent." The reader would pick up on the innocence of nearsightedness even if the main character, ten-year-old Myop, hadn't been named after myopia. Likewise, "The Child Who Favored Daughter" is actually marred by having the father kill his daughter because he confuses her with his dead sister named "Daughter." The hints of incest, the unclear cross-generational identities, and the murky Freudian undercurrents are sufficiently obvious without the daughter/Daughter element: it begins to smack of Abbott and Costello's "Who's on First?" routine after just a few pages. Alice Walker's preference for telling over showing suggests a mistrust of her readers, or her texts, or both.

Alice Hall Petry, "Alice Walker: The Achievement of the Short Fiction," *Modern Language Studies* 19, No. 1 (Winter 1989): 21–22

CHARLES R. LARSON   Fiction and conviction make strange bedfellows. Nor am I convinced that novels that resurrect characters from a writer's earlier work are likely to be as imaginative and as artful as the result of the initial inspiration. But one does not have to read many pages of *Possessing the Secret of Joy* to realize that Alice Walker has not foisted her subject—female circumcision—upon us; instead, this writer of bold artistry challenges us to feel and to think. Here is a novel—and a subject—whose time has surely come. ⟨. . .⟩

The novel's ironic beginning is patently romantic. There is joy in Tashi and Adam's initial lovemaking, in spite of their conflicting backgrounds. Because of her conversion to Christianity, Tashi has not been traditionally circumcised. And Adam, the African-American missionary's son, appears not to harbor the Puritan layers of guilt typical of missionaries at the time—though Walker uses no dates, apparently the 1920s or '30s—the story begins.

What, in fact, can possibly diminish their happiness? The marriage appears destined to become a union of their complementary spirits and yearnings for togetherness.

But then Tashi wavers. As Adam's future wife, in America, shouldn't she attempt to retain as much of her African culture as possible? Should she be circumcised? The operation, she feels, will join her to her sisters, "whom she envisioned as strong, invincible. Completely woman. Completely African." ⟨. . .⟩

⟨. . .⟩ How is it possible, ⟨Tashi⟩ asks herself, that the person who administered her own excision ⟨. . .⟩ could be a woman? The question takes her back to Africa, to her Olinka people, and to the resolution of her fate. Though it would be unfair to reveal the end of her story—Tashi's final act of defiance—a part of her understanding of her ordeal can be noted: "The connection between mutilation and enslavement that is at the root of the domination of women in the world." It's a chilling realization, not simply related to Tashi's own culture, but central to images of female victimization worldwide. Tashi says: "It's in all the movies that terrorize women . . . The man who breaks in. The man with the knife . . . But those of us whose chastity belt was made of leather, or of silk and diamonds, or of fear and not of our own flesh . . . we worry. We are the perfect audience, mesmerized by our unconscious knowledge of what men, with the collaboration of our mothers, do to us."

> Charles R. Larson, "Against the Tyranny of Tradition," *Washington Post Book World*, 5 July 1992, pp. 1, 14

DONNA HAISTY WINCHELL   The Alice Walker of the 1980s and early 1990s comes across as a woman at peace with herself. She has spent half a literary lifetime tracing women's search for self, including her own. Ironically, her harshest critics have focused on her portrayal not of women, but of men. One regret that she has is that such criticism merely succeeds once more in drawing attention away from injustices done to women. Another is that people tend to see only the negative behavior of her male characters.

Walker told Oprah Winfrey in 1989, "Why is it that they only see, they can only identify the negative behavior? . . . I think it's because it's the negative behavior, the macho behavior, that they see as male behavior and that when the men stop using that behavior, when the men become gentle, when the men become people you can talk to, when they are good grandparents, when they are gentle people, they are no longer considered men and there is an inability even to see them." Critics don't often "see," or at least don't remember, that near the end of *The Color Purple*, a reformed Albert asks Celie to marry him again, this time in spirit as well as flesh. They forget that Grange Copeland comes back from his "second life" in New York a new and responsible man—and a loving grandfather. Truman Held takes on the burden that Meridian finally puts down when she walks away, refusing to be a martyr. And Suwelo in *Temple of My Familiar* grows from using Carlotta's body without considering her pain to recognizing that she is far more than blind flesh, that indeed all women are. At the end of the novel, he has left university teaching and is learning carpentry, although he suffers pangs of guilt over the requisite slaughter of trees.

Walker already saw a "new man" beginning in some of her poetry from the 1970s. At first, she thought that new man would be one who, like Christ, put love in front and the necessary clenched fist behind, as she explains in "The Abduction of Saints." However, by the time she wrote the dedication to the 1984 volume that contains this poem, *Good Night, Willie Lee, I'll See You in the Morning*, she had set a slightly different standard for the new man. Her ideal man's rebellion now takes a more subtle form; he doesn't need fists. She calls him simply "the quiet man." Walker considers such a new, nurturing man essential for the survival of the planet.

Donna Haisty Winchell, *Alice Walker* (New York: Twayne, 1992), pp. 132–33

◈ Bibliography

Once. 1968.

The Third Life of Grange Copeland. 1970.

Five Poems. 1972.

Revolutionary Petunias and Other Poems. 1973.

In Love and Trouble: Stories of Black Women. 1973.

Langston Hughes, American Poet. 1974.

Meridian. 1976.

The Women's Center Reid Lectureship, November 11, 1975: Papers (with June Jordan). 1976.

I Love Myself When I Am Laughing . . . and Then Again When I Am Looking Mean and Impressive: A Zora Neale Hurston Reader (editor). 1979.

Good Night, Willie Lee, I'll See You in the Morning. 1979.

Beyond What. 1980.

You Can't Keep a Good Woman Down. 1981.

The Color Purple. 1982.

In Search of Our Mothers' Gardens: Womanist Prose. 1983.

While Love Is Unfashionable. 1984.

Horses Make a Landscape Look More Beautiful. 1984.

The Alice Walker Calendar for 1986. 1985.

To Hell with Dying. 1987.

From Alice Walker. 1988.

Living by the Word: Selected Writings 1973–1987. 1988.

The Temple of My Familiar. 1989.

Finding the Green Stone. 1991.

Her Blue Body Everything We Know: Earthling Poems 1965–1990 Complete. 1991.

Possessing the Secret of Joy. 1992.

Warrior Masks: Female Genital Mutilation and the Sexual Blinding of Women (with Pratibha Parmar). 1993.

Everyday Use. Ed. Barbara Christian. 1994.

John Edgar Wideman
b. 1941

JOHN EDGAR WIDEMAN was born on June 14, 1941, in Washington, D.C., the son of Edgar and Betty (French) Wideman. He spent his early years first in Homewood, a suburb of Pittsburgh, and then in Shadyside, a predominantly white upper-middle-class district in Pittsburgh. Wideman attended the University of Pennsylvania on a scholarship, studying psychology and English and playing basketball. After graduating Phi Beta Kappa in 1963, he attended Oxford University on a Rhodes Scholarship, only the second black American—after Alain Locke early in the century—to win that honor. In 1965 he married Judith Ann Goldman, with whom he raised three children, Jamilla, Jacob, and Danny.

In 1966 Wideman received a B.Phil. from Oxford and began what would be a long and distinguished teaching career. He first joined the faculty of the University of Pennsylvania, where he became professor of English while also founding and directing the Afro-American Studies program and being assistant basketball coach from 1968 to 1972. In 1975 he joined the faculty of the University of Wyoming, remaining there as a professor of English until 1986. Wideman is currently affiliated with the University of Massachusetts at Amherst.

In 1967 Wideman's first novel, *A Glance Away,* appeared. It explores the struggles caused by drug addiction and homosexuality and their effects upon human relationships in a world in which people feel increasingly isolated. In *Hurry Home* (1970), Wideman's second novel, the protagonist searches for meaning against a backdrop of confusion and rootlessness. In both these novels Wideman uses surrealistic and other experimental techniques to probe the imaginative lives of his characters. As an antidote to existential despair, however, Wideman's characters frequently turn to history, both personal and communal. The past provides an anchor for characters directionlessly floating through the present. Neither of Wideman's first two novels is concerned exclusively with racial themes. Both works received considerable, and mostly favorable, attention from reviewers.

Wideman's third novel, *The Lynchers* (1973), as its title suggests, is more centrally focused on race. The novel, dealing with the lives of black people in the Philadelphia ghetto, fared poorly with critics. The communal history of *The Lynchers* is replaced by personal history in *Hiding Place* (1981), in which Wideman returns to his childhood settings and family folklore. Wideman's next novel, *Sent for You Yesterday* (1983), won the PEN/Faulkner Award. These two novels, along with a collection of short fiction, *Damballah* (1981), comprise the Homewood Trilogy and were published in one volume in 1985.

Wideman has continued to write prolifically. His most recent works include *Brothers and Keepers* (1984; nominated for the National Book Award), a memoir about his relationship with his brother, who is in prison; two novels, *Reuben* (1987) and *Philadelphia Fire* (1990); and a collection of short stories, *Fever* (1989). *The Stories of John Edgar Wideman*, a large volume collecting all his short work, appeared in 1992. An autobiographical work, *Fatheralong*, is announced as forthcoming in 1994.

Critical Extracts

ROGER EBERT   John Edgar Wideman's *A Glance Away* does not completely disguise the traces of the writer at work. His craft and plan occasionally become visible at the surface of the novel, blurring the characters beneath. ⟨. . .⟩

Wideman has the materials of a good novel, but his command of language is concealed by a bagful of stylistic tricks. He makes no distinction between quotes and narrative, and while I suppose there's nothing wrong with that, I can't understand why anyone would want to do it now that the innovators of the 1920's have shown it can be done. At the novel's end the three characters come together, drunk, in a hobo jungle, and Wideman presents their thoughts at random. The technique fails; one is not moved but simply confused. Or does it matter anyway whose stream of consciousness is chanting, "Paddy cake Paddy cake"? There are other signs of the phantom English professor lurking in and behind the author: Eliot is quoted, as are nursery rhymes and spirituals; and one scene suddenly turns into a fragment of a play. Emerging intact from the confusion, however, is the well-drawn character of

Thurley, who is memorable and sympathetic as, in his own words, "in religion an aesthetic Catholic, in politics a passive Communist, in sex a resigned anarchist."

Roger Ebert, "First Novels by Young Negroes," *American Scholar* 36, No. 4 (Autumn 1967): 684, 686

JOHN O'BRIEN   INTERVIEWER: Your first two novels, *Glance Away* and *Hurry Home*, are very differently conceived one from the other. The second experiments rather radically with the form of the novel.

WIDEMAN: Well, each book presented different kinds of problems. I would say in the first book, with a close reading, that you would see pretty quickly that I am interested in the formal aspects of the novel. I am doing apprenticeship work, I am going to school to various other writers, using others' techniques, but also trying out some things that I hope are original. I had a real interest in experimenting, in expanding the form of the novel even in the first book. I think then that the second book continues that. The first book was much less self-consciously organized; in the second book I thought a lot about what precisely I wanted to do from page one to the very last page. There was a progression in technique and craft in *Hurry Home*, so that I had a little more certainty about what I could do. I could set up goals or objectives far more consciously in it and I think this is even more true in *The Lynchers* because there I began the book with a completed plot. I could write a section and know that it was something that would be near the end of the novel.

INTERVIEWER: Is it more difficult when you are just beginning a novel to know how the parts will relate to the whole?

WIDEMAN: When you're beginning, even though you may be telling yourself otherwise, the process is very much in bits and pieces. You think there might be connections, but you're not really sure. You never really can be sure until the last word is written and you see what you have. For instance, *A Glance Away* didn't begin as a novel. I wanted to write something long but it didn't come. I kept writing shorter pieces. I had maybe fifteen or twenty shorter pieces just lying around. Then I began to re-read them and I suddenly found that two or three main characters emerged if I cut out about ten of the stories. So it became very natural to think of ways of putting these bits and pieces together. But I tried with all three books to set up a regular work-schedule. In that way, whether or not you have an idea, you're producing something. There is a lot of brute work involved in getting several thousand words down on paper. It takes me time, but you have to do that at some stage, whether the words are very polished or not. You have to get the raw material down.

INTERVIEWER: Do you think of A *Glance Away* as being a realistic novel?

WIDEMAN: It starts off with a warning that it is not going to be totally realistic. The Prologue uses many poetic rather than traditional prose devices for organization. It warns any reader that he is not going to be able to effect a traditional kind of relationship to the material following the Prologue. So it moves pretty quickly away from realistic convention. By the end it attempts to orchestrate on the page the inner thoughts of people and treat those in the same way a conventional novel would treat dialogue; and there are levels of interaction between the characters' minds that permit them to roll over time and place. All of that makes it not at all a realistic novel.

John O'Brien, "John Wideman," *Interviews with Black Writers* (New York: Liveright, 1973), pp. 214–15

MICHAEL G. COOKE   In *Damballah* Wideman shows all the rancor and folly and grief and confusion of black experience that put Wright off, and he shows it with candor and affection. In "Lizabeth: The Caterpillar Story," for example, a father eats the remainder of a caterpillar his baby daughter has started chewing, on the pretext that if he didn't die, neither would she. The scene is presented without revulsion and without humor. It is taken as something with the authority of human feeling and human action, and with total unconcern for any adverse opinion about blacks that it might give rise to. 〈. . .〉 But eating a caterpillar expresses more than a parental love unto death. It tells of a father's readiness to destroy whatever might endanger his child, and his willingness, where it is necessary for her protection, to go into any squalor. Though the act itself is ineffectual, the spirit behind it has a decided power, on the social as well as the symbolic level.

Wideman sets down the equivalent of the caterpillar story, again and again, defying common opinion and common etiquette. "You got to *Go there to Know where,*" one of his characters proclaims. Wideman simply takes us there and immerses us in things. In "The Watermelon Story," a wino is sitting on a stack of watermelons in front of an A & P plate-glass window when the watermelons give way under him and he is flung through the glass and has his arm "chopped off." But the wino survives and passes his time "in the Bum's Forest drinking just as much wine with one arm as he did with two." And this story freely modulates—because "the watermelon" is a corporate noun that includes all the fruit of that name—into the story from "slavery days" about old Rebecca and Isaac who at long last are vouchsafed a baby boy, found inside a watermelon when Isaac cracks it open with "that talking knuckle of his."

The story does not apologize for its miracle, but turns on the skeptical audience: "youall niggers ain't ready. . . . Youall too smarty panted." And it establishes its own pitch of reality with the wonderful picture of "a living breathing baby boy hid up in there smiling back at Isaac, grabbing that crusty knuckle and holding on like it was a titty." The phrase "smiling *back* at Isaac" fully captures Isaac's delight and belief without making an issue of them. And the image of the child "grabbing that crusty knuckle" establishes the child's instincts and health. And yet the scene is unclamorous, sure of its own knowledge, content with its own world.

Michael G. Cooke, *Afro-American Literature in the Twentieth Century* (New Haven: Yale University Press, 1984), pp. 211–12

JACQUELINE BERBEN   *Hiding Place,* John Wideman's 1981 novel about a young black's flight from unjust accusation, reveals the ghetto experience as a honeycomb of psychological and verbal subterfuges, all temporary shelters that must eventually give way before the onslaughts of reality. Wideman shifts back and forth between the narrative devices of indirect and direct interior monologue and dialogue to juxtapose the harsh world of poverty with the realm of dreams and fantasies in which the individual can hide from the unpleasant facts of his life. Language itself is rife with "hiding places" which afford a false sense of security to the unwary. Sincerity speaks in non-verbal forms of communication: gestures, songs, telepathic thoughts, heightened sensitivity, and bonds of kinship. Only names have an equivocal value, now a kind of title to dignity and a mark of permanence, now yet another mask to hide behind and change at will. In this network of deceit, of self-deception and pathological lying, the ability to deal with truth becomes the ultimate test of one's success or failure as a human being. ⟨. . .⟩

Bess, like Tommy, has come to Bruston Hill for its protective powers, to hide from a world that has become too cruel to bear and especially to talk about. Words only bring inexpressible pain. She will not listen to Tommy's troubles because she has heard it all before; she knows trouble and suffering far too intimately for someone else to describe it to her. The tragedy of Bess's life and the source of her resentment against the appellation *Mother Bess* stem from her ironic inability to share in the general fertility of Bruston Hill. Her sterility was all the harder to bear in face of the ease with which all her sisters conceived and gave birth. Easy as dancing. But Bess could not dance, either. She has a man she loved, a man whose touch turned her to "silk and honey" almost like the Biblical promised land where the desert would bear fruit. And their love grew, but no child. Bess who was so good at growing things, who had spent all her life digging in the ground "on her hands and knees or flopped down flat on her belly if nobody was watching," Bess who had long been confident that "anything she planted would grow," who had "cradled" so much "in the black earth," Bess gave her man no son. Then, after they had given up all hope, when they were old "like Abraham and Sarah in the Bible," they had Eugene. But Eugene was killed on Guam, though Bess never accepted the word of the telegram that her man had carried up Bruston Hill. Then it was her man's turn. Twenty years her senior, he passed on and left her alone. So Bess had come back to Bruston Hill to live with her ghosts and await her time to join them in the grave. While she waits, she walls herself in from communication with the outside world that only brings more pain: no mail, no telephone, no radio, and *no* visitors. All hope has been denied her. Since her womb brought forth death, not life, her image of her own "subterranean chamber" deep inside herself is not Tommy's warm cave of life through which run the rivers of his own blood, but a death hole, a grave ⟨. . .⟩ She recognizes the hole of death in her waking consciousness when she pictures her man slipping away from her, when she sees Shirl's dead baby in her white satin coffin, her beautiful "black-eyed Susan black eyes" staring into space. All Bess can find to say about the injustice of it all are the empty words, "Oh Jesus! Oh God Almighty!" Empty words in her mouth because Bess is no longer a Christian and has not been one ever since she lost the illusion of a guiding, protecting paternal hand in her favorite spiritual, "Father, Father along." But the real words were *farther, farther* along and so Bess lost her

God. Words are hypocritical; words can kill a son or even God himself.
One must not listen to words or ever trust in them.

Jacqueline Berben, "Beyond Discourse: The Unspoken Versus Words in the Fiction
of John Edgar Wideman," *Callaloo* 8, No. 3 (Fall 1985): 525, 528

BERNARD W. BELL   Wideman's five novels (*A Glance Away*
[1967], *Hurry Home* [1970], *The Lynchers* [1973], *Hiding Place* [1981], and
Sent for You Yesterday [1983]) and his collection of stories (*Damballah* [1981])
reveal a tension between realistic material and experimentation with form
and style, especially stream-of-consciousness techniques and black speech.
In *A Glance Away*, Wideman says, "I am going to school to various other
writers, using others' techniques, but also trying out some things that I hope
are original." Eliot's Eurocentric influence is apparent in the mood, style,
and characterization of this first novel, which is a quasi-parable on the
resurrection of Edward Lawson, the thirty-year-old black protagonist who
returns to Philadelphia on Easter Sunday, April 20, from a drug rehabilitation
center in the South only to suffer the pain and guilt of his mother's death.
The person driven by his own painful memories to get him through the
night is Robert Thurley, a fictionalized J. Alfred Prufrock, a middle-aged
white homosexual professor of comparative literature who pursues black
lovers and for whom "Eliot was . . . the poet of weariness, of old age."
Although Eliot's specter hangs over most of the book, in the final ten pages
Wideman displaces dialogue with the alternating inner thoughts of Eddie,
Robert, and Brother Small, their albino friend, as they sit in spiritual communion around a small fire in a hobo camp.

Equally Prufrockian in characterization but more nonrepresentational and
experimental in time structure and point of view is *Hurry Home*. Whereas
Thurley, the ineffectual, suffering intellectual in *A Glance Away*, wanders
through the streets and after-hours clubs of Philadelphia, Charles Webb,
the guilt-ridden white writer and intellectual of *Hurry Home*, wanders
through the museums, cafés, and beaches of Spain in a vain search for
redemption from the black son he has never seen because he had abandoned
his black mistress not knowing she was pregnant. Using interior monologue,
letters, journal entries, rapid shifts in time and point of view, surreal
vignettes, mythic associations, linguistic puns, and frequent allusions to
writers and painters, especially Hieronymus Bosch and his triptych of "The

Adoration of the Magi," Wideman is concerned in his second novel with the thin line between reality and fantasy, "between individual and collective experience which permits one to flow into the other." Going to get a haircut for his graduation, Cecil Otis Braithwaite, the protagonist who, aided by the sacrifices of his girlfriend Esther and his scrub-woman mother, is only the second of his race to graduate from the university law school, is symbolically rejected by the black community as a "Humbug magistraitassed uppitty nigger." He, in turn, deserts Esther on their wedding night to go to Spain and Africa, seeking to understand his double-consciousness and to accommodate both the gospels and the Easter song, the "St. John Passion," of Heinrich Schutz. The question that Cecil asks throughout the book is, Why did you do that? As he actually and imaginatively travels back in the past for answers, his personal experience is conflated into the collective history of his race. But after three years of wandering through the corridors of time and foreign countries, reconstructing and reliving the journey of his race from Africa to America, he hurries home in the spring to work in a hair straightening parlor, to rejoin his wife, and to dream. "To go back into one's past," Wideman states, "is in fact dreaming. What is history except people's imaginary recreation." Thus Cecil's actual past and his dream past, like his personal and racial identities, become merged in the course of the novel.

Bernard W. Bell, *The Afro-American Novel and Its Tradition* (Amherst: University of Massachusetts Press, 1987), pp. 307–9.

JAMES W. COLEMAN   During his career as a writer-intellectual, John Edgar Wideman in his personal life has overcome feelings of alienation from the black community and has reorientated himself as a participant in black culture. In his fiction, I contend, Wideman has effected a similar shift, using modernism and postmodernism to bring his intellectual characters out of their isolation and into contact with the needs, concerns, and traditions of black people generally. Before he could write about this shift, Wideman had to inform himself about black culture. An eight-year period of immersion in the works of nineteenth- and twentieth-century authors gave him the resources he needed. Using them, he was able to circumvent modernism's dead-end, pessimistic worldview and at the same time to chart a new course for other, similarly estranged black intellectuals.

I identify three main stages in Wideman's career: the early books (*A Glance Away*, 1967; *Hurry Home*, 1970; and *The Lynchers*, 1973); the Homewood trilogy (*Hiding Place*, 1981; *Damballah*, 1981; and *Sent for You Yesterday*, 1983); and the recent books (*Brothers and Keepers*, 1984; and *Reuben*, 1987).

The early books certainly exhibit differences, but most evident at this point in Wideman's career is his depiction of the black intellectual's isolation from the black community. Wideman was influenced both by the modernist literary treatment of such alienation and, as the circumstances of his life indicate, by his own doubts about the black community and his relationship to it. In his books the black community expresses hostility toward the black intellectual, has interests and concerns that differ from his, and is at times oblivious to him. ⟨. . .⟩

The Homewood Trilogy, which followed Wideman's long period of discovery of and immersion in the work of black writers, shows the black intellectual in a meaningful relationship with the black community and integrates modernism and postmodernism with black traditions by means of a black literary voice. In *Hiding Place* the black intellectual's rapprochement with the black community is tentative, but in *Damballah*, the intellectual characters, often obviously surrogates for Wideman himself, feel impelled to understand their alienation from the community and seek to learn and use its oral rituals. The intellectual in *Sent for You Yesterday* maintains a close relationship with blacks while he constructs the fictions and myth that will allow him to function as a helpful, saving force in the community.

Brothers, Wideman's biographical-autobiographical work, provides the transition that truly releases the black intellectual to pursue the personal, subjective life of the intellectual as he strives to serve his people. In *Brothers*, Wideman the writer-intellectual reintegrates himself into the black family and community, and *Reuben* shows that he has finally established his allegiance and his role as an intellectual. His intellectual interests are those of the community, which he is obliged to help as much as he can. He no longer feels obliged to work through a dead-end, pessimistic modernism, and he no longer experiences anxiety about experimenting as a writer: experimentation that serves the goal of the intellectual is acceptable.

In *Reuben*, a black intellectual prepares himself to help the black community. Reuben, a very bookish individual, perceives that postmodernism is well suited to his purposes (and by implication better suited than modernism). He realizes that all perspectives on life are fictions to a significant extent but views postmodernism as helpful because it can easily be manipulated to create helpful fictions that will counteract the harmful ones perpetrated against blacks by white society.

James W. Coleman, "Introduction," *Blackness and Modernism: The Literary Career of John Edgar Wideman* (Jackson: University Press of Mississippi, 1989), pp. 3–5

RANDALL KENAN   In each story ⟨in *Fever*⟩ some dim memory, some deep urge, some knowledge, some inescapable prophecy reaches through time or space. Voices whisper across voids; calls float over oceans.

These voices he often finds—like a child picking up pebbles on the beach—in fragments of history, news items, his own novels, even Bobby Short! Valaida Snow, the legendary trumpeter of the Jazz Era to whom the Queen of Denmark gave a golden trumpet, supplies perhaps the most chilling voice in "Valaida." "Tell him," she speaks from the grave, "they loved me at home too, a down-home girl from Chattanooga, Tennessee, who turned out the Apollo, not a mumbling word from wino heaven till they were on their feet hollering and clapping for more with the rest of the audience. . . . Yesteryears, yesterhours." But the story turns into a What If: "What if Valaida Snow, who was interned in a Nazi concentration camp for over a year, what if she had saved the life of a 13-year-old boy who would become a survivor? Cut then within the same story to an old man disgusted and indifferent toward life trying to tell the remarkable tale of how he had one day been saved by a "colored woman" to his equally disgusted and indifferent black cleaning woman who "has put on flesh for protection. To soften blows. To ease around corners." The ironies do not merely abound, they cluster, almost fester—he, a Jew, tells her, a black woman, the story on Christmas Eve.

For irony is the tool Wideman is forever honing, sharpening, working with surgical precision. "Hostages," the story of a woman whose husband is a captive of Arab terrorists, becomes an unravelling, a debunking of the concept of "prisoner." Suddenly everything is to be viewed in a new light—marriage, sickness, materialism—and to be seen as imprisoning. An immigrant in a new land; to be black in America; to be a child in the care of parents: Mostly trouble haunts these characters, trouble as in tension between black and white, Arab and Jew, men and women. Wideman manages to transmute that trouble into some of his most challenging and powerful prose yet, in which everything is subject to ridicule or doubt. ⟨. . .⟩

⟨. . .⟩ Wideman's characters all want something, desperately, something they cannot have, something inarticulable and inconceivable. This is the vision, that of a cruel world peopled by victims who go on and on unrequited, unavenged, unloved, that fuels *Fever*. A theme recurs in these stories: the mythic, Talmudic Lamed-Vov: "The Thirty Just Men set apart to suffer the reality humankind cannot bear? Saviors"; "God's hostages"; "Lamed-Vov are sponges drawing mankind's suffering into themselves"; "A thousand years is not long enough to thaw the agony each Lamed-Vov endures." Wideman sees us all as Lamed-Vov—which accounts for these ever-present, insistent, wailing voices, rippling out through time.

Randall Kenan, "A Most Righteous Prayer," *Nation*, 1 January 1990, pp. 25–27

JOHN EDGAR WIDEMAN   Good stories transport us to those extraordinarily diverse regions where individual lives are enacted. For a few minutes we can climb inside another's skin. Mysteriously, the dissolution of ego also sharpens the sense of self, reinforces independence and relativity of point of view. People's lives resist a simple telling, cannot be understood safely, reductively, from some static still point, some universally acknowledged center around which all other lives orbit. Narrative is reciprocal process, regressive and progressive, dynamic. When a culture hardens into heliocentricity, fancies itself the star of creation, when otherness is imagined as a great darkness except for what the star illuminates, it's only a matter of time until the center collapses in upon itself, imploding with sigh and whimper.

Minority writers hold certain, peculiar advantages in circumstances of cultural breakdown, reorientation, transition. We've accumulated centuries of experience dealing with problems of marginality, problems that are suddenly on center stage for the whole of society: inadequacy of language, failure of institutions, a disintegrating metropolitan vision that denies us or swallows us, that attracts and repels, that promises salvation and extinction. We've always been outsiders, orphans, bastard children, hard pressed to make our claims heard. In order to endure slavery and oppression it has been necessary to cultivate the double-consciousness of seer, artist, mother. Beaten down by countles proofs of the inadequacy, the repugnance of our own skin, we've been forced to enter the skins of others, see the world and ourselves through the eyes of others. The reality carried around inside our skulls is a sanctuary. Imagination has evolved as discipline, defense, coping mechanism, counterweight to the falling facts of life. We've learned to confer upon ourselves the power of making up our lives, changing them as we go along.

> John Edgar Wideman, "The Architectonics of Fiction," *Callaloo* 13, No. 1 (Winter 1990): 43

DARRYL PINCKNEY   *Philadelphia Fire*, Wideman's most recent novel, is based on the police action in 1985 against a small collective, Move, that advocated, among other things, destruction of "the system". A police helicopter dropped a bomb on the roof of the fortified house occupied by Move, igniting drums of gasoline stored inside. Eleven members of the collective, five of them children, were killed, scores of homes were destroyed in the fire that burned out of control, and the damage in the neighbourhood was widespread. 〈. . .〉

In *Philadelphia Fire*, the random and institutional violence in the city, the low regard for life among the young, the cynicism and helplessness, transform the positive black perspective of holding on, "the story he must never stop singing", into the saddest of consolations. Disorganized, fractured, inchoate, Wideman's parable about lost children and how adults have ruined the world for the young attempts too much. "Poison works its way through their veins into their brains." The source of the misery is clarified in an essay inserted in the middle of the book that deals with another real life-tragedy: Wideman's younger son currently serving a life sentence for the murder of his room-mate on a camping field trip when he was sixteen. "To take stock, to make sense, to attempt to control or to write a narrative of self—how hopeless any of these tasks must seem, when the self attempting this harrowing business is no more than a shadow." 〈. . .〉

Claude Brown, in *Manchild in the Promised Land*, was frank about the contempt his generation of hoodlums had for what they saw as the back-country, downtrodden ways of their parents. The break between generations was taken for granted when Brown was writing in the early 1960s. *Brothers and Keepers* (1984) helps to explain why Wideman attempts, almost as a pastoral mission, to compensate for this break in the urgent desire to bear witness, to prove the spiritual kinship of the present with the past and restore a kind of pride of ownership. It is as though he wanted to give something back to his immediate family because the attrition of years has taken away so much. So many of the stories and figures in *Brothers and Keepers* have been met before that it reads like a concordance to the Homewood trilogy. Though the book depends on Wideman's eclectic style, it is a non-fiction account of his relationship with his younger brother, who, involved in a robbery in 1975 during which a man was killed, was sentenced to life in prison.

Wideman discusses the brutality of the penal system and the effects of hard time, "a death by inches", but what drives the book is how their lives diverged, what drew his brother to the life of the addict, thief and absentee father while he entered the "square world" of professional status, marriage to a white woman, and children in the back of the station wagon. Wideman takes himself to task for staking too much of what he was on what he would become, for looking forward to the day when he could look down on Homewood, and for merely teaching books about black consciousness in the quiet of the classroom while his brother was living it in the "real world". In trying to come to terms with the waste, he reaches to define his brother as a rebel, one of the young black men of the 1960s who had "dynamite growing out of their skulls".

Wideman confesses that he was embarrassed when his brother loudly sang along to a soul radio station in front of his white wife. In a previous book, Wideman had admitted to his brother in the preface that as a child he was reluctant to be seen enjoying watermelon from fear that to do so would mark him as an "instant nigger", "black and drippy lipped". It is as though Wideman must pay for the shame he once felt at his working-class roots by fervently embracing a concept of blackness "that would come to rest in the eyes; blackness a way of seeing and being seen", much like one of his characters who thinks that having a string of babies by a number of men is a liberation from the notion that "crossing t's and dotting i's had something to do with becoming a human being and blackness was the chaos you had to whip into shape in order to be a person who counted".

Motivated by family tragedy, Wideman corrected his assumptions. But, as it turned out, this embrace could be reduced to an abstraction by real-life events in your own safe back yard. His brother's case, then that of his son—the irony is not that the curse of the ghetto followed Wideman into his middle-class exile. The meaning, if there is one, is that the trouble is

arbitrary, indiscriminate; or that the two Americas are not as far apart as
we like to think, or that disorder does not depend on class.

Darryl Pinckney, " 'Cos I'm a So-o-oul Man," *Times Literary Supplement*, 23 August
1991, pp. 19–20

JAMES WOOD   Wideman is at his most literary when attempting to
be most "oral", and he is most natural when calmly accepting the traditional
burdens and formalities of third-person narration. In "Backseat", he writes
autobiographically about the Wideman family in Pittsburgh, and about the
death of his grandmother. The story opens with a fine, conventional evocation of lovemaking in the back of a 1946 Lincoln Continental ("We made
love in the belly of the whale"). The story makes good, plain progress, until
Wideman again attempts his oral stutter, his imitation of a mind at thought,
imagining his grandmother in hospital: "Skin and bones. She's down to
skin and bone. Wasting away. We thought she'd live forever. She'd be sick,
real sick but she always came back. Flesh has deserted her now." But that
last droopy sentence belongs not to thought but to bad adolescent poetry.
⟨. . .⟩
    Yet, for all this, Wideman is worth staying with. He has moments of
aeration, sudden openings of natural power. Sometimes these are visual, as
when in "Conceit", a man watching a band dressed in black tie sees "how
the starched white shirtfronts sever their dark heads. Canonballs dropped
in the snow." Elsewhere, lovely strange words appear: jook, brammed, sassing,
splib. More often, the moments of feeling are achieved, as in Dreiser's
fiction, in spite of a sluggish language. At the end of the title-story ⟨"All
Stories Are True"⟩, after much meandering, everything suddenly tightens.
We are standing in a prison, and the narrator notices that a leaf is being
blown high up over the prison walls. Others notice it, and soon people are
cheering: "that leaf had a whole lot of fans when it sailed over the wall.
Would have thought people cheering for the Steelers of somebody's lottery
number hit. . . . After watching it a while you know that leaf was flying out
of here on its mind. Every little whip and twist and bounce starts to matter. . . . Whole visiting yard whooping and hollering when it finally blew
over the wall." In a second, Wideman's weaknesses have become virtues:
we are all pulled along the slow rope of oral narration, but this time without
frustration, for a moment of delicacy is building, and we need to feel it

grow; above all, Wideman's sentimentality—and this is a sentimental passage—seems courageous, not an excuse.

> James Wood, "The Voices of Homewood," *Times Literary Supplement*, 7 May 1993,
> p. 21

▣ *Bibliography*

A Glance Away. 1967.

Hurry Home. 1970.

The Lynchers. 1973.

Damballah. 1981.

Hiding Place. 1981.

Sent for You Yesterday. 1983.

Brothers and Keepers. 1984.

The Homewood Trilogy 〈*Damballah, Hiding Place, Sent for You Yesterday*〉. 1985.

Reuben. 1987.

Fever. 1989.

Philadelphia Fire. 1990.

The Stories of John Edgar Wideman. 1992.